THE COLLECTED ESSAYS OF

BARBARA HARDY

Volume One

THE COLLECTED ESSAYS OF

BARBARA HARDY

Professor of English, Birkbeck College
University of London

Volume One

Narrators and Novelists

THE HARVESTER PRESS · SUSSEX

BARNES & NOBLE BOOKS · NEW JERSEY

First published in Great Britain in 1987 by
THE HARVESTER PRESS LTD
Publisher: John Spiers
16 Ship Street, Brighton, Sussex
and in the USA by
BARNES & NOBLE BOOKS
81 Adams Drive, Totowa, New Jersey 07512

British Library Cataloguing in Publication Data

Hardy, Barbara
  Narrators and novelists: the collected
  essays of Barbara Hardy
  1. English fiction—History and
  criticism
  I. Title
  823'.009   PR821

  ISBN 0-7108-1004-0

Library of Congress Cataloging in Publication Data

Hardy, Barbara
  Narrators and novelists.

  1. English fiction—History and criticism. 2. Narration.
(Rhetoric) I. Title.
PR823.H26   1987   823'.009   87-11385
ISBN 0-389-20738-1 (v. 1)

Typeset in 10 on 12pt Plantin by C. R. Barber (Highlands) Ltd,
Fort William, Scotland

Printed and bound in Great Britain by
Biddles Ltd, Guildford and King's Lynn

In affectionate memory
of
Geoffrey Tillotson

Contents

Acknowledgments

I have been and am grateful to the following friends for help, encouragement, and criticism: F. W. Bateson, Laurel Brake, James Britton, Helen Corke, Martin Dodsworth, Janet El-Rayess, Richard Ellmann, Graham Handley, Ernest Hardy, Samuel Hynes, Nancy Martin and Michael Slater. I am indebted to many students at Birkbeck and Royal Holloway College. I wish to thank, as always, the staff of Birkbeck library for all their help. My admiration and affection for Geoffrey Tillotson, my colleague at Birkbeck for fifteen years, is recorded in the dedication.

Preface

Narrators and Novelists is a collection of essays given some unity by a sense of narrative as a form of inquiry. That inquiry is personal, impassioned, and particularised—at least in the fiction discussed here. Much of this book shows a taste for close analysis of the novel's rich mixed medium. Practical criticism is not yet quite out of date, and I still find no substitute, in teaching and criticism, for a close and careful reading of the text, with an awareness of individual response. To distrust the text may be the end of study—at times, and for various reasons—but to distrust the text without ever having trusted it seems hollow or specious. And close reading need not be simply empirical, or enclosed. There is a myth that the decades after the Second World War treated the text as a sacred object, self-contained, insulated and contextless, but the critics from whose work I learnt, William Empson, L. C. Knights, and Winifred Nowottny, for instance, practised a close analysis that was alert to history, biography, and other works of art. Their virtues are not cloistered and I value their example.

Most of these essays are concerned with the novelist's effort to make sense of human life, an effort which is most valued, by the critic concerned with evaluation, when it is least confident and simplifying, most tentative and experimental, inclining to entertain doubt and nuance. My earliest work on the Victorian novel was an attempt to discuss fictional structures and languages as vehicles for such trials and errors. When I began to look at George Eliot's fiction I was probably too uncritically dependent on concepts of realism, and on distinctions between art and 'life', but not merely concerned with the novel as a reflection or affirmation of life. George Eliot's art used to be disparaged as loose, casual, and subordinated to social or moral argument, and my formal analysis of her texts attempted to propose a more flexible and complex approach to fictional structures. Since then I have become more explicitly interested in modes of narrative investigation. My essay on Thomas Hardy, for instance, considers him at his most implicit and least discursive, offering a muted model for the analysis of imagination. The first chapter in this volume, on narrative as art and primary social and psychic activity, is concerned with ways in which novels reflect, and reflect on, forms of art and forms outside art, and sees a continuity between what we call art and what we call not-art. The essay on objects is not a contribution to a theory of mimesis but examines the novelist's instruments of inquiry. Surfaces and environments are regarded not merely as imitations of surfaces and environments in social life, but structures and paradigms. Literary investigations are impassioned: Laclos's *Les Liaisons Dangereuses* and Conrad's *Lord Jim* think feelingly about feeling. Laclos's great novel transcends the pornographic solicitations of its narrative tensions and sensational scenes in discovering psychological and social effects and causes. In my discussions of reflexiveness I do not see art as introvertedly aesthetic but as creatively two-faced, scrutinising its forms and languages but also analysing the forms and languages of that life we call ordinary.

The novelist's art is not only impassioned, but particularised, accreting its details in a process of ordering, classifying, judging, dissolving, declassifying and doubting. My interest in the particulars of fiction is, I hope, controlled not only by an interest in narrative inquiry, but by a longstanding interest in form, shown here in an early essay on Joyce Cary, and later on in more elaborate discussions of Joyce and Beckett.

The book is a miscellany, bringing together changing views, derived from the formal and the informal intellectual activities of teaching and learning. Along with more academic pieces, I have included a toast for a Dickens dinner, a note on Mrs Ramsay's bad housekeeping, a broadcast talk on Laclos, and reviews of Susan Ferrier and Alan Sillitoe, reminders of special occasions and special enthusiasms. I have often been tempted to revise argument and analysis but have resisted such urges, and made only corrections and stylistic changes. Most of these essays were first commissioned or requested by colleagues, as lectures or contributions to books, and the collection recalls for me many pleasures of teaching, travelling, talking, and listening.

1. The Nature of Narrative

Narrative, like lyric or dance, is not to be regarded as an aesthetic invention used by artists to control, manipulate and order experience, but as a primary act of mind transferred to art from life. The novel heightens, isolates and analyses the narrative motions of human consciousness. Novelists have been more concerned with this element of fiction than critics, and the point of this essay is to suggest that we go to novels to find out about narrative. Novelists have for a long time known enough about the narrative mode to be able to work in it, criticise it, and play with it. Sterne juggles, shows off, and teases us in a form which draws special attention to its own nature—and ever since, novelists have been dislocating, inverting, attenuating and analysing narrative. The uses and dislocations exist in a pre-aesthetic state in routine acts of human consciousness, and the novelists' analysis is not narrowly literary but extends to the whole range of psychic narratives.

I take for granted the ways in which storytelling engages our interest, curiosity, fear, tensions, expectation and sense of order. What concerns me here are the qualities which fictional narrative shares with the inner and outer storytelling that plays a major role in our sleeping and waking lives. We dream in narrative, daydream in narrative, remember, anticipate, hope, despair, believe, doubt, plan, revise, criticise, construct, gossip, learn, hate and love by narrative. In order to live, we make up stories about ourselves and others, about the personal as well as the social past and future.

This long, incomplete and obvious list not only points to the narrative structure of acts of mind but suggests the deficiency of our commonly posited antagonism between dream and realistic vision. Educationalists still suggest that the process of maturation involves

a movement out of the fantasy-life into a vision of life 'as it is.'
Teachers have even constructed syllabuses on the assumption that
we begin with fairytales and daydreams and work gradually into
realistic modes. John Stuart Mill, his feelings restored by the poetry
of Wordsworth, took the love of narrative to be characteristic of the
infancy of men and societies. F. R. Leavis and his disciples are stern
about immature and indulgent fantasy in literature. There is a
widespread, dubious, but understandable assumption on the part of
wishful believers in life-enhancement that human beings begin by
telling themselves fairytales and end by telling truths.

If we apply some introspection it looks rather as if we go on
oscillating between fairytale and truth, dream and waking. Fantasy-
life does not come to an end at eighteen but goes on working with the
more superficially 'life-orientated' modes of planning, faithful
remembering and rational appraisal. We can distinguish the
extremes of cut-off indulgent fantasy and faithful document, but
the many intermediate states blur the distinction and are
compounded of both fantasy and realism. The element of dream can
be sterile and dangerously in-turned; it can also penetrate deeply
and accept a wide range of disturbing and irrational experience that
cannot easily, if at all, be accepted, ordered, understood or
reconstructed coherently and dispassionately. Dream can
debilitate, but its subversive discontents are vital for personal and
social development. It can provide escape or a look at the unwished-
for worst. It lends imagination to the otherwise limited motions of
faithful memory and rational planning. It acts on future, joining it
with past. It creates, maintains and transforms our relationships: we
come to know each other by telling, untelling, believing and
disbelieving stories about each other's pasts, futures and identities.
Dream probes and questions what can be the static and overly
rational stories about past, future and identity, and is in the process
itself steadied and rationally eroded. We tell stories in order to
escape from the stubbornness of identity, as Randall Jarrell reminds
us:

> What some escape to, some escape: if we find Swann's
> Way better than our own, and trudge on at the back
> Of the north wind to—to—somewhere east
> Of the sun, west of the moon, it is because we live
>
> By trading another's sorrow for our own; another's
> Impossibilities, still unbelieved in, for our own. . . .

Here, in 'Children Selecting Books in a Library', he argues that to be mature involves escape, or rehearses a non-attachment to self which is perfected in death. Thus we may be engaged in telling ourselves stories in a constant attempt to exchange identity and history, though many of us stay in love with ourselves, sufficiently self-attached to rewrite the other stories for our own purposes. But 'escaping' and 'escaping to' form only a part of narrative activity and function. We tell stories in order to change, remaking the past in a constant and not always barren *esprit d'escalier*. The polarity between fantasy and reality is another instance of convenient fiction: we look back to go forward or to stay in a past-centred obsession. Like most works of fiction, personal history is made up of fantasy and realism, production and idling.

We often tend to see the novel as competing with the world of happenings. I prefer to see it as the continuation, in disguising and isolating art, of the remembering, dreaming and planning that is imposed outside art on the uncertain, attenuated, interrupted and unpredictable or meaningless flow of happenings. Real life may have the disjointedness of a series of short stories, told by someone like Katherine Mansfield, but seldom has the continuity of a novel. Recollection of happenings, which removes certain parts for various conscious and unconscious motives, is the best life-model for the novel. We do not grow out of telling stories.

What consequences are involved in seeing fictional narrative as continuous with narrative action and reaction? One might be the erosion of our favourite distinction between fantasy and reality. The best fantasists, as we know from introspection and *Emma*, work in starkly realistic terms, staying in the drawing-room, using the minutiae of everyday dress and dialogue. Another consequence would be an increased attentiveness to the combination of reminiscence and anticipation, interpenetrating each other and complicating the temporal relations of beginning, middle and end as they do indeed in our play of consciousness, which is more like the loose-leaf novel than the Aristotelian progress. Another consequence would be the recognition that while twentieth-century interior monologues are more realistic in form than their Victorian predecessors, earlier novelists represent or symbolise the inner narrative in indirect and less mimetically accurate modes. Joyce, Proust, and Beckett use the stream of consciousness in ways which force us to acknowledge the continuities of narrative I have spoken of, but eighteenth and nineteenth-century novelists use the multiple plot, the shifting point of view, the combined impersonal and personal narrative, the person-centred third-person novel, and so on, to represent the same confused and complex fluency of recording. Such earlier novels mime the sheer variety of mental narration, often most explicitly.

Out of many such interests, I take the self-conscious representation of narrative as a starting-point. Art-forms frequently and unsurprisingly discuss and explore the subject of their own mode. Narratives and dramas are often *about* making up stories and playing roles. The novel is introverted in this sense, not because novels tend to be about novels, but because they tend to be about the larger narrative structure of consciousness, and the value and dangers involved in narrative modes of invention, dream, causal projection, and so on. Sterne shows this introversion in a highly literary way, and his play, like most, is based on certainties, or at all events starts off from theories which are locally or temporarily entertained as exploratory hypotheses. When in *Tristram Shandy* he plays with the complexities of authorial voice, generality, omniscience, completion, chronological order, and biography, he reveals the complexities of such conventions by exaggeration, distortion, suspension and isolation. Our attention is engaged with such narrative means in a play which temporarily and wittily presents them as ends. In order to perform such virtuoso acts of distortion and separation Sterne has had to identify, judge and analyse as persistently and closely as any Hypercritic. Narrative—analysed and judged in the chronological displacements—is revealed as a coherence and a solicitation of curiosity, a movement towards completion. The very incoherence, the tantalising, and the incompleteness unbare characteristics of narrative and also mime the complexity of the process in the primary act of consciousness. Tristram is both a novelist and an informal presenter, his medium close to the medium of interior monologue. He 'unrealistically' interrupts his story over and over again, refuses to let us read straight through, frustrates and plays with our desire to learn, know, keep to the point and come to a conclusion. The form is only unrealistic or artifical when contrasted with other narratives; set beside the multiplicity and complexity of psychic narration it is close to life. Unrealistic, rather, is the story that has its say for good long stretches, the story that is isolated, the story that gets finished.

One characteristic of most novels is the sheer number of narratives they contain, and *Tristram Shandy's* many anecdotes, stories, tall tales, travelogues, and so forth are small and artificial conventional stories that draw attention to the force of the main meandering.

Beckett is perhaps the novelist closest to Sterne in his marvellous combination of anecdote with discontinuous, self-defeating story. Joyce seems to me to mime the life-narrative much less faithfully, and to impose a mannered control on fluency and incompleteness, though I know this is open to argument. But all three provide us with lucid criticism of narrative as well as with great narratives. They have analysed well enough to play. Less realistic novelists, like the Victorians, seem to be caught between the assured conventionality of an earlier age of fiction and the assured brave dislocations of the next. They too are sufficiently in touch with the forms of narrative in consciousness, using them implicitly and analysing them explicitly, to be worth a look in this context. Fielding and Sterne, in their individual ways, contrast the neatness of artistic narrative with the flux and fits and starts, the untidiness and incompleteness of inner action. The Brontës, Thackeray, early Dickens, George Eliot, and even Henry James, tend to divide action evenly between many stories, and to avoid an encapsulated model of artificial narrative like Sterne's anecdotes or the comic epic or the inset story. Their interest in narrative tends to show itself in discussion. But there may be less obvious connections between their narrative forms and narrative acts of mind. Charlotte and Emily Brontë sometimes drive a lyric wedge between the narrative parts of their novels, and their use of different narrators or points of view reflects the tension between inner and outer vision, between wishing and accepting events. The socially directed novels of Thackeray, Mrs Gaskell and Dickens show an insistence on the connections and collisions between separate stories, though this is sometimes blurred by the Providential pattern. George Eliot and Henry James, for all their differences in intensity, can combine a deep central core of complex inner narrative—Dorothea's or Rowland Mallett's—with a briefer treatment of another opposing or antagonistic story. James of course differs from all the others I have mentioned in the way he centres the narrative on one register of consciousness while avoiding a first-person novel. Charlotte Brontë and Dickens are especially attached to narrative based on memory; George Eliot and Henry James to the reports of immediate apprehension. Taking in the present might be said to be the basic stance in their major novels. All the novelists I mention not only reflect narrative forms but also discuss them.

James likes to show the working of sensibility and intelligence in the present happening, but as he so often centres the interest in a spectator, he can show and exploit a slight but subtle and important gap between happening and interpretation: the narrative contains a narrative of what happens counterpointed on a narrative of what seems to be happening, or what the spectator tells himself is happening. The gap is also present but on an enormous scale and with vast irony in *Tom Jones* and *Wuthering Heights*. One of James's great achievements is to narrow the gap so that many readers never see it at all, and all readers have to work uncomfortably hard to see it. One of his major themes is the relation between what happened and what was reported, expected, believed, dreamed and falsified. The self-contemplating narrative of fiction is nowhere subtler and more explicit than in *The Ambassadors*.

Let us begin with the *locus classicus*, Strether by the river:

What he saw was exactly the right thing—a boat advancing round the bend and containing a man who held the paddles and a lady, at the stern, with a pink parasol. It was suddenly as if these figures, or something like them, had been wanted in the picture, had been wanted more or less all day, and had now drifted into sight, with the slow current, on purpose to fill up the measure. They came down slowly, floating down, evidently directed to the landing-place near their spectator and presenting themselves to him not less clearly as the two persons for whom his hostess was already preparing a meal. For two very happy persons he found himself straightway taking them—a young man in shirt-sleeves, a young woman easy and fair, who had pulled pleasantly up from some other place, and being acquainted with the neighborhood, had known what this particular retreat could offer them. The air quite thickened, at their approach, with further intimations; the intimation that they were expert, familiar, frequent—that this wouldn't at all events be the first time.

(Book Ten, IV.)

David Lodge, in *The Language of Fiction*, quotes Wittgenstein's saying, 'The limits of my language are the limits of my world.' Mediated through the limits of James's language are the limits of his narrative, but he is explicitly aware of such limitations, and they form at least a major part of his subject. Our narratives are of course limited by our sensibility, inhibitions, language, history, intelligence, inclinations to wish, hope, pray, believe, dream. *The Ambassadors*, like most great novels, is concerned with the powers and limitations of narrative, and so Strether is shown here, as elsewhere, seeing and telling. He has been seeing these same characters and telling himself stories about them for a long time, and here he is, seeing them for the first time with the truly alienated vision of the stranger. He is therefore made to show his sensibilities as narrator. We are about to see—not for the last time, indeed, in this novel that goes on moving—a climactic collision between what he wants to tell and what he has to see. We see his impulse to order and his impulse to praise, first in the pure form of a vision of people who mean nothing to him. The imagery is pictorial and even impressionistic, deriving as it does from the generalised imagery of painters, painting and aesthetic vision, and from the localised context of the remembered unbought Lambinet. But this is the kind of picture the impressionists did not paint, the kind that tells a story. James, like Lawrence, seems often to write about artists so that he may and yet need not be writing about novelists. Here the implications, for all the trembling visual delicacy and radiance, are plainly narrative. The figures are 'as if' wanted in the picture but they come to break down the picture's static composition, do not stay, like figures cut through by the frame, on the edge of the impressionist landscape. They continue to move, to come nearer and loom larger, they cease to be compositionally appropriate to the picture and become people. The stories Strether tells are elegant configurations, and who should know more than Strether's creator about the special temptations of aesthetic arrangement in narrative? But Strether is also moved to tell stories out of curiosity: he does not know enough, he is kept guessing, there are secrets and mysteries. He is lied to by Little Bilham and left by Maria Gostrey, who runs away rather than lie or stop telling the story. Maria says at the end that Strether has been vague. He has also, of course, been benevolent. He is more like a Dickens than a James, trying to see the best in people, wanting his characters to be moral as well as dashing. James's method is to show the special bent of Strether's vague and curious benevolence almost unobtrusively set in a routine process of consciousness. What is there in this passage that is coloured by the viewpoint of Strether and his storytelling? He straightway takes the couple for 'very happy persons' on the pretty slight evidence of their dress, their youth, the day, the boating, and nothing else. He sees them as having pulled 'pleasantly' from somewhere else. But much of what he says and thinks is rightly inferred from what is before him. Strether is not a narrator like Emma, who projects her wishful fantasies and interpretations on to highly intransigent materials. Strether needs more malleable stuff to work on. Just as Jane Austen tells us, as well as shows us, that Emma is 'an imaginist', so James gives us many explicit clues, long after we might have ceased to need them. Here he tells us that Strether's inventiveness is active: 'the air quite thickened, at their approach, with further intimations.' The scene is of course created for a narrator by a narrator and the last stroke of irony is that the air was indeed quite right to thicken.

Strether is not the only narrator, only the chief one. Most novels concerned with the nature of narrative—that is, most novels— create tensions between narrators. In *To the Lighthouse*, we have Mr Ramsay, the realist who will not use fantasy and lies even to comfort a child, and Mrs Ramsay, who will, but who also reads James the terrible fairy-story of *The Fisherman's Wife*, thus making it clear that she is no mere sentimental protector of the child. In *The Mill on the Floss* we have the narrow moralising realism of Tom Tulliver, the narrow, powerful fantasy of Stephen's desire, and the strengths and weaknesses of dream, moral scheme, and emotional continuity, in Maggie. In *The Ambassadors* Strether's benevolently coloured vagueness is contrasted with Maria's truthtelling, Little Bilham's kind lies, and Chad's dazzling evasions and omissions, which show him a master of the kind of narrative that will make him succeed in advertising. We also have within single characters the attempt to attend to what really happens and the desire to change by the pressure of wish and faith. This often takes the most subtle form of the benevolent story: Strether, Isabel Archer and Dorothea Brooke do not move from selfish fantasies towards life as it really is but from self-abnegatory fantasies towards a different story. There is a conflict between the story they tell themselves—about marrying Casaubon, helping society, marrying Gilbert Osmond, not marrying Lord Warburton, living hard no matter how, and so forth—and the harder, more realistic story their author has written for them. Yet in a sense the story these heroic characters try to live does shape their lives too. The ironies are blurred and complex.

Dreams are productive when they lead to productive conflicts. Stories need not be just lies.

But there are novelists who show a larger discrepancy between the inner narrative and the novel. Gissing and Hardy write about characters very like the heroic figures in James and George Eliot—but characters who do not succeed in making their fantasy in any sense productive, who indeed fail most bitterly by the imaginative energy involved in telling the story of life as they wish to lead it. Tess is a passive instance, involved and manipulated by her family's narrative, in all its socially significant and pathetic crudeness, rather than by her own energies. Jude is the classical instance of failure of imagination, since the tale he tells himself can have no substance and would have been better untold. Gissing's heroes are often like Hardy's. In *Born in Exile* the hero creates an enterprising narrative and role, explicitly and intelligently attempting to give society what it wants in order to take what he wants. Gissing shows the social impulse to lie, in the extreme inventiveness of the man who is essentially a novelist's creation, who researches for his lie, dresses for it, moves into the right environment, and acts it out, right to the point of collapse. He shows here, as in *New Grub Street*, the failure to impose and sustain a certain kind of story, though in *Born in Exile* the breakdown is weak, coming out of accidental, though probable, discovery, rather than out of socially and psychologically expressive action. Gissing diverts the interest and misses a fine opportunity, failing to finish his story properly, like his hero. Indeed, the two failures may be related. Gissing may fail because he cannot carry through a story about a man who lives a lie—or rather, about a man of such imagination and humanity. His novels are indeed full of more simplified minor characters, like some of the successful writers in *New Grub Street*, who lie successfully by finding the right formula and telling the right story to themselves and others in the right place at the right time and in the right style.

There are also novelists and novels who are more optimistic about the stories people tell, who show the productiveness of fantasy. In Joyce and Beckett we see the healing power or the sheer survival of mythmaking, of telling stories about past and future and identity, even in the face of a dislocation of time and identity. The nostalgias and unrealities and comfort of the dream of youth, love and past happiness, for instance, are set against Molly Bloom's sexually obsessed repetitions—another narrative novelists did not invent—

and against the harshness of infidelity and impotence and the grander nostalgias of the *Odyssey*. In Beckett the human beings tell stories in the least promising circumstances, in the mud, dragging the sacks, jabbed and jabbing: they tell the incoherent story of life as they feel its pressures, with the odd sweet flash of what seems to be memory. The novels of Beckett are about the incorrigibility of narrative, and indeed the pessimistic novelist who wrote a story in which narrative as an act of mind had collapsed would clearly be telling lies about the relation of his own creativity to his own pessimism. Novelists are expected to show the story going on. But in Beckett the productiveness of story, joke, memory or dream is rudimentary, spasmodic, often absurd. Narrative survives, no more.

There are novelists who are less clearly in command of the relation between the storytelling of their characters and the novel in which the stories are told and discussed. Jane Austen creates novels in which characters learn to imagine scrupulously, and feel correctly, in response to the sense of probability. Her novels might be said to describe the difference between writing a Gothic novel and a novel by Jane Austen, to reveal the assimilation of so much parody and criticism of the wrong kind of story. But Mrs Gaskell, Dickens and George Eliot write novels which set out to show a similar process of learning how to dispense with fantasy but which in the end succumb to fantasy after all. And here too, as in Gissing, is a kind of understandable inconsistency: they are attempting what they know, even if they fail.

In *North and South* we have a *Bildungsroman* in which Margaret Hale tells herself a story, a fable about North and South. The novel tests, corrects and dispels this story and others. The narrative is full of supporting cases, not just of blatant and apparently deliberate instances of differences between North and South, but of people telling stories. Bessy Higgins—dying of poverty and consumption—tells the common story of Heaven, which her father sees as the sustaining fantasy she needs—the opiate of the people. Mr Hale tells himself a story about leading a new life in the North. Mrs Thornton tells a story about North and South too, and a more interesting and personally-coloured story about her son and the marriage he may make. Margaret also tells other stories. One is about saving her brother's reputation and bringing about a family reunion. Whenever character comes up against character there is an immediate narrative reaction, and the marked social and regional contrast encourages social fable, though the significant narratives that are tried and dispelled are moral and psychological. Mrs Gaskell is sometimes said to be a rather mechanical and sensational plot-maker, but I have been struck by the way the heavily plotted parts of this novel (almost like sensation-novels in capsule form) eventually have the effect of showing up the falsity and sensationalism of the stories the characters tell. The story about Margaret's brother brings out not only her fantasy of rescue and reunion but also the lie that she has told herself about her own moral principles and the lie that Thornton has told himself about her moral nature. Mrs Gaskell was clearly interested in the way we tell high moral tales about ourselves and each other and our institutions. This novel takes us and the characters through the complex process of adjusting and rejecting untrue and unreal stories. Through but not beyond.

It ends with the reconciliation of Margaret and Thornton, which subsidises his new liberalised attitudes and activities, and with the fabulous story of the financial failure and the lucky legacy. The novel which criticises sensational narrative ends with the plotting of the sensation novel, and we run up against a concluding fable after all, one which resembles the stories that have been tested and found wanting, in its falsity and its ready usableness.

Such a self-division is not a weakness peculiar to Mrs Gaskell. We find it in Dickens and George Eliot too. They write novels about growing away from the romantic daydream into a realistic acceptance, but most of their novels—except perhaps *Middlemarch*—end with the dream-conclusion and wish-fulfilment. *David Copperfield* tells the story of a novelist who learns to discipline his heart, and though there is an interesting lack of connection between his development as a novelist and his development as a man, he certainly thinks he learns to stop dreaming by hearing other people's stories and finding the traps and dangers of his own. This is to express the course of the novel too simply and lucidly. The brilliant parodies of calf-love are anticipations, both literary and psychological, of David's blindness, and we follow him into the 'real' world. Unfortunately, neither the Wordsworthian imitation of natural sublimities in Switzerland nor the saintly and rocklike qualities of Agnes act convincingly to clear the heady air, and the final harmony of financial, professional, moral and domestic successes seems more dreamlike and unreal than anything that has gone before. Not only do we move towards a concluding dream after criticising the dangers of dreaming, but we move further and further away from the real world, while more and more is salvaged by plot and idealised invocation. *David Copperfield* is Dickens's most divided novel, I believe, but a similar self-destructiveness and contradiction exists in most of his other books.

Dickens's attempt to criticise fantasy may often fail because of his personal dependence on sexual fantasy, and because he seems to have been trapped within a fairly common Victorian conflict between faith in the individual and despair about society. Almost the reverse might be said of George Eliot, but she too illustrates the attempt to supplant fantasy by realism, and an interestingly uncontrolled reversion to fantasy. As in Dickens, her characters tell stories to each other, to themselves, try to impose the stories, try to live by them, try to 'escape or escape to'. She puts an enormous energy of imagination and intelligence into a critical analysis of the stories we tell about life. There is no doubt about the life-enhancing realism she sees as her end: it is unfantastic and realistic. She speaks of gradually losing poetry and accepting prose, and all her novels explore the moral consequences of sterile dreaming and productive realism. She shows an interpenetration of many narrative modes that does not come into earlier English novels: of social myth, the literary fantasy, the sustained and culture-fed fantasy, the imaginative fantasy (Maggie's), the ethically noble fantasy (Dorothea's), and the feeble but still potent fantasy (Hetty's), and the tempting nightmare (Gwendolen's). As an analyst of narrative she stands with Stendhal and Flaubert. But in one novel she too succumbs as Mrs Gaskell and Dickens succumb.

We follow Maggie Tulliver's progress through the dreamworld of a child's fantasy-life, to varied deprivations, sufficiently individualised and sufficiently common. We follow her through the solicitations and failure of the fantasies of literature, myth, music, religion and sexual desire. George Eliot not only analyses the individual qualities of the different stories Maggie listens to and tells herself, but shows their mutual influence, correction, tension and interpenetration. Maggie's fantasies are not knocked down like ninepins, but leave their traces even when they have been explicitly discarded: we see her giving up the nourishing fantasies of wish-fulfilling childish story, Romantic poetry and Scott, and Thomas à

Kempis, but eventually each is shown to be a remaining influence, for both good and evil. But at the end, after such a searching and scrupulous analysis, and after taking her heroine into a solitude few Victorian fictional characters ever know, she too falls back into fantasy: the answer to prayer, the healing flood, the return to the past, forgiveness, the brother's embrace, and—most subtle illusion—forgiveness and understanding newborn in Tom's eyes. The novel refuses the prose realities, and saves its heroine from the pains of fresh starts and conflicts by invoking the very narrative consolation it has been concerned to analyse and deny.

Are such failures Victorian weaknesses? The proximity of Providence? We might perhaps look again at Proust, Forster, Virginia Woolf, and even Joyce, and find something like the narrative solution which retreats into fantasy. How often do we as students of politics, self, or literature, make the move from realism back to fantasy again, and translate the despair and pain as stoicism, the madness as aesthetic eloquence, the disorder as a new order? It is hard to stop telling stories.

First published in *Novel*, Fall 1968, in the series 'Towards a Poetics of Fiction' and revised for my book *Tellers and Listeners* (Athlone Press, London, 1975).

2. Objects in Novels

Caricaturists seize eagerly on accessory objects, feeling them to be an important part of the appearance and even the essence of a character, visual, memorable, and an aid to making people more object-like. A public figure may be conveniently turned into a thing, by being brought closer to a hat, a cigar or a pipe. Such identification of person with object turns up frequently in literature. As we remember novels, we tend first to remember their people: Robinson Crusoe, Pamela, Oliver Twist, the Micawbers, Thomas Mann's Hans Castorp, Sartre's Roquentin, Ursula and Gudrun, Leopold Bloom and Holden Caulfield. But we may promptly think of their accessories and accoutrements: Crusoe's hair-covered clothes, clumsy pots and boat made too far from the sea; Pamela's essential pen and ink; Oliver Twist's empty and defiant porridge bowl; the Micawbers' chops and drink, and the object-like twins taking turns at Mrs Micawber's bosom; Hans Castorp's pencil and thermometer; Roquentin's pieces of paper; Ursula and Gudrun's coloured stockings; Leopold Bloom's lemon soap and potato; Holden Caulfield's baseball glove, written on by his dead brother. When we think of characters with whom objects are vividly identified as adjuncts or important possessions, a pattern emerges: most of the objects are essential to survival. Crusoe and Pamela would have died without their clothes, vessels, and writing materials. The energy and resilience of the Micawbers, Oliver, and Holden Caulfield, whose physical and moral survival is no easy matter, are demonstrated by their way with things.

Clothes, food, notebooks, pens, brushes, domestic objects, are vital to our lives, as extensions of body and mind, tools of the trade, and survival kits, like those in Beckett's *How It Is*, where the characters have sacks to carry tins, tins to hold food, and tin-openers, to open tins and to jab each other, in attack and attachment. Clearly, such extensions are what we need. One may not even give a lecture without enough objects to overflow a tray in 'Kim's Game', a watch, paper, books, a typewriter, spectacles, clothing, cars, buses, trains and aeroplanes. Some of these objects provide an environment which enlarges and enhances, others restrict and confine. Our limbs are not clever or strong or ferocious enough, and we extend their powers with machines. Our bodies are covered with protective clothing. Our food and shelter are provided by an elaborate array of complicated objects that feed and service each other. But what is creative and enlarging may also be restrictive.

Mrs Gamp's umbrella was so much a part of her character that it gave a name to the language. It animatedly provides an instance of the extension of character:

> It was a troublesome matter to adjust Mrs. Gamp's luggage to her satisfaction; for every package belonging to that lady had the inconvenient property of requiring to be put in a boot by itself, and to have no other luggage near it, on pain of actions at law for heavy damages against the proprietors of the coach. The umbrella with the circular patch was particularly hard to be got rid of, and several times thrust out its battered brass nozzle from improper crevices and chinks, to the great terror of the other passengers. Indeed, in her intense anxiety to find a haven of refuge for this chattel, Mrs. Gamp so often moved it, in the course of five minutes, that it seemed not one umbrella but fifty. At length it was lost, or said to be; and for the next five minutes she was face to face with the coachman, go wherever he might, protesting that it should be 'made good', though she took the question to the House of Commons.
>
> (*Martin Chuzzlewit*, Ch. 29)

The umbrella is like its owner, violent, aggressive, and self-important. Her way with it, morally and comically, is her way with the world. Woman and object blend into each other, through Dickens' brilliant animistic sense which makes memorable and uncomfortably vivacious[1] so many objects, like the door-knocker on Scrooge's house, the grave-stones in *Great Expectations*, and the junk in the old curiosity shop, on which the narrator-character reflects analytically as he pictures Nell sleeping peacefully in her bizarre surroundings:

> We are so much in the habit of allowing impressions to be made upon us by external objects, which should be produced by reflection alone, but which, without such visible aids, often escape us, that I am not sure I should have been so thoroughly possessed by this one subject, but for the heaps of fantastic things I had seen huddled together in the curiosity-dealer's warehouse. These, crowding on my mind, in connection with the child, and gathering round her, as it were, brought her condition palpably before me.
>
> (*The Old Curiosity Shop*, Ch. 1)

He goes on meditating on her future, turning the objects into 'a crowd of grotesque companions', with Nell 'the only pure, fresh, youthful object in the throng'.

Nell sleeps unabashed by the old, the twisted, the grotesque, and the rusty things, but the chamber of strange and aged objects, collected appropriately and rapaciously by her old, twisted, worn-out grandfather, is her environment. It determines and constricts her. Dickens makes in passing the interesting technical observation about the power of visual objects, and he uses them, as so often, to fix and symbolise the world in which innocence finds it hard to survive. But the objects around us do not exist just as symbols; their physical burdens may weigh us down and hamper our movements. Mrs Gamp extended and expressed herself through her things, Nell is impeded by hers, as is another heroine, Isabel Archer, in Henry James's *The Portrait of a Lady*. Isabel is innocent, poor, romantic, and believes in freedom. Her attempt to be free shows up the power of that inanimate world of which Gilbert Osmond, her husband, is so powerful a devotee. Isabel's early desire to get along without possessions and decorations, to lead a free and unconditioned life, a gloriously unshelled existence like that of a newborn chick, is rebuked by Madame Merle, worldly speaker for the object world, in which she moves unspontaneously and stealthily, manipulated and manipulating in the service of the false gods of money and possessions:

> "When you've lived as long as I you'll see that every human being has his shell and that you must take the shell into account.

By the shell I mean the whole envelope of circumstances. There's no such thing as an isolated man or woman; we're each of us made up of some cluster of appurtenances. What shall we call our 'self'? Where does it begin? Where does it end? It overflows into everything that belongs to us—and then it flows back again. I know a large part of myself is in the clothes I choose to wear. I've a great respect for *things*! One's self—for other people—is one's expression of one's self; and one's house, one's furniture, one's garments, the books one reads, the company one keeps—these things are all expressive."

(*The Portrait of a Lady*, Ch. 19)

Isabel demurs: 'Nothing that belongs to me is any measure of me; everything's on the contrary a limit, a barrier, and a perfectly arbitrary one.' Neither Madame Merle nor Isabel is quite right. Madame Merle fails to observe the horror implicit in her own metaphor of selfhood flowing into what belongs to us, and 'then . . . back again,' with all the contamination and reification that may imply. Isabel is wrong in saying that the limits and barriers are arbitrary. She is to discover, as we mostly do, that we cannot ignore the social envelope, and that it envelops the intention to be free. Thus we see her after her marriage to the sterile dilettante, at one of their evenings, 'poor human-hearted Isabel', woman weighed down by her clothes, enclosed within a woman's social envelope. Like Dorothea Brooke, and many women inside and outside novels she feels imprisoned by house, furniture, clothes, and conventions, that do not express her, but enclose her, or, worse, absorb her into their mechanisms. Objects become deadly in Henry James. He knew as precisely as his great predecessor, Thackeray, that there is a cruel sense in which, as Lady Kew says to Ethel Newcome in *The Newcomes*, 'We belong to our belongings'. For other instances we might go to *Women in Love*, where in an attempt not to belong to the belongings of a past time, conventions, and institutions, Ursula and Birkin refuse to take the Jane Austen chair they have bought. We may also observe, as Lawrence failed to, that they give it to a less free and mobile couple. In his Preface to *The Spoils of Poynton* Henry James spoke of the germ of history and his recognition of the ruling passion expressed in the spoils. The Things, he decided early on, would be central to the story, typical of our society's passion for things. He slyly plays with the metaphor 'thing' as he talks about the real things:

One thing was 'in it,' in the sordid situation, on the first blush, and one thing only—though this, in its limited way, no doubt, a curious enough value: the sharp light it might project on that most modern of our current passions, the fierce appetite for the upholsterer's and joiner's and brazier's work, the chairs and tables, the cabinets and presses, the material odds and ends, of the more labouring ages.

He brooded on the Balzacian problem of doing the things. 'They would have to be presented . . . painted . . . something would have to be done for them. . . .'

Balzac is invoked in the discussion of things by another novelist, as one who presided over the presentation of things in the nineteenth-century novel. In his essay, 'A Future for the Novel', Alain Robbe-Grillet has this to say:

Objectivity in the ordinary sense of the word—total impersonality of observation—is all too obviously an illusion. But *freedom* of observation should be possible, and yet it is not. At every moment, a continuous fringe of culture (psychology, ethics, metaphysics, etc.) is added to things, giving them a less alien aspect, one that is more comprehensible, more reassuring. Sometimes the camouflage is complete: a gesture vanishes from our mind, supplanted by the emotions which supposedly produced it, and we remember a landscape as *austere* or *calm* without being able to evoke a single outline, a single determining element. Even if we immediately think, 'That's literary,' we don't try to react against the thought. We accept the fact that what is *literary* (the word has become pejorative) functions like a grid or screen set with bits of different coloured glass that fracture our field of vision into tiny assimilable facets.

And if something resists this systematic appropriation of the visual, if an element of the world breaks the glass, without finding any place in the interpretative screen, we can always make use of our convenient category of 'the absurd' in order to absorb this awkward residue.

But the world is neither significant nor absurd. It *is*, quite simply. That, in any case, is the most remarkable thing about it. . . . Around us, defying the noisy pack of our animistic or protective adjectives, things *are there*, their surfaces are distinct and smooth, *intact*, neither suspiciously brilliant nor transparent. All our literature has not yet succeeded in eroding their smallest corner, in flattening their slightest curve.[2]

Robbe-Grillet suggests that the intransigent thingness of the object-world is thrust on our attention, transformed in dimension and colour, by the cinema, an art engaged, heir of the novel as it is, in using images to signify ethics, psychology and metaphysics, but which can't help presenting the visual excess, the 'hard, unalterable, eternally present' objects, 'mocking their own meaning'. There is a sense in which Henry James is guilty of what Robbe-Grillet calls signification. Every adornment on the furniture, every splash on the marble floor, every turn of the screw, amounts to meaning, is expressive of a society, a time, a human nature, a relationship, a story. Nevertheless, the Victorians weren't quite as naive as Robbe-Grillet thinks. They were aware, as they performed their characteristic act of bestowing meaning on the object-world, that this was precisely what they were doing. In George Eliot and Henry James, there is an important gap between the object-world and the animating human presence. That gap is a small one; Robbe-Grillet cannot be entirely right about the mocking of meaning. Objects do express certain significations, those of their manufacture, their history, their purchase, their price, their origin in capital and labour. They were made by people for people. This is of course not true of natural objects, and some of the coldest and most frightening objects outside us are 'natural', that is, mineral or the most mineral-like bits of vegetable, or parts of animals and vegetables, made objects by detachment and dilapidation. (Surrealist art frequently mingles the man-made and the natural objects.) When dealing with the world of man-made objects, James and George Eliot resist the opportunity and the temptation to make them totally significant.

They do this in two ways: by showing the act of significance-making within character, and by showing a loss of significance. The simplest example of each kind may be found in George Eliot, who has her own way of revealing disenchantment—her word for lack of centrality or the sense that the exterior world, as Robbe-Grillet says, has lost its interiority. She shows light falling starkly on familiar objects, chairs, tables, chests of drawers and draining significance from them.[3] She also shows how meaning is conferred on objects:

Yet even in this stage of withering a little incident happened, which showed that the sap of affection was not all gone. It was one of his daily tasks to fetch his water from a well a couple of fields off, and for this purpose, ever since he came to Raveloe, he had had a brown earthenware pot, which he held as his most precious utensil, among the very few conveniences he had granted himself. It had been his companion for twelve years, always standing on the same spot, always lending its handle to him in the early morning, so that its form had an expression for him of willing helpfulness, and the impress of its handle on his palm gave a satisfaction mingled with that of having the fresh clear water. One day as he was returning from the well, he stumbled against the step of the stile, and his brown pot, falling with force against the stones that overarched the ditch below him, was broken in three pieces. Silas picked up the pieces and carried them home with grief in his heart. The brown pot could never be of use to him any more, but he stuck the bits together and propped the ruin in its old place for a memorial.

(Silas Marner, Ch. 2)

Even with an object whose inherent function is plainly valuable, the life-giving one of carrying water, a bestowal of extra significance is possible. Silas has lost the human world, and turns for companionship to the coins who turn to him. Their faces are not loved, as they are by some misers (Anna's father, Tellwright, in *Anna of the Five Towns*, for example), for their monetary value, but as the faces of friends. The object world is given a needed humanity or interiority. The novelist, however, clearly sees the nature of the imaginative act of transference, how it works, and why. It is Silas who loves the things, coins and jugs, not George Eliot. Well-worn anthropomorphic metaphors—expression, handle, face—are revived, to show relationship. Silas creates it:

. . . the money had come to mark off his weaving into periods, and the money not only grew, but it remained with him. He began to think it was conscious of him, as his loom was, and he would on no account have exchanged those coins, which had become his familiars, for other coins with unknown faces. (Ch. 2)

The pathetic fallacy is analysed, not relied upon.

Turning back now to *The Spoils of Poynton* we see a more elaborate analysis. James is using objects in two ways. No novelist, not even Robbe-Grillet, can avoid the representation of the social surface, typical of time, place, class, purchasing-power. (*Jealousy*'s deadpan landscape presents a twentieth-century wealthy couple on a banana plantation.) The other use of objects is also unavoidable, or avoidable only by a gross act of distortion which far from rendering things as they *are* tears them violently apart from human making, caring, preserving and adoring. One of the odd things in the heavily filled object-fields of Robbe-Grillet is the separateness of objects. No one seems to have cared for them, to have given them to anyone. Human beings are related to objects by the obsessed gaze of the jealous eye, which is the source of Robbe-Grillet's own romantic animation of objects.

In the *Spoils* James cunningly combines a few particulars with a generalised impression. This is how we first see and feel the objects in Poynton, through the eyes and emotions of Fleda Vetch who

> discovered for herself that Poynton was the record of a life. It was written in great syllables of colour and form, the tongues of other countries and the hands of rare artists. It was all France and Italy, with their ages composed to rest. For England you looked out of old windows—it was England that was the wide embrace. While outside, on the low terraces, she contradicted gardeners and refined on nature, Mrs. Gereth left her guest to finger fondly the brasses that Louis Quinze might have thumbed, to sit with Venetian velvets just held in a loving palm, to hang over cases of enamels and pass and repass before cabinets. There were not many pictures—the panels and the stuffs were themselves the picture; and in all the great wainscoted house there was not an inch of pasted paper. (Ch. III)

However, while taste and style are applauded, mere possessions, even of supreme aesthetic and historic interest, are not the point. James expressly disclaims 'avidity'. Even though Mrs Gereth is fearful of the intrusion of Mona's 'Little belongings and hoards—cheap gimcracks' thrust in 'on top of my treasures', the sanctuary is valued for private reasons, as created by husband and wife, from energy and intelligence rather than mere money:

> 'I could give up everything without a pang, I think, to a person I could trust, I could respect. . . . The best things here, as you know, are the things your father and I collected, things all that we worked for and waited for and suffered for . . . almost starved for! They were our religion, they were our life, they were *us*!' (Ch. III)

The pervasive sense of the things as spoils in a desperate battle is impressive, but it is joined with the sense of their sacredness as memorial. This is clearly brought out when Mrs Gereth's sense of value and order creates another sanctuary out of the maiden aunt's possessions at Ricks. This making of a new harmony makes plain not only the subordination of monetary and aesthetic value, but also explains what Mrs Gereth means by saying that the objects need love and care. Fleda comes to comprehend such caring as she embarks on a life of similar sad maidenhood, after losing both the spoils of Poynton and Owen Gereth:

> 'Ah, the little melancholy, tender, tell-tale things: how can they *not* speak to you and find a way to your heart? It's not the great chorus of Poynton; but you're not, I'm sure, either so proud or so broken as to be reached by nothing but that. This is a voice so gentle, so human, so feminine—a faint far-away voice with the little quaver of a heart-break. You've listened to it unawares. . . .
> 'If there were more there would be too many to convey the impression in which half the beauty resides—the impression somehow of something dreamed and missed, something reduced, relinquished, resigned: the poetry, as it were, of something sensibly *gone*. . . . something here that will never be in the inventory. . . .
> ' . . . a kind of fourth dimension. . . . a perfume, a touch. It's a soul, a story, a life.' (Ch. XXI)

The women of course see the point that there will be ghosts like this at Poynton too. But James does not allow this to happen. Fleda is, unlike the maiden aunt, offered a treasure as souvenir, the gem of the collection, 'the thing in the whole house that's most beautiful and precious' and the gift is offered with passion; it is also accepted with passion, in a perfect understanding and reciprocity:

> Would she act upon his offer? She would act with secret rapture. To have as her own something splendid that he had given her, of which the gift had been his signed desire, would be a greater joy than the greatest she had believed to be left her. . . . a thousand times yes—her choice should know no scruple. . . . it should be one of the finest because it was in the finest he saw his symbol. (Ch. XXII)

James destroys Poynton, in one of those splendid symbolic

burnings in Victorian fiction, but unlike the burnings in Brontë and Meredith, it settles nothing except the question of symbolism. There are many possible reasons for the ending, and I propose that amongst them is James's sense that to rescue a symbol from such loss, while tempting, is inadequate. The novel asserts the old and common value of the keepsake, the souvenir, the object that not only commemorates a time past but was designed, by a donor for a beloved, to be such a memorial. It incorporates also that equally old and common sense that memorials are fragile and heart-breaking. After such losses, what souvenirs?

Throughout this drama, James sees the human beings creating complicity, while observing, of course, that there is a reciprocity in the relation of person and object. As Madame Merle said, we flow into the envelope and then flow back. When we flow back, we take some of the object stuff with us. In a way, the burning at the end of the *Spoils* stops this process, as well as ensuring that the objects themselves will die and not survive without love. It is the human beings who do this.

Human beings love objects, and use objects in their relationships. *The Golden Bowl* exhibits the object playing a role in a personal drama, crucial to plot and as active in symbolism. Its first appearance is as solid and objective as Robbe-Grillet might require, and it even resembles his *choses* in presenting an enigmatic appearance, which may mean this or that. In a world of speculation, purchase and connoisseurship, however, appearances are supplemented by prices, and as soon as Amerigo is told the price he knows there must be something wrong. Given the nature of the object, crystal covered with gold-leaf, that something must be a crack. Here is the bowl as it first emerges from its case in the Bloomsbury shop:

> . . . he extracted a square box, of some twenty inches in height, covered with worn-looking leather. He placed the box on the counter, pushed back a pair of small hooks, lifted the lid and removed from its nest a drinking-vessel larger than a common cup, yet not of exorbitant size, and formed, to appearance, either of old fine gold or of some material once richly gilt. He handled it with tenderness, with ceremony, making a place for it on a small satin mat. 'My Golden Bowl,' he observed—and it sounded on his lips as if it said everything. He left the important object—for as 'important' it did somehow present itself—to produce its

certain effect. Simple but singularly elegant, it stood on a circular foot, a short pedestal with a slightly spreading base, and, though not of signal depth, justified its title by the charm of its shape as well as by the tone of its surface. It might have been a large goblet diminished, to the enhancement of its happy curve, by half its original height. As formed of solid gold it was impressive; it seemed indeed to warn off the prudent admirer. Charlotte, with care, immediately took it up, while the Prince, who had after a minute shifted his position again, regarded it from a distance. (Book I, Ch. VI)

The golden bowl relates to the symbol of life in Ecclesiastes, and also becomes a commodity whose movement on the market is eloquent. The shopkeeper sells it to Maggie, but repents and the repentance discloses the story of Amerigo's and Charlotte's visit to his shop. Fanny Assingham throws it to the ground and exposes its weakness. Maggie sticks together the three pieces and presents the assembly to Amerigo, as a signal of discovery and an image of a patched-up triangle. The bowl is clearly hard-worked. But it resembles many other objects in the everyday drama of donation portrayed by nineteenth-century novels. There is the silver knife in *Mansfield Park* which Fanny Price gives to her sister, healing a rift, and demonstrating her own promotion from the status of taker to giver. It is an object which most sensitively signals moral change in a novel full of significant presents, some loving, some thoughtful, some careless, some seductive. There are the significant fairings of *Vanity Fair*, stolen, scrounged, given in love, solicitation, and exhibitionism: a dictionary, a bouquet, a white muslin dress, a French officer's epaulets, medal (Cross of the Legion of Honour) and sword-hilt, 'relics from the field of battle' which Becky Sharp sends hopefully to Miss Crawley, her aunt-in-law, pretending that they were Rawdon's spoils, though in reality Becky has bought them, Thackeray tells us, 'for a few francs, from one of the innumerable pedlars . . . of the war.'[4] Our ceremonies of donation,[5] like our symbol-making, are part of everyday life, adopted as devices by fiction.

The novelist analyses the social and emotional significance of objects. But objects are of course part of the novelist's technique. Certain objects perform a function or possess an identity *because* they exist in a novel. The object may be there to give the ring of truth, to clink or clang noisily in a silent world, to protrude in a flat

land of two dimensions. It proffers its particularity, a counter of
weight and promise. All it can really do is to shift us, illusorily, from
one plane of imitation to another, but in so doing, it has its own
mimetic strength. It can also undermine mimesis by drawing
attention to it. The varying ways in which the object can assert
solidity and particularity, making a sudden appearance to vouch for
reality, yet mocking realism, is strikingly visible, indeed almost
tangible, in the behaviour of two coins. The first comes from Scott
Fitzgerald's unfinished novel, *The Last Tycoon*:

> 'Skip the dialogue for a minute,' said Stahr. 'Granted your
> dialogue is more graceful than what these hacks can write—that's
> why we brought you out here. But let's imagine something that
> isn't either bad dialogue or jumping down a well. Has your office
> got a stove in it that lights with a match?'
> 'I think it has,' said Boxley stiffly, '—but I never use it.'
> 'Suppose you're in your office. You've been fighting duels or
> writing all day and you're too tired to fight or write any more.
> You're sitting there staring—dull, like we all get sometimes. A
> pretty stenographer that you've seen before comes into the room
> and you watch her idly. She doesn't see you, though you're
> very close to her. She takes off her gloves, opens her purse and
> dumps it out on a table—'
> Stahr stood up, tossing his key-ring on his desk.
> 'She has two dimes and a nickel—and a cardboard match box.
> She leaves the nickel on the desk, puts the two dimes back into
> her purse and takes her black gloves to the stove, opens it and
> puts them inside. There is one match in the match box and she
> starts to light it kneeling by the stove. You notice that there's a
> stiff wind blowing in the window—but just then your telephone
> rings. The girl picks it up, says hello—listens—and says
> deliberately into the phone, "I've never owned a pair of black
> gloves in my life." She hangs up, kneels by the stove again, and
> just as she lights the match, you glance around very suddenly and
> see that there's another man in the office, watching every move
> the girl makes—'
> Stahr paused. He picked up his keys and put them in his
> pocket.
> 'Go on,' said Boxley, smiling. 'What happens?'
> 'I don't know,' said Stahr. 'I was just making pictures.'
> Boxley felt he was being put in the wrong.
> 'It's just melodrama,' he said.
> 'Not necessarily,' said Stahr. 'In any case, nobody has moved

violently or talked cheap dialogue or had any facial expression at all. There was only one bad line, and a writer like you could improve it. But you were interested.'

'What was the nickel for?' asked Boxley evasively.

'I don't know,' said Stahr. Suddenly he laughed. 'Oh, yes—the nickel was for the movies.'

The two invisible attendants seemed to release Boxley. He relaxed, leaned back in his chair and laughed.

'What in hell do you pay me for?' he demanded. 'I don't understand the damn stuff.'

'You will,' said Stahr grinning, 'or you wouldn't have asked about the nickel.' (Ch. III)

Here the novel is analysing the function of assertive objects, particularising and seizing attention, in the film. But the analysis of cinematic art brings the solidity and arbitrary appearance of an object into the novel. Stahr's key-ring, which is the stand-in for the objects he is imagining, is tossed on the desk and picked up again, as any object casually and arbitrarily found in his pocket might have been handled, and so particularly solid-seeming, innocent of meaning. Just an object.

My second coin, a ten-franc piece from Gide's *The Counterfeiters*, works in almost the opposite way, by coincidence, coming pat upon its cue. Edouard, the novel's novelist, also writing a novel which may be called *The Counterfeiters*, though it is growing beyond that title as he ruminates on it in mind and in notebooks, tries to give an instance of his theme. He wants to show the 'struggle between what reality offers him and what he himself desires to make of it':

'Has it ever happened to you to hold a counterfeit coin in your hands?' he asked at last.

'Yes,' said Bernard; but the two women's 'No' drowned his voice.

'Well, imagine a false ten-franc piece. In reality it's not worth two sous. But it will be worth ten francs as long as no one recognizes it to be false. So if I start from the idea that . . .'

'But why start from an idea?' interrupted Bernard impatiently. 'If you were to start from a fact and make a good exposition of it, the idea would come of its own accord to inhabit it. If I were writing *The Counterfeiters* I should begin by showing the counterfeit coin—the little ten-franc piece you were speaking of just now.' (Part II, Ch. III)

And Bernard pulls a small coin out of his pocket and throws it on to the table. The novelist dexterously brings together stubborn 'outside' particularity, Bernard's 'real' coin, unexpected and not exactly as Edouard has imagined it (worth a little more than two sous, we notice), with the more abstract idea Edouard is talking about. The struggle between what the world gives and what the novelist wants, in advance, to make, is instantly dramatised. Bernard goes on, rather like Stahr:

> 'Just hear how true it rings. Almost the same sound as the real one. One would swear it was gold. I was taken in by it this morning, just as the grocer who passed it on to me had been taken in himself, he told me. It isn't quite the same weight, I think; but it has the brightness and the sound of a real piece; it is coated with gold, so that, all the same, it is worth a little more than two sous; but it's made of glass. It'll wear transparent. No; don't rub it; you'll spoil it. One can almost see through it, as it is.' (Part II, Ch. III)

That last sentence oscillates functionally between literal and metaphorical meanings. The 'real' counterfeit coin suits Gide's book, though not Edouard's, as it effectively disturbs the illusion, like Cleopatra's reference to the boy-actor who 'will' perform, and in fact is, performing her story. It shifts us from one level to another. There is a small but functionally conspicuous creak as we change gear, to remind us that reality is elusive and recedes from our avid and cunning grasp. It reminds us of that hard world of uncooperative existence which Robbe-Grillet yearns for, as well as brilliantly solving the novelist's problem of how to make us see the invisible, touch the intangible. 'Don't rub it' is a dramatic rendering of appearances. No wonder that Edouard ends by admitting to Bernard that 'the reality' interests but also 'disturbs' him.

The rendering of these objects is part of the special themes of film-making and novel-writing, in these two aesthetically self-conscious novels, part too of the general problem of particularity's reluctant marriage to abstraction. The dramatisation of the object-world takes another form in the novels of Arnold Bennett, unfairly derided by Virginia Woolf for their inert rendering of human nature in terms of its envelope of things and their prices and origins. If we look at Edwin Clayhanger building his house or Anna Tellwright painting a plate in a pottery, we can see that person and object are vitally related. Anna is intoxicated by the making and doing, is proud of painting the rim round the plate, is drawn to a man by responding strongly to the objects he creates. Edwin is overpowered by the thought of building his house. Bennett creates the relation between man and object while seeing the selection and dramatisation which is performed by the man. While Anna falls in love with the busy factory turning, the novelist reminds us that some of these girls in the painting-shop died of lead-poisoning.

If the novel renders the appearance of the object-world with particular solicitude, in order to imitate solidity or to show the process of such imitation, it can also dislocate the object-world. The novel can show what Sartre calls the 'dilapidation' of the surrealists: in the portrayal of madness, as in Maupassant's story, 'Le Horla', where mirrors do not reflect, where water and milk stealthily vanish from the glasses; in the comic Saponiad of *Ulysses*, where Bloom's voyage is accompanied by the wanderings of his lemon soap; in the creation of bizarre objects like Kafka's star-shaped reel; or in Roquentin's nausea, in *Nausea*, largely shown through the object-world, and suitably illustrated on the cover of the Penguin edition by Salvador Dali's painting, 'The Triangular Hour', with its transformations and dislocations of objects, man-made and natural. Roquentin feels nauseated by the cardboard box, the pebble, the doorknob, the Autodidact's face and hand, by a glass of beer, a piece of paper. Sartre brings out with special emphasis the *feel* of objects:

I am very fond of picking up chestnuts, old rags, and especially pieces of paper. I find it pleasant to pick them up, to close my hand over them; for two pins I would put them to my mouth as children do. Anny used to fly into a rage when I picked up by one corner pieces of paper which were heavy and rich-looking but probably soiled with excrement. In summer or early autumn, you can find in gardens pieces of newspapers baked by the sun, as dry and brittle as dead leaves, and so yellow you might think they had been dipped in picric acid. Other pieces of paper, in winter, are pulped, crumpled, stained; they return to the earth. Others which are new and even shiny, white and palpitating, are as sedate as swans, but the earth has already ensnared them from below. They twist and tear themselves away from the mud, but only to fall a little farther on, this time for good. All these pieces of paper are worth picking up. Sometimes I simply feel them, looking at them closely; at other times I tear them to hear the long crackling noise they make, or else, if they are very wet, I set fire to them, something which is not easy to do; then I wipe the muddy palms of my hands on a wall or a tree trunk.

So, today, I was looking at the fawn-coloured boots of a cavalry officer who was coming out of the barracks. As I followed them with my eyes, I saw a piece of paper lying beside a puddle. I thought that the officer was going to crush the paper into the mud with his heel, but no: with a single step he strode over paper and puddle. I went up to it: it was a lined page, probably torn out of a school notebook. The rain had drenched and twisted it, and it was covered with blisters and swellings, like a burnt hand. The red line of the margin had blurred into a pink smear; the ink had run in places. The bottom of the page was hidden by a crust of mud. I bent down, already looking forward to touching this fresh and tender pulp which would roll into grey balls in my fingers. . . . I couldn't do it.

I stayed in a bent position for a moment, I read: 'Dictation: The White Owl', then I straightened up, empty-handed. I am no longer free, I can no longer do what I want.

Objects ought not to *touch*, since they are not alive. You use them, you put them back in place, you live among them: they are useful, nothing more. But they touch me, it's unbearable. I am afraid of entering in contact with them, just as if they were living animals.

Now I see; I remember better what I felt the other day on the sea-shore when I was holding that pebble. It was a sort of sweet disgust. How unpleasant it was! And it came from the pebble, I'm sure of that, it passed from the pebble into my hands. Yes, that's it, that's exactly it: a sort of nausea in the hands.

(*Nausea*, Diary entry for 29 January 1932.)

Sartre is of course a convenient target for Robbe-Grillet, who analyses his complicity with the object-world. That world may lie at the other extreme of the pathetic fallacy from Robbe-Grillet's impassive renderings of surfaces, which are equally obsessive and personally expressive. Sartre is sickened by alien existence; the narrator in Robbe-Grillet's *Jealousy* is maddened and the curious reader of *The Voyeur* mystified by similar object-enigmas. It does not seem clear that the New Novel, any more than the older novel, renders the world of appearances as entirely alien. How can it? Novels are written by human beings, and the world of objects, loved, hated, preserved, broken, understood, misunderstood, penetrated or inviolate, has to be shown as part of the environment. Despite the difficulty that we cannot see fictional objects, as we can see the objects in the paintings of great still-life painters like Chardin or Morandi, or touch them, as we can in sculpture, we can still be put in close touch with what Lawrence calls the thingness of things. If we take the object-world too much for granted, literature can restore its significance or its lack of significance. The novel can create a second coming of *things*, beautiful or functional, lucid or inscrutable, friendly or obstructive, outside ourselves but connected with us, for better or for worse; adjuncts to life, means of life, ways to death, guns, bibles, jugs, plates, jewels, toys, clothes, stones. The novels show not only our psychological, aesthetic and social relation with objects but probe a little what Wordsworth called the life of things.

First published in *Genre*, Winter 1977.

Notes

1. See especially Dorothy Van Ghent's *The English Novel: Form and Function* (Holt, Rinehart and Winston, New York, 1956) and W. J. Harvey, *Character and the Novel* (Chatto and Windus, London, 1965).
2. *For a New Novel: Essays on Fiction* (Grove Press, New York, 1965); published as *Pour un nouveau roman* (Editions de Minuit, Paris, 1963).
3. I have discussed this subject more fully in *The Novels of George Eliot: A Study in Form* (Athlone Press, London, 1959).
4. For further discussion of Thackeray's handling of objects, see Barbara Hardy, *The Exposure of Luxury: Radical Themes in Thackeray*, (Peter Owen, London, 1972).
5. For discussion of Jane Austen's treatment of donation, see Barbara Hardy, *A Reading of Jane Austen* (Athlone Press, London, 1975).

3. Analysts of Feeling: Joseph Conrad, James Joyce and Samuel Beckett

If we think of the novel as realistic, aiming at verisimilitude or creating an imitation of life, or if we consider realism to be a means rather than an end, it is important to consider the representation of feeling. If we think about the novel's modes of conducting a moral and psychological inquiry, it is essential to look at the representation of human emotion and passion. If we look at language, structures and technique, it is necessary to see that the representation of feeling, the attempt to rouse our feelings, and the attempt to create structures of feelings, are a part of the organisation of fiction.

More novelists than critics have been concerned with the question of representing feeling in fiction. George Eliot was the guest of honour at a dinner party in Cambridge, celebrating the Boat Race, where she was asked by the great Sophocles scholar R. C. Jebb how Sophocles had influenced her. It was one of those ideal conversations one would like to have overheard. The answer was as good as the question. George Eliot replied, 'In the delineation of the great primitive emotions.'[1] Much later, D. H. Lawrence insisted that if we wanted to understand our feelings we should 'look at the real novels, and listen in to the cries of the characters as they wander in the dark woods of their destiny'.[2]

The novelist represents characters who feel. The novelist also deals indirectly or directly, with the question of an authorial feeling and is necessarily aware (and this awareness often comes out explicitly as well as implicitly) of the reader's feeling. The novel is an affective medium. Novelists very often incorporate into the narration, the action, and the presentation of character, that sense of the oddity of literary response. A colleague once said to me, when we had been talking about the death of Paul Dombey, 'Isn't it extraordinary that one should feel for a structure of words?' Novelists sometimes deal with the very question of our extraordinary feeling for fictions. It is one of the themes of Conrad's novel *Lord Jim*. Conrad used his narrator Marlow to engage in an analysis and discussion of the way we feel for other people's stories, and the reasons for our feeling. He is interested in language, in the relation between what we feel and what we say. Looking at his models, his fictitious characters, Conrad stands back and allows Marlow to comment precisely on the relationship between what we may call style and what we may call sensibility. Here are two passages in which Marlow is commenting on the way Jim speaks. Jim is a young Englishman who has wanted to be a romantic hero, and has instead been a murderous traitor, and coward. Here he is remembering and confessing:

> He spoke slowly; he remembered swiftly and with extreme vividness; he could have reproduced like an echo the moaning of the engineer for the better information of these men who wanted facts. After his first feeling of revolt he had come round to the view that only a meticulous precision of statement would bring out the true horror behind the appalling face of things. (Ch. 4)

Throughout this account of Jim's true confessions, Marlow is not only responding as the great compassionate narrator of modern fiction, but is observing with an intelligent and analytic sense of form, style and utterance.

And again, in a passage which carries with it the charge of a powerful simile:

> He wanted to go on talking for truth's sake, perhaps for his own sake also; and while his utterance was deliberate, his mind positively flew round and round the serried circle of facts that had surged up all about him to cut him off from the rest of the kind: it was like a creature that, finding itself imprisoned within an enclosure of high stakes, dashes round and round, distracted in the night, trying to find a weak spot, a crevice, a place to scale, some opening through which it may squeeze itself and escape. This awful activity of mind made him hesitate at times in his speech. . . . (Ch. 4)

The image of the imprisoned creature incisively fixes what Marlow calls the 'awful activity'; the vivid passage is implicitly analytic. Conrad is manipulating complex effects, relating a cool and clear language to an internal frenzy. Jim's feeling about his treachery is entirely assimilated to his feelings about truthful telling; he tries to understand as he tries to make himself understood. Even the final omission points register emotional stress. Conrad's narrative insists on the complexity of the affective medium.

What the narrator brings out here can stand for, and is part of, the novelist's analysis. In his attempt to understand, Marlow describes Jim as creating images which make a medium for feeling. The novelist impresses us at the same time with a sense of the observer's and the character's feeling, and with a sense of a predicament for which we as readers are required to feel. There is very strongly present throughout *Lord Jim* the sense of the difficulty we have in reading our own and other people's feelings. Although there are times when people may say what they feel, truthtelling is no guarantee that the listener will know what they feel. What the character is doing here acts as a model for that peculiar and powerful kind of psychological analysis which the novel provides.

On one more occasion when Jim is telling his story to Marlow, face to face, there is the prominent sense that the narrator is trying to read a character in the way that the reader is trying to read the fiction. Marlow says of Jim:

> He was not speaking to me, he was only speaking before me, in a dispute with an invisible personality, an antagonistic and inseparable partner of his existence—another possessor of his soul. These were issued beyond the competency of a court of inquiry: it was a subtle and momentous quarrel as to the true essence of life, and did not want a judge. He wanted an ally, a helper, an accomplice. (Ch. 8)

Here the rhetoric goes back to the beginning of the novel, in Bunyan's *Pilgrim's Progress*, which represents the inner life through allegory, emblem and image. It is characteristic of Conrad, the author of the story *The Secret Sharer*, that he should articulate that sense of a division within a tormented character. But although this analysis of character is congenial to Conrad, and here done in the trope of an invisible sharer of the soul, it is something traditional, and central in English fiction. Just as the Morality Play analyses the individual into components in order to define and dramatise moral dilemma and moral collision, so the novel uses the mode of allegory both in order to analyse and to show the process of self-struggle. The novel can show the process of an attempt to feel and to make out the nature of the self that feels. This is the kind of investigation which we desire to carry out, and are yet not competent to carry out; we feel we know what is going on inside us, but our inside actions are not wholly accessible to us. This portrayal of experimental hesitancy and indeterminacy is brilliantly typical of Conrad's narrative inquiry.

Conrad dramatises this ambitious and frustrated attempt to analyse. In doing so, he sometimes reveals an ability to pinpoint feelings and passions. For instance, fear. In the following passage Conrad takes a cliché and transforms it. We say, 'don't be afraid— have no fear', emptying the emotional terms of emotion; he takes the phrase 'have no fear', and uses it literally, playfully, and seriously. He permutes it, and in doing so conveys the sense of someone possessed by fear. Abstraction is particularised.

> Nothing easier than to say, Have no fear! Nothing more difficult. How does one kill fear, I wonder? How do you shoot a spectre through the heart, slash off its spectral head, take it by its spectral throat? It is an enterprise you rush into while you dream, and are glad to make your escape with wet hair and every limb shaking. The bullet is not run, the blade not forged, the man not born; even the winged words of truth drop at your feet like lumps of lead. You require for such a desperate encounter an enchanted and poisoned shaft, dipped in a lie too subtle to be found on earth. An enterprise for a dream, my masters! (Ch. 33)

This powerful and subtle passage is not actually a part of the particularisation of character and action, but a piece of vivid imagistic general discourse. Throughout *Lord Jim* (and in other novels too), Marlow is used to establish the point of view of someone trying to understand the nature of feeling, in general and in particular. The structure is highly convoluted. Marlow fixes the point of view of someone trying to make out another man's attempt to comprehend his own feelings, also in general and in particular. Furthermore, Marlow is also the imaginary storyteller who is telling the story to an imaginary group of listeners. Every now and then he appeals to his listeners. He says, for instance:

And it's easy enough to talk of Master Jim, after a good spread, two hundred feet above the sea-level, with a box of decent cigars handy, on a blessed evening of freshness and starlight that would make the best of us forget we are only on sufferance here and have to pick our way in cross lights . . . (Ch. 5)

It is an excursion from the narrative which acts as an intense reminder of the oddity of literary response. We enjoy in some detachment the tragic story of human suffering, like the listeners within the novel, two hundred feet above the sea level with a box of cigars handy. The listeners are an ironic image for the separation of reader and character. The reader is placed at an even greater distance from narrator, listeners, characters, and novelist, and may also be smoking, drinking, or eating as well as laughing and pitying.

On one occasion Marlow admits that the sense of tragedy itself is not the only response to Jim's tragedy. Tragedy is a word which is not absolute, and the response within the novel to Jim is too complex to be called tragic. Marlow says that Jim's thoughts of suicide are not just tragic, but tragic and funny:

It was tragic enough and funny enough in all conscience to call aloud for compassion, and in what was I better than the rest of us to refuse him my pity? (Ch. 11)

This is a comment on a character within the story, by a character within the story, which reminds us of the literary enterprise, and our affective response to it. We are made to recognise the nature of our compassion, to see that in responding to life and in responding to that part of life we call literature, the combination of something tragic with something funny may evoke that compassion.

James Joyce and Samuel Beckett bring together, as no English novelists of our time do with such commanding success, 'something tragic and something funny'. Joyce and Beckett are the two great novelists who are both tragic and comic. Joyce began in *Dubliners* with styles of scrupulous meanness which show his adroit and imaginative use of understatement and avoid sentimentality. Unlike George Eliot in *Scenes of Clerical Life*, he refuses to canvass for the pitiable lives he creates. Frank O'Connor accuses him of creating puppets and caricatures, but no caricatures were endowed with such inner affective existence as the Dubliners. They wish, long, imagine, like themselves, are ambitious, get drunk on alcohol, poetry, music and sex, are religious, savage, angry, frustrated, jealous, patient, heartbroken, loving. They have a full impassioned life. 'Clay', for instance, the story of the little laundress, uses a quiet and unemotional language which strongly evokes the sense of compassion. The characters in the story are callous to Maria, who is not fully aware of the world around her, and is pleased with her own little image and little life. As so often in *Dubliners* Joyce shows the littleness of people as funny and tragic, through a medium which is ridiculing and compassionate.

When he turned from the most objective and detached language of feeling to the most subjective mode, in *A Portrait of the Artist as a Young Man*, it was to devise another and quite different form for feeling. This time the danger lay not in patronising compassion or belittling cruelty, but in an indulgent identification with the dreams and feelings of Stephen Dedalus. Joyce manages to be neither too excited nor too cold. He makes a full use of the free indirect style, which allowed him to keep as close as possible to Stephen's mind and feelings without losing detachment. Furthermore, he extended the free indirect style to the point of parody, so the stages of Stephen's development are given the appropriate languages, of infantilism, schoolboy slang, the portentous style of nineteeth-century translators of Dumas, Elizabethan floridity and colour, and so on until the narrative can move into the first-person eclecticism of Stephen's journal.

Joyce is able, for instance, to use the language of Dumas's *The Count of Monte Cristo* to represent what E. M. Forster would call the 'inflamed feelings' of adolescent romantic fantasy. Stephen's self-dramatising desire, ambition and solitude are bookish, archaic, sentimental, overwrought. Style is criticised, but also appraised as an indication of a genuine response to bookishness, archaism and high vague language. Joyce writes critically, using parody and detachment, and sympathetically, because he is using decorum, an appropriate style. The style is shown as right for the hero's development and Joyce's cumulative and unified novel: what is felt here, is to be felt again, and has been felt before—the right story for the time, the feeling of 'strange unrest,' of loneliness, of 'tender influence' and of the desire for substantiation and transfiguration, not yet sufficiently sexualised, but to become so:

He returned to Mercedes and, as he brooded upon her image, a

strange unrest crept into his blood. Sometimes a fever gathered
within him and led him to rove alone in the evening along the
quiet avenue. The peace of the gardens and the kindly lights in
the windows poured a tender influence into his restless heart.
The noise of children at play annoyed him and their silly voices
made him feel, even more keenly than he had felt at Clongowes,
that he was different from others. He did not want to play. He
wanted to meet in the real world the unsubstantial image which
his soul so constantly beheld. He did not know where to seek it or
how, but a premonition which led him on told him that this
image would, without any overt act of his, encounter him. They
would meet quietly as if they had known each other and had
made their tryst, perhaps at one of the gates or in some more
secret place. They would be alone, surrounded by darkness and
silence: and in that moment of supreme tenderness he would be
transfigured. He would fade into something impalpable under
her eyes and then in a moment, he would be transfigured.
Weakness and timidity and inexperience would fall from him in
that magic moment. (Ch. 2)

Here, as in the great parodies in *Ulysses*, Joyce fixes unerringly on
weaknesses of emotional language even while he successfully uses
them to represent emotion. The stylistic medium he is using is the
language which says what the feelings are, instead of enacting
them—'a strange unrest . . . a fever gathered . . . a tender influence
. . . a supreme tenderness'. The phrases are thin, well-worn, as in
'fall from him in that magic moment', but this is the language for
felt, if romantic, fever, and Joyce manages to convey the inflation,
vagueness and derivativeness of the emotion through vague and
literary style. As I use the word 'vague' I am quoting from *A
Portrait of the Artist*. Stephen comes into his own, when he comes at
the end of the novel to write his journal, and starts using the first
person. He writes and also inspects his writing, judging one of the
journal entries, which is intense, florid and throbbingly eloquent:
'vague words for a vague emotion'.

Leopold Bloom is loving, generous, pacific, charitable, energetic,
creative and compassionate. His warmth comes after Stephen's
coldness, his cheerfulness after Stephen's gloom. In many ways his
secular virtue resembles that of the heroes and heroines of Dickens
and George Eliot, but Joyce's controls of form and style are more
wary and ironic than any used before him. The controlling image of

Ulysses both enlarges and reduces Bloom, who can appear heroic and mock-heroic. There are local controls as well, like the narrative shifts in the *Cyclops* episode. In earlier episodes Bloom's humane virtues are demonstrated in the conventional modes of action and language. He gives, pities and loves—his children, his wife, his own past, the world around, acquaintances, the newly dead, beggars and birds. He reflects in a style which is inventive, intelligent and creative: his story telling is not public, like that of Ulysses, but private. Wherever he goes, his imagination reaches out, negating itself, to imagine the lives of everyone he meets—the skivvy in the butcher's shop, the chemist, and the blind man. Joyce does not show this negative capability as Bloom's only way of response: he is saved from losing himself in the outer world by his constant flow back to personal desires and demands. He never loses definition. His sympathetic images and narratives are grounded in self: he concludes after the effort to imagine or read the blind man's story that 'somehow you can't cotton on to them someway'. He can be alive in memory, but also in the present: a shadow over the sun or a light-revealing cloud will change his mood and sentiments. He is preserved from losing shape in softness or sentimentality.

Like Ulysses, Bloom must kill the Cyclops, his one-eyed giant. The 'technic' of the Cyclops episode is described in the Gorman-Gilbert schema as 'gigantism'. Bloom's assertions, however, must be kept in their place, and not magnified. His claims are large: 'I belong to a race . . . that is hated and persecuted', 'I'm talking about injustice', 'that's not life for men and women, insult and hatred', and 'Love . . . the opposite of hatred' all courageously assert beleaguered values. In the hostile context of nationalism, cynicism and sentimentality sound loud voices. Joyce makes hostilities into a proper environment for heroism: it prompts and provokes the assertions of love, which are not made loosely or gratuitously but under strain and pressure. The unsympathetic voices create effects of parody, exaggeration and inflation which make Bloom's plainness stand out as sincerity. Oppositions, alternatives and extremes are at his elbow. Bloom not only vanishes shyly and prudently after his declaration of love, but when his back is turned is put down by sentimental variations:

Love loves to love love. Nurse loves the new chemist. Constable 14A loves Mary Kelly. Gerty MacDowell loves the boy that has the bicycle. M. B. loves a fair gentleman. Li Chi Han lovey up kissy Cha Pu Chow. Jumbo, the elephant, loves Alice, the elephant. Old Mr. Verschoyle with the ear trumpet loves Old Mrs. Verschoyle with the turnedin eye. The man in the brown macintosh loves a lady who is dead. His Majesty the King loves Her Majesty the Queen. Mrs. Norman W. Tupper loves officer Taylor. You love a certain person. And this person loves that other person because everybody loves somebody but God loves everybody. (12)

The assertion of love and peace is ridiculed, by the fair and foul means of showing degradations of love. The reasons for being shy of the word 'love' are created through comedy. At the other extreme of inflation, comes the conclusion:

And they beheld Him in the chariot, clothed upon in the glory of the brightness, having raiment as of the sun, fair as the moon and terrible that for awe they durst not look upon Him. And there came a voice out of heaven, calling; *Elijah! Elijah!* And he answered with a main cry: *Abba! Adonai!* And they beheld Him even Him, ben Bloom Elijah, amid clouds of angels ascend to the glory of the brightness at an angle of fortyfive degrees over Donohoe's in Little Green Street like a shot off a shovel. (12)

The parody of rising ends with a fall, in a shot off the shovel. Like Sterne's picture of the captive in *A Sentimental Journey*, the magnification can't be kept up. In Joyce, as in Sterne, sentiment is analysed, degraded, mocked and travestied, to protect and relieve it from sentimentality.

Both Joyce and Beckett use the comic mode for representation of serious and solemn feelings. As they deploy it, it is a good analytic mode, forcing us to respond by inverting the process of rhetorical decorum. They create a clash of modes, which forces the sense of discrepancy, and acts as analysis or the provocation of analysis. Beckett can of course show and evoke compassion directly and simply, as he does in 'Dante and the Lobster', from *More Pricks Than Kicks*. Belacqua is an ignorant lobster-eater who has not realised that lobsters are prepared for table by being boiled alive;

'What are you going to do?' he cried.
'Boil the beast' she said, 'what else?'

'But it's not dead' protested Belacqua 'you can't boil it like that.'

She looked at him in astonishment. Had he taken leave of his senses.

'Have sense' she said sharply, 'lobsters are always boiled alive. They must be.' She caught up the lobster and laid it on its back. It trembled. 'They feel nothing' she said.

In the depths of the sea it had crept into the cruel pot. For hours, in the midst of its enemies, it had breathed secretly. It had survived the Frenchwoman's cat and his witless clutch. Now it was going alive into scalding water. It had to. Take into the air my quiet breath.

Belacqua looked at the old parchment of her face, grey in the dim kitchen.

'You make a fuss' she said angrily 'and upset me and then lash into it for your dinner.'

She lifted the lobster clear of the table. It had about thirty seconds to live.

Well, thought Belacqua, it's a quick death, God help us all. It is not.

The story unashamedly uses a nakedly appealing language, 'In the depths of the sea it had crept into the cruel pot', and at the end, most audaciously, three of the simplest and shortest words in the English language, 'It is not'. The story makes a moral statement of extreme originality. But Beckett can join humour with his pathos. Like Conrad, he creates narrators who analyse and analyse feelingly. They can analyse fearfully, and they can analyse with the insufficiently discussed emotion of justified self-pity, the compassion that one is from time to time entitled to feel for oneself. They also analyse, as befits analysts, in an attempt to detach themselves from emotion. On the second page of *Malone Dies* we have a strong and typical example of the vertiginously flexible agility of Beckett's emotional medium. The narrator, Malone, proposes to do what we all do, tell himself stories, as he is dying:

While waiting I shall tell myself stories, if I can. They will not be the same kind of stories as hitherto, that is all. They will be neither beautiful nor ugly, they will be calm, there will be no ugliness or beauty or fever in them any more, they will be almost lifeless, like the teller. What was that I said? It does not matter. I look forward to their giving me great satisfaction, some satisfaction. I am satisfied, there, I have enough, I am repaid, I need nothing more. Let me say before I go any further that I forgive nobody. I wish them all an atrocious life and then the fires and ice of hell and in the execrable generations to come an honoured name.

This characteristic shift from calm to anger is in itself a comic form. In this instance, the transition is from lyricised nostalgia to restraint, though restraint is demanded with expressive urgency:

It also tells me, this voice I am only just beginning to know, that the memory of this work brought scrupulously to a close will help me to endure the long anguish of vagrancy and freedom. Does this mean I shall one day be banished from my house, from my garden, lose my trees, my lawns, my birds of which the least is known to me and the way all its own it has of singing, of flying, of coming up to me or fleeing at my coming, lose and be banished from the absurd comforts of my home where all is snug and neat and all those things at hand without which I could not bear being a man, where my enemies cannot reach me, which it was my life's work to build, to adorn, to perfect, to keep? I am too old to lose all this, and begin again, I am too old! Quiet Moran, quiet. No emotion, please.

(*Molloy**, p. 132) (Calder, London, 1959)

Beckett can parody the loss of emotional control through such transformations and exaggerations. They are parts of his ordering process. Like Joyce, too, he is fond of a compressed and intense form of narrative, used with brilliance and virtuosity. Joyce is good at showing Leopold Bloom's creativity through his stream of consciousness. He makes up stories about all the people he meets; as he helps the blind man across the road he imagines what it would be like to be blind, and the act of imagination generates narrative. Such compressed narrative is one of Beckett's key rhetorical figures. The example I conclude with is a sliver of memory from *How It Is**. Even the speed and telegraphese of *The Unnamable* looks prolix beside the tautness of this narrative, an unusual novel related in lyrically stanzaic paragraphs. In this passage, the narrator remembers the past, not quite knowing whether he is remembering or imagining:

samples whatever comes remembered imagined no knowing life above life here God in heaven yes or no if he loved me a little if

* The novel has no chapter-divisions.

Pim loved me a little yes or no if I loved him a little in the dark the mud in spite of all a little affection find someone at last someone find you at last live together glued together love each other a little love a little without being loved be loved a little without loving answer that leave it vague leave it dark

(p. 82) (Calder, London, 1964)

Beckett's love stories are fragmented and the fragmentation gives one a sense of the emotional life being both rendered and scrutinised, in extremely adverse conditions. It is a long way from the company of Marlow's listeners, two hundred feet above sea level with their cigars, to the company of crawlers in the mud in *How It Is*, equipped with their economical survival kit, the sack of tins and the tin opener which you can use for the several purposes of opening the tin to feed yourself and sticking it into the next body for aggression and communication. But the permutations and repetitions move to assimilate the reader, and annihilate distance. Although Beckett's world is minimally (in *How It Is*) or lavishly (in the trilogy) a world of grotesque and distorted circumstances, it is one in which the characters feel and constantly speculate on the nature of feeling, to shock and solicit a reader's response.

First published in *The Rikkyo Review*, (Tokyo) No. 46, 1986.

Notes

1. Gordon S. Haight, *George Eliot. A Biography* (Clarendon Press, Oxford, 1968).
2. 'The Novel and the Feelings', *Phoenix: The Posthumous Papers of D. H. Lawrence* (Heinemann, London, 1936).

4. *Robinson Crusoe*: the Child and the Adult Reader

Robinson Crusoe is a marvellous story and a complex novel. Unlike those other great books which appeal to all ages—*Don Quixote, A Pilgrim's Progress, Gulliver's Travels*—its appeal is one and indivisible. When we grow up, we discover profundities and complexities we missed in Cervantes, Bunyan and Swift, and look back on the childhood charm as simple and easy, a mere selection from a vast and rich experience. But although there are some things in *Robinson Crusoe* which are omitted in abridgement, or skipped by children, many of the important things can be appreciated and shared by people at all ages. The story of Robinson Crusoe's religious conversion to a faith in Providence is an important subject and structural principle, but it is of little interest to the child, and it is not the centre of the book's power and originality. Henry James once tenderly described the grown man's response to Stevenson's *Treasure Island* as being like reading the story over a boy's shoulder. When we re-read *Robinson Crusoe*, it is to remember and include the experience of the child. We are still moved and gratified by the fantasy of defiance, escape, solitude, making and making-believe, companionship, rescue and survival. *Robinson Crusoe* is a fuller and deeper novel than *Treasure Island*, and no one outgrows it. At a time when books are written either for adults or children, it offers particular pleasure.

It is a great adventure story, with many perils—storm, shipwreck, cannibals, wild animals, war and exposure. What makes its adventures more than mere thrills is the presence, at the heart of the action, of the adventurous human being. The dangers and exploits of Robinson Crusoe are linked with great narrative skill in a pattern of tension, expectation, and surprise, kept up in an astonishingly sustained creation of excitement. More important, they are presented from the inside as well as the outside. There is a chain of events, with a circulation of feeling. The adventures are not baldly or externally related, events that are important only as events. They happen to a particularised person, and the tension is not only our breath-held expectation of the next event, it is Robinson Crusoe's. Clearly, our fear is created through his fear, our relief, curiosity and courage provoked and particularised by character.

The actual description of the shipwreck shows Defoe at his most excitedly reticent, sensing the effectiveness of a description of action so overwhelming that much can, and should, be taken for granted in the reader's response. But the response is there, as it has been imagined:

. . . the Land look'd more frightful than the Sea.

After we had row'd, or rather driven, about a League and a Half, as we reckon'd it, a raging Wave, Mountain-like, came rowling a-stern of us, and plainly bad us expect the *Coup de Grace.* In a word, it took us with such a Fury, that it overset the Boat at once; and separating us as well from the Boat as from one another, gave us not time hardly to say, O God! for we were all swallowed up in a Moment.

Nothing can describe the Confusion of Thought which I felt when I sunk into the Water; for tho' I swam very well, yet I could not deliver my self from the Waves so as to draw Breath, till that Wave having driven me, or rather carried me a vast Way on towards the Shore, and having spent it self, went back, and left me upon the Land almost dry, but half-dead with the Water I took in. I had so much Presence of Mind as well as Breath left, that seeing my self nearer the main Land than I expected, I got upon my Feet, and endeavoured to make on towards the Land as fast as I could, before another Wave should return, and take me up again. But I soon found it was impossible to avoid it; for I saw the Sea come after me as high as a great Hill, and as furious as an Enemy which I had no Means or Strength to contend with; my Business was to hold my Breath, and raise my self upon the Water, if I could; and so by swimming to preserve my Breathing, and Pilot my self towards the Shore, if possible; my greatest Concern now being, that the Sea, as it would carry me a great

Way towards the Shore when it came on, might not carry me
back again with it when it gave back towards the Sea.
(pp. 49–50, Shakespeare Head Edition, Blackwell Oxford, 1927)*

We would all feel similarly overwhelmed by the mountainous
raging wave. But what happens is happening to someone capable of
confusion and self-possession, and we have Robinson Crusoe's
special sensations, retrospectively chronicled in a detail which
makes the experience vivid, concrete, and particular, but
deliberated with linguistic and rational awareness: 'Nothing can
describe' and 'my Business was to hold my Breath'.

When he has landed on the island, there is room for feeling as well
as sensation; once more, the language is reflective and even
reflexive:

> I was now landed, and safe on Shore, and began to look up and
> thank God that my Life was sav'd in a Case wherein there was
> some Minutes before scarce any room to hope. I believe it is
> impossible to express to the Life what the Extasies and
> Transports of the Soul are, when it is so sav'd, as I may say, out of
> the very Grave; and I do not wonder now at that Custom, *viz.*
> that when a Malefactor who has the Halter about his Neck is tyed
> up, and just going to be turn'd off, and has a Reprieve brought to
> him; I say, I do not wonder that they bring a Surgeon with it, to
> let him blood that very Moment they tell him of it, that the
> Surprise may not drive the Animal Spirits from the Heart, and
> overwhelm him:
>
>   'For sudden Joys, like Griefs, confound at first.'
>
> I walk'd about on the Shore, lifting up my Hands, and my whole
> Being, as I may say, wrapt up in the Contemplation of my
> Deliverance, making a Thousand Gestures and Motions which I
> cannot describe, reflecting upon all my Comrades that were
> drown'd, and that there should not be one Soul sav'd but my self;
> for, as for them, I never saw them afterwards, or any Sign of
> them, except three of their Hats, one Cap, and two Shoes that
> were not Fellows. (pp. 51–52)

Defoe is in fact so interested in his first emotional response that he
describes it three times, changing it a little as he shifts his

*The novel has no chapter-divisions

perspective. One account is immediate and breathless, another more leisurely and written in his journal, suggesting lavish space for reflection as well as physically realised immediate response. The current of feeling links all the adventures of Robinson Crusoe; it is continuous and varied, it moves flatly, curves steeply, pulses regularly and irregularly, and is one of the qualities that transform an adventure into a psychological novel. It is impossible to say whether this emotional current is as important to the child as to the grown-up. The child often seems capable of supplying his own emotion, of making a direct identification, even where storytellers provide only a violent stimulus of action, with a blankness of feeling and character. Such a response, if I am right about its quality, is rather like the adult's response to melodrama or pornography. But for the adult reader, there is no doubt that the embedding of action in emotional cause and effect makes all the difference. The adventures are internal as well as external. Take the most surprising thing that happens in the whole novel.

> It happen'd one Day about Noon going towards my Boat, I was exceedingly surpriz'd with the Print of a Man's naked Foot on the Shore, which was very plain to be seen in the Sand. I stood like one Thunder-struck, or as if I had seen an Apparition; I listen'd, I look'd round me, I could hear nothing, nor see any Thing; I went up to a rising Ground to look farther; I went up the Shore and down the Shore, but it was all one, I could see no other Impression but that one. I went to it again to see if there were any more, and to observe if it might not be my Fancy; but there was no Room for that, for there was exactly the very Print of a Foot, Toes, Heel, and every Part of a Foot; how it came thither I knew not, nor could in the least imagine. But after innumerable fluttering Thoughts, like a Man perfectly confus'd and out of my self, I came Home to my Fortification, not feeling, as we say, the Ground I went on, but terrify'd to the last Degree, looking behind me at every two or three Steps, mistaking every Bush and Tree, and fancying every Stump at a Distance to be a Man; nor is it possible to describe how many various Shapes affrighted Imagination represented Things to me in, how many wild Ideas were found every Moment in my Fancy, and what strange unaccountable Whimsies came into my Thoughts by the Way. (pp. 177–8)

Defoe's way of describing feeling is various, its variety deceptively miming naivety. At times Robinson Crusoe tells us what he felt, 'after innumerable fluttering thoughts' and 'terrify'd to the last degree', and at times he stresses the strength of feeling by saying it is indescribable, 'nor is it possible to describe'. But there are effective details, like the mistaking of bushes, trees and stumps, which not only perfectly record the general infection of terror, but give it substance and shape. Most powerful of all is the account, behaviouristically simple, of event and action. Robinson Crusoe sees 'the print of a man's naked foot', very plain. And once he has seen it, he listens, looks, goes up and down the shore, and then— perfect detail, perfect restraint—goes back to make sure it really was a footprint. The various ways of dramatising and narrating feeling join in giving us the impact of the event on the nerves, on the senses, and on the intelligence, of the hero. Beyond the hero, revealed in linguistic self-consciousness, is the skilled novelist who creates the excited but rational narrator.

Some of the most startling scenes are deliberately surprising: they dwell on terror to move into anti-climax. The episode of the parrot who calls 'Robin Crusoe' when Crusoe least expects him, or the episode of the frightful old goat, are good examples of Defoe's humour and realism. Life on this desert island has real terrors of nightmare, fresh shipwreck, and cannibal feasts, but these are accompanied by what can be called more mundane threats, which relieve the 'sensational' crises and ground them in something that approximates to ordinary experience. Defoe's blend of the ordinary with the extraordinary is an essential feature of his genius. It also permits him to show Crusoe under constant nervous strain, but not always in a state of high crisis.

Character depends on more than the drama of the affective life, and Robinson Crusoe, like Odysseus, has brains as well as physical courage. We like our heroes—and heroines—to survive through intelligence. In that early swimming scene, we saw how the hero was not totally overwhelmed, but controlled his breath and movements. The story of Crusoe's survival is the story of an intelligent man, to be believed in, admired and emulated, as he plans, explores, adapts his resources to the needs and requirements of the island and its seasons, using his supplies cleverly and economically. In many ways, *Robinson Crusoe* is the story of a game, and a story which resembles a game. Crusoe has both skill and luck, though Defoe's word for luck is Providence. Like many games, the island models a simple environment with rules, laws, limits and hazards. Of course, since this is a story, not a game, and the story of a game played with and by Providence, its rules change, or our view of them changes. Once Robinson Crusoe has got used to solitude, he is terrified, then delighted, by alien human presences. Once he and Friday have got used to their idyll *à deux*, more company turns up, the desert island becomes positively crowded, and the end is in sight. Defoe's continuous creation of adventure, of course, doesn't stop here, and both the end of the novel, and its two sequels, show the indefatigability of hero and novelist. But the central interest is an interest in the story of the island.

We delight in Crusoe's cleverness, as he settles in, surrounds himself with necessaries and luxuries, salvages things from the wreck, and uses the raw materials to provide shelter, food, clothes, furniture, writing materials, a calendar, and other aids to survival. The game changes from games that are played with imaginary environments to constructional games. The child's brick-building, jigsaws and imitations of the manufactured adult world, are both fun and learning. Defoe's precise and careful descriptions of making are sometimes blueprints for doing it yourself. I am not suggesting that we learn from the making in the novel, but rather that we associate ourselves with Crusoe's learning. His achievements are not only, as Ian Watt has insisted in *The Rise of the Novel* (Chatto; London, 1957), steps in technological development, but are games, too, to be played painstakingly, clumsily, sufficiently, like the making of planks (one plank each tree); ingeniously but also stupidly, like the building of the first boat; and by scientific observation and experiment, like the making of cooking pots. Crusoe is the one who learns, by trial and by error. And some things he never learns to make, like a thing so important to writers— ink. The borderlines of skill and clumsiness, achievement and failure, make the environment game credible and exciting. The making of a thing, like the building of the card-castle, meccano-bridge, or lego-house, is a feat, another kind of adventure, and a form of experiment. Robinson Crusoe stands between the child at play and the grown-up artisan.

Children do not only make replicas and models, they also use things to make makeshift and make-believe worlds, secret places, private habitations. Robinson Crusoe makes several houses, and lucidly reminds us of the psychological need for the making. Like the imaginary houses, refuges and secret gardens we all make, here and there, and everywhere, are Robinson Crusoe's magazines, castles, town- and country-houses. They are really made and really make-believe, so giving us a double delight. They are nests, without either mates or babies, and they resemble play-houses, real and imaginary. Crusoe loves caves and tree-houses, for their physical shelter and imaginative gratification. They are serious playthings. His dwellings meet deep psychological needs for privacy, comfort, seclusion. They are cosy wombs.

The secret houses are full of things, and though the things are necessary to Robinson Crusoe, they have a special charm. The identity and accumulation of things is fascinating to the child, for reasons both obvious and arcane. The child gets to know the use of things, but the childhood feeling for objects, happily not vanishing completely in adult life, has a sense of the individuality of objects, radiant, funny, startling or terrifying. Robinson Crusoe caters to the lively interest in individual things. We see the making, almost from scratch, of the world of things we take for granted, except on desert islands. We see the special qualities of Crusoe's resourcefulness, patience, good temper, intelligence and piety, as he makes and handles things. But there remains something, too, of that extra delight in the individual faces of things, which is gratified by the flotsam and jetsam of the island. There are odds and ends, like three little things Crusoe has with him when he is first swept on to the island—a knife, a pipe, and a little tobacco in a box. There is all the joy of salvage and treasure-hunting in a whole wreck, with its goods at his disposal:

> I got on Board the Ship, as before, and prepar'd a second Raft, and having had Experience of the first, I neither made this so unweildly, or loaded it so hard, but yet I brought away several Things very useful to me; at first, in the Carpenter's Stores I found two or three Bags full of Nails and Spikes, a great Skrew-Jack, a Dozen or two of Hatchets, and above all, that most useful Thing call'd a Grindstone; all these I secur'd together, with several Things belonging to the Gunner, particularly two or three Iron Crows, and two Barrels of Musquet Bullets, seven Musquets, and another fowling Piece, with some small Quantity of Powder more; a large Bag full of small Shot, and a great Roll of Sheet Lead. But this last was so heavy I could not hoise it up to get it over the Ship's Side. (p. 61)

There is all the pleasure of finding the larder full of food:

> . . . I found a great Hogshead of Bread and three large Runlets of
> Rum or Spirits, and a Box of Sugar, and a Barrel of fine-Flower;
> this was surprizing to me, because I had given over expecting any
> more Provisions, except what was spoil'd by the Water: I soon
> empty'd the Hogshead of that Bread, and wrapt it up Parcel by
> Parcel in Pieces of the Sails, which I cut out; and in a Word, I got
> all this safe on Shore also. (p. 63)

There is all the pleasure of rummaging amongst miscellaneous,
useful, and useless things:

> . . . I discover'd a Locker with Drawers in it, in one of which I
> found two or three Razors, and one Pair of large Sizzers, with
> some ten or a Dozen of good Knives and Forks; in another I
> found about Thirty six Pounds value in Money, some European
> Coin, some Brasil, some Pieces of Eight, some Gold, some Silver.
> (p. 64)

And there is the invention and fun of dressing up:

> I had a great high shapeless Cap, made of a Goat's Skin, with a
> Flap hanging down behind, as well to keep the sun from me as to
> shoot the Rain off from running into my Neck; nothing being so
> hurtful in these Climates as the Rain upon the Flesh under the
> Cloaths.
> I had a short Jacket of Goat-skin, the Skirts coming down to
> about the middle of my thighs, and a Pair of open-knee'd
> Breeches of the same: the Breeches were made of the Skin of an
> old He-goat, whose Hair hung down such a Length on either side
> that like Pantaloons it reach'd to the middle of my Legs;
> Stockings and Shoes I had none, but had made me a Pair of
> some-things, I scarce know what to call them, like Buskins to flap
> over my Legs and lace on either Side like Spatter-dashes; but of a
> most barbarous Shape, as indeed were all the rest of my Cloaths.
> I had on a broad Belt of Goat's-Skin dry'd, which I drew
> together with two Thongs of the same, instead of Buckles, and in
> a kind of a Frog on either Side of this, instead of a Sword and a
> Dagger, hung a little Saw and a Hatchet, one on one Side, one on
> the other. (pp. 172–3)

To the child, things have a peculiar and pure fascination. To the adult, their economic meanings and moral ironies take over. Both child and adult enjoy the things, the same things, the things Defoe specifies so solidly. And just as adult and child enjoy the sense of discovery, accumulation and manufacture, so, too, both enjoy the strong, if less solid, satisfactions of a world of fantasy. Robinson Crusoe makes believe one dwelling is home, one is a fortress, one a castle, one a country-house. He plays king with his domestic animals as living toys. (His parrots are pets but also speak his name and break his speech-solitude.) Later on, he enacts more practically and dangerously the fantasies of kingship and colonisation, but in the early days the fantasy is strongly rooted in childhood needs for privacy, controllable companionship, isolation, self-discovery and escape.

Defoe is pretty clear and conscious about his fantasy. Robinson Crusoe is the youngest son, the third son of fairy-story and folk-tale. Despite the warnings and persuasions of his 'ancient' father, he longs to drop out of 'the middle station of life'. He does, running away from home and parents to seek his fortune, to find not only a fortune, but himself. Although the religious vision and conversion is the part of the novel least read by children, the actual experience of self-discovery seems to be perfectly accessible. There is the pleasure of the escape from middle-class commercial success to risk and adventure. (True, the adventures have commercial significance, and the gold Crusoe despises is put away for a rainy day, but the limits of escape sound their own ring of wry truthfulness.) The deepest gratification of Defoe's fantasy of escape, freedom and adventure, is the self-contained and manageable desert island. It is bordered by sea, big enough to map, explore and range, small enough to seem like the perfect imaginary home, estate and kingdom. Its wild life is not too troublesome, and Crusoe learns to cultivate its soil. As survival becomes less desperate, luxuries and pleasures are possible. Crusoe enjoys making and playing, comes to terms with weather, keeps pets and even herds. After he learns that the island sanctuary is not a sanctuary, but visited by cannibals, another fantasy comes to replace the first, that of innocent companionship. Crusoe has a best friend. His happiness with Friday is as perfect as is possible, he says, in our sublunary state.

Just as the boys in William Golding's *Lord of the Flies* seem in some ways to re-enact stages of cultural and religious development, so *Robinson Crusoe* enacts the pre-sexual idyll of solitude and friendship. (The pre-sexual idyll was also pre-Freudian, and can be proposed as anti-Freudian to be sure; the seeking out of island solitudes, like Yeats's Innisfree, has become associated with auto-erotic reverie. The friendship with Man Friday has inevitably been seen as a homosexual love.) Whatever the psychological interpretations, however, Defoe's overt presentation is strikingly non-sexual. Since he could be sexually candid, gross, and prurient when he chose, as in *Moll Flanders* and *Roxana*, he probably deliberated the absence of sexuality in *Robinson Crusoe*. (*The Journal of the Plague Year* is another remarkable sexless novel, but its form and subject have been obstacles too great for popularity with child readers.) Crusoe's island is a world of matter-of-fact making, adventure and companionship, which offers either its innocence or its blandness to the innocence or blandness of childhood. Its fantasy is strong, but it is not a sexual fantasy. Man Friday is scarcely an aphrodisiac image, for all his charm.

Violent adventure, a game of making environments and things, a fantasy of escape, solitude, and self-possession: the hero of these adventures, creations and dreams, is Crusoe, whose simplicity makes him just the right hero for a story that appeals to the child. Crusoe's simplicity is one of nature, not caricature. His simplicity is healthy and vital, compared with that of crude or gross supermen. It is compatible with intelligence and a (fairly) rich emotional life. Although Crusoe is contaminated with capitalist energy and imperial pride, he also possessed admirable qualities of good humour and friendliness. Unlike the heroes so brilliantly analysed by David Holbrook in his essay on C. S. Lewis in *Children's literature in education* (No. 10, March 1973), Crusoe is loving, self-critical and moral. When he longs to destroy the cannibals, second thoughts rebuke him, and his aggressiveness is rationally and imaginatively restrained. The novel has violence in it, but it is neither sensational nor amoral in presentation. We are never crudely stimulated by fear or hostility, but shown the workings of fear and hostility in Robinson Crusoe. He is simple enough to be Everyman, and simple enough to have an unmysterious emotional life which is accessible to the child, but sufficiently vivid and various for the adult. Though there are no women on the island (in Part One) Crusoe is not a sexist hero, and does traditional woman's work, as well as man's.

Defoe insisted that his novel was modest and serious, and both modesty and seriousness make it a whole and profound story of adventure. He also urged its religious application, and said that to abridge this story was to leave it 'naked of its brightest ornaments'. This is arguable. Even if we abridge or ignore some passages of religious meditation and interpretation, the moral force of character resides not in doctrinal detail, but in that modesty and seriousness we find in Robinson Crusoe the man. Defoe's commentary on the novel also insisted, as we all know, on the factual accuracy and truth of his fiction: 'The editor believes the thing to be a just history of fact; neither is there any appearance of fiction in it'. This convention or illusion of verisimilitude may or may not delight children—some of the book's charm may lie in the harmony of verisimilitude with the glamour of dream. (Only the very young child asks if stories are true.) But there is another aspect of the disclaimer which seems important. Defoe's artlessness, I believe, has a double appeal. The story and the character shine through a transparent medium, radiantly and purely, with no assertion of decoration or artifice. There *is* artifice, but as always in Defoe, it is most thoroughly concealed and assimilated. The simplicity of story and language is enhanced by the relaxation of rhetoric. There is a directness and modesty which can delight the adult by its restraint, and never irritate the child. If we want the borderline between fact and fiction blurred, then we will find that excellent blurring in *Robinson Crusoe*. Its adventures, its solid world and objects, its manifold fantasy, its simple but individual hero, are presented in perfectly candid form and style. But the novel has all the cunning and advantage of art. Of all great novels, *Robinson Crusoe* is the novel we can share most easily and completely with our children.

First published in *Children's literature in education*, Vol. 8, No. 1, Spring, 1977.

Note

1.   I have discussed the religion in the novel in *The Appropriate Form* (Athlone Press, London, 1964).

5. *Les Liaisons Dangereuses*: Transcending Pornography

This is a novel about dangerous relationships. What is dangerous is more than getting to know dangerous people, who are out to conquer and corrupt. This danger is only a part of Choderlos de Laclos's story, a story told in a way both old and new, traditional and individual. Its narrative method determines and shapes the subject-matter or theme.

In *Les Liaisons Dangereuses* people communicate in ways which are familiar, inside and outside fiction. The characters gossip, record the events of the day, plan, inform, imagine, remember, fantasise, tell the truth, tell lies, betray, blackmail, confide and confess. They perform all these acts of narration in letters, and the correspondence itself forms a medium admirably designed to bring out and develop certain subjects: intimacy, treachery, complicity, secrecy and publicity. Secrets are dangerously shared, dangerously preserved, and dangerously revealed. The letters are also important props and instruments in the plot. Madame de Merteuil sensitively calls them dangerous. Their physical existence is strongly emphasised; how they are written, how they are delivered, how they are addressed, how they are copied, how Madame de Tourvel's last letter disintegrates, how the letters are used in the final revenge—all these things are crucial, in this novel which explores, as it unfolds, the dangers of writing things down, of sending and showing letters to certain people, of reading certain letters, and of using them for certain purposes. It is a novel which creates, and in creating analyses, a dangerous correspondence. At the heart of the web of communication woven by Laclos are the major characters and plot-makers, the Vicomte de Valmont and his mistress, Madame de Merteuil.

Their correspondence is not simply a brilliant and intricate device for constructing the story of an intrigue in a way which excites us through irony, contrast, suspense and shock. It is also an imaginative analysis of an intimate relationship, depending on affinity, need, distance, absence and remote control. We cannot comprehend the implications of this central relationship, unless we recognise the peculiarity of the central correspondence. (And *vice versa*.) The novel displays and analyses the passions of pride, power, jealousy and desire, but it also displays and analyses the ways in which these passions are communicated. In some ways the correspondence is an intimate discussion of pride, power and desire, and in some ways it is—as its imagery keeps reminding us—a battlefield, a theatre of war, in which passions clash. It is also an erotic correspondence, in which the lovers make love. Valmont and Madame de Merteuil begin by making love and end by making war, and both love and war are proposed, started, developed, elaborated and concluded in the letters they write, through the dangerous complicity of an epistolary correspondence.

Valmont and Madame de Merteuil are not isolated power maniacs, but are shown to be shaped by social attitudes to marriage, fidelity, virginity, education, prostitution, and the double standard of sexual conduct. The forms and languages used by the characters are seen to be shaped by institutions, conventions, manners and morals. They are part of the subversive underground which lies beneath a polite surface and which, like many underground movements, soon becomes corruptly conventional and orthodox. The figure of the rake, for instance, is both romantically rebellious and conservatively conventional. The rake is subversive, attacking vulnerable conventions of virginity, married virtue, and reputation, but his role is in the end a conventional one. What he does is expected of a man, and flaunted by him, as evidence of his aggressive masculinity, wit and intelligence. But male gallantry is exposed as courting exposure. It needs to be boasted about and depends on publicity. For the woman, it is another matter: in this society depending on the double standard, she is forced to stay underground. Unlike the man she cannot flaunt her promiscuity, but needs secrecy. This is why the confidential and clandestine nature of the narration in these letters is crucial, and why Valmont is so necessary to Madame de Merteuil. His is the only ear in which she can whisper her boasts and unlike his, her boasts are secrets.

Valmont boasts, and sometimes excites, in salacious step-by-step detail of his conquests, telling Madame de Merteuil, in serial narrative, of the quick pushover seduction of Cécile, and the more difficult and unpredictably complex slow persuasion of Madame de Tourvel. Madame de Merteuil's stories of her lovers, while equally contemptuous and confident, are much less complete in sexual detail, though their very evasions, often teasing, carry their own charge of erotic suggestiveness. The difference between the man's full confidences and the woman's inhibited narrative may show that Laclos was restricted by convention, or that he was realistically reflecting a social difference, emphasising what is—only relatively, of course—a greater expressive constriction for a woman, even for this woman. (It is also true that they believe they can enjoy the erotic game of seducing and telling, and underestimate the interference of jealousy.) But in many ways the lovers either seem, or are, equal, and evenly matched. He is a rake, and she emulates his role. She imitates his callous conquests, and his pride in conquest.

It is historically inevitable that we, as readers of the nineteen-eighties, two hundred years after Laclos,[1] should be especially sensitive to his feminist theme, but it seems central to the novel. Madame de Merteuil is monstrously callous and cruel and, unlike Valmont, has no redeeming personal features. He has at least his unexpected and reluctant love and admiration of Madame de Tourvel and of her virtue, and a certain perverted loyalty and allegiance to Madame de Merteuil herself. (The novel shows the existence of a kind of honour amongst thieves, bawds, pandars and seducers.) Madame de Merteuil lacks sympathetic moral qualities, but she offers the example of a woman who understandably and explicably rejects her woman's place and role. She longs, and tries, to free herself from the limits which society imposes on her, but she cannot disconnect herself from the conditions which create her, however clearly she discerns them. The rake's gallantry has become orthodox and the woman's way is, at first sight, less orthodox. But she too finds—or shows—that rebellions become conformist. Madame de Merteuil wants to cut out her own path, and redefine a woman's role; she formulates her aim with force and clarity:

> 'My principles . . . are not, like other women's principles, given
> at hazard, accepted without reflection and followed from habit;
> they are the result of my profound meditations; I created them
> and I can say that I am my own work.'[2] (Letter LXXXI)

This extract comes from a most original and central passage of storytelling in this novel full of stories. She writes her autobiography, and offers it to her lover, ironically and aggressively. The point of view of each storyteller is shown to be restricted; and however intelligent and confident the liberated woman is as she narrates her life and principles, there are things about herself as a product of her society, a private person shaped by a larger public life, which she cannot see. Her very boldness and boastfulness draw our attention to the mistake which she makes about the extent to which she can be free. She is conspicuously blind to her own conservatism.

In a sense, it is admirable to try to live by your own ideas and principles, to create your own life, to exchange the conventional woman's role for something less false, passive and restricted. She tells most movingly how she hated the feeling of losing her individuality and tried to guard her one possession, her inner life:

> 'I was still very young and practically without any interest; but I only possessed my thoughts and I felt indignant that they might be snatched from me or surprised in me against my will.' (*loc. cit.*)

But she comes to believe—perhaps rightly, for her time—that the only alternative to being a woman, enslaved by convention, rule and pattern, as young girl, as wife, and as widow, is to take the man's role as her model. Her role-model is that of the rake. Her actions, her competitiveness, even her favourite metaphors of war make this frighteningly plain. Her principles of freedom, independence, originality and revolt, are corrupted. She cannot really be her own work; she can*not* create herself. (Because nobody can.) She merely finds new distortions and degradations to replace the old ones. She mistakes novelty for revolution.

As the novel offers its subtle social analysis, it combines a rational appeal to intellect with a manipulative erotic persuasion. *Les Liaisons Dangereuses* has a claim to be one of the most pornographic—perhaps the most pornographic—of all novels outside the actual genre of pornography, a remarkably ironic achievement for an Enlightenment novel. In pornography proper, there cannot be individualised characters or actions, only blanks suitably packaged and programmed to provide the reader with erotic stimulus. Far from creating stereotyped images, this novel certainly creates full particularity and individuality in its major characters, and even the minor ones, like Cécile or Danceny, are clearly and conveniently displayed as social examples. The novel is far too realistic, psychologically and socially, to be simply erotic, but its structure and language have some of the salient and definitive characteristics of pornography.

Its form mimes tumescence and detumescence. There is narrative foreplay: an initial tension prepares and slowly develops the climaxes of its various seductions. There are sexual variations and perversions, games and scenarios. Many local scenes are carefully contrived and shaped for erotic effect. There is the slowly staged seduction of Madame de Tourvel, and the quicker, more brutal, seduction of Cécile. There are suggestions of homosexual feeling, obvious in the relationship of Madame de Merteuil and Cécile, and suggested on one occasion in Valmont. There is individualised sado-masochism in Valmont's brutal account of Cécile's miscarriage and his nastily playful notion of immediately making her pregnant again. There is the scene—certainly no less cruel for being amusing—in which Valmont writes a hypocritical letter, filled with double meanings, to Madame de Tourvel, on the back of the girl Emilie, whom he uses as a writing-desk. Madame de Merteuil is erotically supplied with these stories and stimulants.

Even though all these are stock tensions and variations, the novel places its erotic appeals and allures in a special way. It uses certain effects common to pornography but particularised in ways which are subtly exploratory and analytic. It transcends the medium which it imitates. In placing and explaining pornographic effects, it calls attention to dangers of erotic communication, and its erotic tension, shock, salacious detail, permutations and climaxes, are not directed simply, or wholly, at providing the reader with excitement or stimulant, but are provided, within the novel, for the excitement of one character by another. The excited reader observes excited readers. The materials are salacious, but the novel investigates the working of its provocations and enjoyments. Forms, languages, causes and effects are revealed in a socially and psychologically inquiring spirit. This is erotic narrative and narrative inquiry.

Pornography's reduction of people into objects, for instance, is clearly brought out, in social cause and in psychological effect. Fantasy turns into action, as sexual fantasy has a way of doing. We decide that the reduction of people into objects by Madame de Merteuil and Valmont is less innocent, and more horrifying, than the reductions in pornography, as we also see the transformation of ideas into acts. Individual feelings and passions are shown, in corrupted and destroyed victims. Individual passions are shown, too, in the oppressors. Madame de Merteuil requires her lover to perform his seductions and inform her fully about them, in a special kind of commissioned erotic writing which depends on the conversion of sexual scenarios into destructive realities. Sexual games can go wrong, and go too far, and they do both in *Les Liaisons Dangereuses*. Sex won't stay in the head. Acting becomes action. Sadism leads to torture and death. The lovers' game of sexual teasing and complicity turns sour, cruel and murderous. Complacency plays at jealousy, but becomes the real thing. The erotic game has been played for political as well as sexual motives and the woman's rake's fantasy, contempt for other women, competitiveness and sadism, become deadly serious, then mortal. The lovers write the most dangerous letters of all, terminal challenges and declarations of war. Valmont demands that Madame de Merteuil should reject Danceny, and keep her assignation with him, but the request dangerously asserts what he sees as his man's rights and dangerously betrays his feeling for Madame de Tourvel, the 'beautiful and sensitive woman . . . at this very moment . . . perhaps dying of love and regret'[3] (Letter CLI).

Madame de Merteuil's reply to his challenge is characteristically irrational, but plays—and plays well—with reasons: 'Do you know why I never remarried? . . . because I would not allow anyone the right to criticise my actions. . . . you write the most marital letter one could ever behold. . . . how can one fail a person to whom one owes nothing?' (Letter CLII). These are excellent questions, and key questions in this novel, originating in Laclos's feminist recognition of the woman's desire for freedom, independence and fidelity to herself. She has been using Valmont as an object, not as an ally, and he comes to recognise this at last, as she goads him, with words, to challenge her—in *words*, since only men are allowed the dubious honours of real weapons. He says, 'A word will do' and—at last physically rejecting the conventions of this letter writing—she scrawls the word on his own letter, 'War' (Letter CLIII).

She has used the image of Samson and Delilah, seeing herself as the dangerous woman in possession of woman's weapon, 'scissors'.

But at the end, when the pillars of the community are pulled down, she casts herself in the role of Samson rather than Delilah. Despite her degrading woman's punishments, she has succeeded in the man's power game. The game was dangerous, and its success disgraceful. Her emulation, fight for freedom, politicisation of the woman's cause, are all made historically understandable and seductive to the reader. In reading we are made to feel a dangerous, and instructive, complicity. The novel involves us in its dangerous communications as it performs an economically shocking act of elucidation—and experiment.

This is a slightly revised version of a radio talk commissioned by the Open University for a course on 'The Enlightenment', and first broadcast in 1980.

Notes

1.   We must remember that *Les Liaisons Dangereuses* is written on the eve of the French Revolution, analyses the pre-revolutionary situation, and is itself revolutionary.
2.   References are to the translation by Richard Aldington, *Dangerous Acquaintances* (Routledge & Kegan Paul, London, 1924 and 1981).
3.   There is a sub-text in the novel, anti-sexist on behalf of men, in which Valmont shows the role-restrictions imposed on a man's affective experience, and acts against the grain of his feelings for Madame de Tourvel.

6. Susan Ferrier's *Marriage* and *The Inheritance*

The novelist's profession was the only one open to homebound, middle-class and under-educated women at the beginning of the last century but entry was jealously guarded by traditional practitioners and patrons. Even after the successes of Fanny Burney and Jane Austen, Monk Lewis was thrown into 'great perturbation' by the rumour that Susan Ferrier wrote or was about to write novels. He trembled 'lest she should fail in this bookmaking' since 'as a rule I have an aversion, a pity, and contempt for all female scribblers. The needle, not the pen, is the instrument they should handle, and the only one they ever use dexterously'; but he conceded, 'I must except, however, their love-letters which are sometimes full of pleasing conceit: but this is the only subject they should ever attempt to write about' (quoted in John A. Doyle, *Memoir and Correspondence of Susan Ferrier*, Murray, London, 1898). He was spared having to repeat or eat his words by dying just before *Marriage* came out in 1818.

As the only unmarried daughter, Susan Ferrier devoted herself to her father James, about whom she wrote a brief, moving sketch for her nephew, which was later published with her letters. Asked not to bring him library books written by women, she read to him from the manuscript of *Marriage*, carefully hiding it from his sight, and was rewarded by enthusiasm, refusal to believe it was written by a woman, and fatherly tears when told she was its author. This well-worn tender anecdote needs the sub-text of her dry description of daughterly devotion, when she had to refuse an invitation from her friend Charlotte Clavering: 'My father I never see, except at meals, but then my company is just as indispensable as the tablecloth or chairs, or, in short, any other luxury which custom has converted

into necessity.' Walter Scott saw her as 'a sister shadow'—
unpatronisingly, since he was imagining himself as a phantom in the
same sentence—and helped her to change her publisher and
improve terms. When Blackwood made a belated offer for her third
novel, *Destiny*, she turned him down with the tart reminder, 'I
should never have thought of offering a future work to you after
being told the second edition of my former one was "Dead stock".'

Judge Irvine, in the Three Rivers Books edition, seems less than
accurate in placing the origin of the fiction in those 'deliciously
splashy walks at noon and . . . enchanting orgies at midnight'
recalled by Susan Ferrier in writing to Charlotte Clavering. The
idea of a collaboration, the first novel, *Marriage*, and Susan's
subsequent career had their origin in the needs of separation and the
satisfactions of correspondence. Writing letters was the source and
seedbed of the novels. One of Richardson's insights about letters—
and who knew more about them than he did?—is buried in a shrewd
observation in which Mr B attributes Pamela's education in
language to her epistolary exercises. The correspondence of Susan
Ferrier and Charlotte Clavering, edited by John A. Doyle and
published in 1898 with other letters and a memoir of the novelist,
should recall the fictional correspondence of Clarissa and Anna
Howe, as they created sisterly bonding within patriarchal bondage.

They are letters which should be reprinted, sprightly, clever,
intelligently and fluently communicative, arch and facetious,
generating a flow of images, anecdotes and projects. Susan Ferrier
throws off the odd careless funny poem, writes exuberantly about
her pen's exuberance and thinks of writing about the adventures of a
pen. Charlotte suggests regular exchange and collaboration, Susan
is amused, considers, modifies plans, to be criticised and approved
in her turn. Charlotte contributed one of the inset stories to
Marriage, which Susan revised, abridged and duly acknowledged.
In a darkly guarded masculine culture, the correspondence let in
light. The exchange teems and grows. Jokes become ideas, fantasies
are made actual, amateurs evolve into professionals, comic
affectation becomes pastiche. The familiar correspondence is a
workshop. Susan teases Charlotte about her taste for 'the horrible
and the astonishing', for red ink violence, 'vile catastrophe' and the
Gothic nonsense of 'raw heads and bones'. Half-serious, she
deprecates her own 'grovelling' sense of the real. The banter
develops into an intelligent and sustained argument about the art of

fiction. As bubbles solidify into paragraphs and chapters, the critical sense is educated. Susan approves a situation or a scene but comes to argue the need for background and exposition. Charlotte dislikes too much fashionable Frenchifying and deprecates renderings of high life which are mere imitations of fictional stereotypes.

The artist needs and gets a richer nourishment than talk about craft. Susan Ferrier's powers of grotesque caricature, rank domestic farce and pungent satire grow through gossip. The habit of unabashed backbiting and fault finding—which Susan praised as the most reliable of human pleasures—is fostered by an intimacy as frank and malicious as the exchanges of Jane and Cassandra Austen. Susan writes about love, marriage and family life with a pen much sharper than any needle imagined by Monk Lewis. She finds affectation hilarious, and tells a story about the mealy-mouthed daughter of Henry Mackenzie, author of *The Man of Feeling* ('begotten, born, and bred in such a delicate, elegant, chaste, modest, refined, sentimental manner as baffles the description of a poor ignorant homespun maiden like me') who gave an evasive answer to a little sister ignorant of the word 'bastard', to meet nemesis when the child told an inquiring lady that she was sewing a shirt 'for her sister's bastard'. She pretends to mistake a pregnant wife for her husband's 'monstrous swelled leg', observes that someone is marrying a deaf husband who is not to be pitied, mocks two 'little infatuated foolies' suffering from 'that passion so *miscalled*' love, and is scornful when criticised for writing to a man about cutting corns. The best jokes are at the expense of men. She imagines one erring husband punished by transmigration, 'his soul will certainly be transfixed into the body of a nursery-maid with the care of ten children, two of them teething'. She replies to Charlotte's praise of a 'perfect man': 'I've lately discovered that I had the felicity of dancing with this prodigy about two years ago, and I remember I then thought him a *perfect child*, and could have patted his head and set him on my knee and fed him with sweetmeats for being a good boy and a pretty dancer.'

In spite of repeated masculine approvals of the small, closed social experience which fostered satire and grotesque portraiture, the restrictions of her cultural environment encouraged moral stereotype, unreal romance and high-flown passions as an inhospitable medium for her abilities. In spite of Monk Lewis's recommendation that women should write only about love, it is because they are love-stories that her novels are uneven and only patchily readable. Judge Irvine advises the reader to skip the sententious digressions, but this is easier said than done. The novelist has a way of slipping in a crisis or catastrophe at short notice. The mind may well flag or stray during an excursion on feeling or morality and miss a vital death or a fatal declaration. In spite of a good insight (in the letters) about people showing themselves in talk, she surrounds and smothers that talk with long and repetitive generalisations about her characters and life in general. The fault is compounded by her maddening habit of winding up such digressions by invitation to the reader's experience or imagination, in a terrible demonstration and travesty of Lessing's pregnant moment. Her novels are about four times as long as they should be, deal vacuously with passion and conflict, and lack tension and preparation. When she attempts prolepsis, as she does in the very funny episodes of Miss Grizzy's dream in *Marriage*, or Miss Pratt's arrival in a hearse in *The Inheritance*, tragic event comes so violently hugger-mugger at the heels of omen that climax is ludicrous and bathetic.

Her well-known judgement that Jane Austen's *Emma*, which she admired, 'had no story whatsoever', underlines her lack of structural sense. She wrote at a time when romantic conclusions, moral patterns and mechanical religious demonstration were the precondition for any woman novelist not possessed of the artistic courage of a Jane Austen. What Saintsbury insisted on calling her 'genius' was very severely compromised. We should probably not make too much of her preference for anonymity during most, though not all, of her career, since anonymity was then not exceptional. But there were good reasons, whether she knew them or not, for avoidance of publicity. Perhaps there were good reasons, too, for the nature of the early critical reception. Lord Jeffrey disappointed her by neglecting her 'bantlings', another review in the *Quarterly* made only a passing reference to the name of one character, Mrs Downe Wright, in *Marriage*. Christopher North admired her briefly for revealing the tragic decay of Highland chieftainship.

John Doyle rightly argued that she was much closer to Fanny Burney, in defects as well as merits, than to Jane Austen. But the traditional comparison with Jane Austen is inevitable. Many of her characters, caricatures, couplings and situations are shadows of Jane Austen's originals, and the famous first sentence of *The Inheritance*, 'It is a truth, universally acknowledged, that there is no passion so deeply rooted in human nature as that of pride' is a rash, endearing tribute. Like her insistent and unpointed assimilations of Shakespeare, in narrators and characters, this is an inconvenient reminder of irony, wit and subtlety.

Susan Ferrier's genius did not find the right medium, but it is genius, of a kind. The experience of reading the novels is punishing, but it has its rewards. The sharp and spiteful stories in the letters expand into brilliant grotesque sketches of idiosyncratic individuals, pairs, families and social groups.

The serious characters speak a weak and lofty language, are endlessly explicated, and wheel through a series of obvious moves and mysteries. But the comic characters are given racy individual speech, and are mostly freed from the demands of plot. The vivid images in the letters of 'fusty dowagers and musty mousers' and 'all the old tabbies in town . . . sitting on their sofas with *white sashes* on, ready to faint away at the sight of a man' and ladies 'playing whist to the death' spring into particularity. The art of fault finding produces the spinster Miss Pratt, in *The Inheritance*, who combines characteristics of Mrs Norris, Miss Bates and Mrs Gamp, but is all herself, in her busyness, bossiness, inaccurate gossip, guestly rapaciousness and invisible nephew, Anthony Whyte. Another eccentric with an accessory male is Lady Maclaughlan, in *Marriage*, who is blessed with two sinister cats, Gil Blas and Tom Jones, and a shrivelled, sick, polite, portable husband, Sir Sampson, an ancestor of Grandfather Smallweed. She is a rough-and-ready guest and hostess, performing in scenes of festive farce with a warming touch of heart. Uncle Adam Ramsay in *The Inheritance*, another crusty eccentric with a heart of gold, is one of the few approved novel-readers in the novels, so shamefacedly addicted to *Guy Mannering* that he can't go home until he has read to the end.

Another sweet-sour character, product of Susan Ferrier's own brand of regulated love-and-hate, is Mrs Violet Macshake in *Marriage*, a rude receiver of presents but hospitable and generous, liable to follow painful plain-speaking with a gift of diamond earrings. Her line in good-old-days nostalgia shows the force of Susan Ferrier's Scots vernacular. It races in such a strong current that the dialect is part of the fun, and needs no glossing:

I hae heard my mither tell what a bonny ploy was at her waddin. I canna tell ye hoo mony was at it; mair nor the room wad haud, ye may be sure. . . . An' the bride's goon was a shewed ow'r wi favours, frae the tap doon to the tail, an' aw roond the neck, an' aboot the sleeves; and, as soon as the ceremony was ow'r ilk ane ran till her, an' rugget an' rave at her for the favours, till they hardly left the claise upon her back. . . . An' was nae that something like a waddin? It was worth while to be married i' thae days—he, he! (Ch. 34)

Like Fanny Burney and Jane Austen, she compounds social caricature by groupings. She surrounds Mrs Fairbairn, a senseless motherly mother, with accessory accomplices and victims and places Miss Jacky, a spinster 'all over sense', as one of a grotesque series of sisters. Mrs Pullens is a show-off hostess and housekeeper, flaunting useless sales bargains, last season's badly preserved vegetables, and dishes disguised as 'what they were not', and given appropriately complacent guests.

Susan Ferrier is as good as Thackeray at literary affectation, and in a hilarious party at Mrs Bluemits' house (where nothing is spoken but 'conversation') homespun bluestockings perform enthusiastic feats of practical criticism over the dogs in Byron's poetry, and his use of the image 'crunch'. (One of Susan Ferrier's letters passionately exclaims that 'Childe Harold' 'is enough to make a woman fly into the arms of a tiger.') She patterns and ritualises comic type in the twinned alliances of the two Miss Bells, one needle-pointed in the follies of courtship and idiocies of marriage with her long-suffering Major, the other in a pseuds' match with a theatre-mad cit. (Susan was a snob.) Some of her stylised accumulations of cutting images are not unlike the rhetorical roll-calls of distortions and follies in *Our Mutual Friend*.

But there is no assimilation, no perspective, no organising principle of opinion or idea. At certain moments she gives herself away by feverishly dashing off lists of character-descriptions in talk, as if she couldn't find any more space for that needling pen's darts, but could not bear to restrain them. Where her novels express or imply system, as the first two vaguely attempt, and the last, *Destiny*, achieves in its Providential pattern, there is a mechanical and sentimental imposition, at odds with her comic reason. Not that she is alone in this, but where Dickens fails to integrate conventional Christian optimism with radical political satire, in *Bleak House*, for example, Susan Ferrier's fragmentations are far more frequent and far more gross. Had she been born into different choices, she might have concentrated her genius in the essays and sketches of a brilliant journalist. But her failures, as well as her successes, are part of feminist literary history.

First published in *The Times Literary Supplement*, 7 June 1985.

Note

1. References are to the Three Rivers Books edns. (Bampton, Oxfordshire, 1985).

7. Charles Dickens Remembered: a Toast

When we remember great writers, formally and festively, personally and privately, the memory is a blend of the mind that remembers and the mind that is being remembered. To carry memories with us through life, as we do in the case of books and authors we read when young, go on re-reading, and never stop reading until we close our last book, is to create a track on which we travel backwards and forwards in time. We cannot always claim to travel back reliably to the original event. Trying to recover some early memories of Dickens, I was struck again by what has often seemed to be the uncannily appropriate form and tone of memory. Memory has a chameleon's property of taking on local colour. At times it can even seem as if the very scene and situation invoked by memory had been imagined by the writer we remember.

I remember the first time I finished George Eliot's *The Mill on the Floss* and began to weep over the deliciously companionable drowning of Tom and Maggie in each other's arms, then crept into the comfort of my mother's bed for an agonised but luxuriating cry, an authentic Maggie Tulliver tearstorm. I remember taking my first Henry James novel out of a dusty little Welsh library, full of dusty theological books, presided over by a sweet faded librarian, wearing old-fashioned coils of faded fair hair over her ears, who might have been the governess in '*The Turn of The Screw* or the heroine of 'In the Cage'. I remember reading Proust, novelist of sickness and sleep, in a hospital bed.

My first acquaintance with Dickens, at least in my appropriate retrospects, is sharply visual. I remember the green cover of my mother's copy of *Our Mutual Friend*, with her maiden name inscribed on the flyleaf. I find it unreadable but next come across my first readable Dickens, those two enchanted stories where the children never grow up, *Oliver Twist* and *The Old Curiosity Shop*, and perhaps—memory dims here—*David Copperfield*, in rather cardboardy red bindings with meretricious gold on the spines, a black and white whorl pattern on the endpapers, borrowed from a bookshelf in the arm of an uncle's impressively smart thirties armchair. Perhaps it didn't strike me like that at the time. Perhaps the visual images have been picked out and heightened as I have read and re-read Dickens's marvellous accounts of a young child's powers of observation and memory. (Long before the psychologists of our time he suggested that we remember what we fixedly and attentively observe.)

Moments in our individual lives are connected and refreshed by such acts of memory. So too are our relations with people who share the same memories in a common and refreshing fellowship like the one we are enjoying tonight. This formed and formal fellowship is part of a larger, more public unity and continuity, that formal and published memory we call our literary tradition.

Dickens is the Inimitable. Probably the least successfully imitated of great writers, he declines to melt or merge in the words, shapes and stories of others. Yet other writers cannot leave him alone.

About the time that James Joyce was finishing his first novel *A Portrait of the Artist as a Young Man* he had to write an essay[1] on Dickens for an examination at the University of Padua in order to get an official qualification for teaching English in Italy. In it he wrote that Dickens had entered into the language more than any other writer since Shakespeare. He enters into more than language, becoming assimilated also into the forms and imaginations of other writers. His successors have probably been haunted by him even more than by Shakespeare, because Dickens is odder, more idiosyncratic and less universal than Shakespeare. Joyce himself wrote a parody of Dickens in *Ulysses*, as part of a great burlesque history of language and literature, but it is one of the palest and frailest sections of that great novel. It is a parody which breaks the first rule of parody—that it should be stronger than its original, which it must heighten and exaggerate. Dickens is such a magnifier of life that his parodists and parodies turn pale and frail beside the original, instead of reducing him to pallor and feebleness. But when Joyce lets Dickens appear in his own strength, it is a different story.

Ulysses and *Finnegans Wake* are full of comic and affectionate reminiscences, from the joking but irreverently probing distortions of titles, like 'Doveyed Covetfilles' and 'The Old Cupiosity Ship' to his possibly conscious adapation of Jingle's extrovert, staccato narrative style for Leopold Bloom's introspective stream of consciousness and Flora Finching's and Mrs Lirriper's unpunctuated garrulousness for Molly Bloom. Joyce and Dickens co-exist gloriously. And like all memory Joyce's reminiscence of Dickens isn't always deliberate or conscious. The river Liffey flows and merges with the eternal ocean in *Finnegans Wake* in a way all Dickensians immediately recognise, but Samuel Beckett had to draw Joyce's attention to Dickens's river.[2] Joyce must have been pleased, liking to join his voice with ancestral voices, especially those who prophesy peace and love.

Dickens is best remembered by other writers when remembered easily and naturally, and when given his head. That good Dickensian Angus Wilson can rely on the associations of the world 'Quilpish' (in *Anglo-Saxon Attitudes*), when out to convey nastiness swiftly, or can economically convey the narrator's prudent sense of reality (in *The Old Men at the Zoo*) by proclaiming that he never found it possible to believe in Micawber's Australian triumph. Like Joyce's Dickens, Wilson's is a critic's and a novelist's Dickens, as well as the common reader's Dickens. As he reflects and distorts the fog and damp of *Bleak House* at the beginning of *As If By Magic* he does more than recapitulate for the purposes of beginning his novel. He establishes a continuity of social fogginess, introduces and reinforces his theme of art's powerful but limited magic. He has himself testified to the inspiration of Dickens's vitality, too large, powerful and general to be pinned down by definition.

Between Joyce, at the beginning of the century, and Wilson, in our own time, come several distinguished and distinctive writers who remember Dickens. T. S. Eliot was haunted by Dickensian words and rhythms. One haunting appears appropriately enough in the comic book *Old Possum's Book of Practical Cats*, where Possum remembers Podsnap. In the most famous chapter of *Our Mutual Friend*, celebrating one of the most famous dinner-parties in Dickens, Podsnappery finds its unforgettable expression. As Podsnap informs the company, and especially that enlightened European, the foreign gentleman, of Providence's careful bestowal of the British Constitution, the foreign gentleman begins to question, 'And ozer countries?' only to be interrupted by Podsnap's pedagogic clemency, 'We do not say Ozer; we say Other: the letters are "T" and "H"; You say Tay and Aish, You Know' and 'The sound is "th"—"th"!' The foreign gentleman trying again with 'And other countries . . . They do how?' feeds Podsnap's style and inspiration: 'They do, Sir . . . they do—I am sorry to be obliged to say it—*as* they do'. Podsnap's British triumph is remembered and converted by Mr Eliot, another enlightened foreigner, into the comment on the incorrigible and perverse cat, the Rum Tum Tugger, who inconveniently and perversely prefers a flat to a house and pheasant to grouse, but who has to be accepted, for 'He will do/As he do do/And there's no doing anything about it!'

The descent of Podsnap was pointed out by Mrs Valerie Eliot in her 1971 facsimile edition of the original version of Eliot's *The Waste Land*, a book which revealed another even odder Dickensian reminiscence. Students of Eliot and Dickens were astonished to find that in the original draft, much longer, more urban, more Cockney, and more satirical than the one Eliot published in 1922, the most prominent presiding Muse was not Frazer, Jessie Weston, Shakespeare, Marvell, Webster, the Bible, Baudelaire, Virgil, Spenser, Ovid or Dante, but Dickens, who was not even mentioned in the notes which illuminate the published *Waste Land*, after Eliot revised it with the help of Ezra Pound. The first two books had the title taken from Betty Higden's memorable words about Sloppy's reading of the newspapers: 'He do the police in different voices', perfect for the poem about London squalor, crowds, bridges, churches, chimes, pubs, underworld and river, and also perfect for Eliot's 'modernist device' (mildly anticipated in *Bleak House*) of juxtaposing different voices and viewpoints. Perhaps the interest in Betty's Cockney 'he do the police' effected the transfer from Podsnap's correct 'they do' to the Rum Tum Tugger's 'he do'. Sloppy would have been as astonished at his elevation into a Muse as Podsnap indignant at his lowering metamorphosis into a cat. Sloppy, alas, disappeared from the revised version of Eliot's poem, but we can be grateful to the Golden Dustman of scholarship, which as it rummages in its dust-heaps, sometimes unearths genuine legacies like this Dickensian treasure.

Evelyn Waugh, another great comic writer who laughs while he satirises urban life, profitably took his epigraph and title, in *A Handful of Dust*, that sad, grisly and bitter book, from Eliot's *The*

Waste Land, which included the words, 'I will show you fear in a handful of dust'. (Eliot had taken it from John Donne's *Devotions upon Emergent Occasions* [1624].) As well as remembering Eliot, he remembered Dickens. Perhaps Dickens was evoked unconsciously together with the dust. He is present at the beginning of the novel, in a cultivated and easy Dickensian description of an intricately hideous Gothic pile as 'authentic Pecksniff', the family joke originating in an acid aunt's comment that the house must have been built from the plans purloined by Pecksniff from his pupil's design for an orphanage. The Dickens memory goes deeper than this; the novel ends with the strangest invocation of Dickens in modern literature. The hero, Tony Last, who has lost wife, son, family estate and England, ends as a captive reader of Dickens in a Brazilian village, doomed to read forever to the eager, crazy, illiterate Dickensian Mr Todd, with his collection of all Dickens's novels except two (unnamed) which have been eaten by ants. At first he amuses Tony who, like many Dickensians, prides himself on his Dickens readings, by wonderfully obvious observations, 'Dedlock is a proud man' and 'Mrs Jellyby does not take enough care of her children'. He also amazes him by sinister misplaced response to the description of the outcasts in Tom-All-Alone's, which makes him weep with laughter. Finally he condemns Tony to the torture of Dickens' readings every afternoon, for the rest of his life. After they are all read, which will take two years, Todd tells Tony, they can begin again: 'I have heard them all several times by now, but I never get tired; there is always more to be learned and noticed, so many characters, so many changes of scene, so many words. . . . Each time I think I find more to enjoy and admire.' A joke against Dickens? The tables turned on Dickens' fans? I think not. Few other novelists would turn up in a set (only slightly ant-eaten) in a mud hut on the Amazon. A relic of decayed Englishness. No other novelist would bring together so ironically the illiterate Todd— himself a Dickens-like caricature of the most appalling kind—and the educated Tony. Most important, Waugh is letting Dickens appear at the right time in the right place, in an ending as grotesque and gruesome as spontaneous combustion, or Miss Havisham's wedding-cake, or Wegg's leg. The grotesque effect here, however, has its own futility. Dickens and Waugh join their darker visions.

Our Mutual Friend haunted the memory and imagination of a later satirical novelist, whose picture of England is even blacker and bleaker than Dickens's or Waugh's. Like Joyce and Eliot, George Orwell is particularly haunted by the richness and inventiveness of Dickens's language. With the sensibility and tact of a good novelist and a good Dickens critic, he chooses Dickens as the only novelist specified in the list of writers doomed to be translated, or cut down (by the first or second decade of the twenty-first century) into Newspeak, that mindshrunk and mindshrinking new language. Entirely appropriate that Dickens should be chosen to survive, as a prestigious remnant and travesty of the Great Tradition, as a name indestructible even in *1984*, and yet particularly terrible that his fertility of language should be picked for sterilisation by the Fiction Department, coldly listed in the appendix which ends the novel with its chilling documentary report. Orwell is fully incorporating Dickens into his novel, for it begins with a proof and invocation of Dickens's richness, powers and play, in a chapter describing a gritty, dust-bringing wind, a whirl of dust and swirl of paper, the detritus and bad breath of the city which, even in 1984, still has rotten, crazily shored-up nineteenth-century houses standing— bleak houses indeed. This time it is Chapter 12 of *Our Mutual Friend* which is recalled, the chapter which also describes a cold and bitter spring, sawdust and paper currency. The odour and dirt of Dickens is as potent as the memory of post-war, austere Britain. Just to clinch the recall, Orwell has his dust-heaps too, refashioned in 1949, the date of the novel's publication, and located in war-stricken London, chief city of Airstrip One, in 1984, in 'bombed sites' where 'the plasterdust swirled in the air and the willowherb straggled over the heaps of rubble'.

Orwell, Waugh, Eliot, Wilson and Joyce do not imitate their great predecessor, but let him assert himself, in a full reminiscence of his individuality, power and humanity. They all assume a conscious or an unconscious recognition of his presence, relying, as they can rely, on the fellowship of Dickens readers, the strength of our memories, and the memory of Dickens.

This chapter is the text of the Dickens toast given at the London Birthday Dinner, 1977, and was published in the *Dickensian*, Vol. 73, 1977.

Notes

1. Published in *Journal of Modern Literature*, Vol. 5, No. 1, February 1976.
2. I am indebted to Richard Ellmann and Samuel Beckett for this information.

8. Mrs Gaskell: Novelist of Sensibility

Although there are two places—Knutsford in Cheshire, and Manchester—which provided sources and images for much of Elizabeth Gaskell's writing, hers was not a life which can be obviously mined for constructive criticism. We have to observe the background of Unitarianism, on her father's side and her husband's, her domesticity, her social contacts with the industrial world and the literary world, in the North, in London and in Europe. We need to insist on her close and sympathetic knowledge of the lives of the poor. Her letters show how she and her daughters were exhausted and appalled by their relief work in Manchester during the cotton famine of the early eighteen sixties, for instance. And there are many points of detail in the novels that can be traced back to a direct or indirect biographical source, like the change of faith of Mr Hale in *North and South*, which transforms but uses her own father's conscientious resignation from the Unitarian ministry, or the celebrated anecdotes about the cow's flannel coat and the cat who swallowed the lace in *Cranford*. But if there were crises in her emotional and intellectual life, like the crises which mark the lives and the art of Dickens, Thackeray and George Eliot, they remain invisible. Hers is a remarkable and various body of novels and stories which have to be looked at in and for themselves.

This is of course not to deny that her most important works are potent social expressions both in their steady and complete presentation of a society in whole and parts, as in *Cranford* and *Wives and Daughters*, and as criticisms and appeals, showing a view of contemporary society, its suffering, irrationality and injustice, in that clear but never impersonal mirror which she holds up to her time. Certain critics, rightly reacting against an older pretty persistent view of her art as the product of a minor, charming, but slender talent, emphasised the eloquence of her sociological thinking and feeling, and both Kathleen Tillotson, in *Novels of the 1840s*, (Clarendon Press, Oxford, 1954), and Edgar Wright, in *Mrs Gaskell: The Basis for Reassessment* (O.U.P., London 1965), have examined her handling of social facts. Both Wright and Arthur Pollard stressed her importance as a psychological novelist, whose social analysis depends very markedly on a realistic handling of the language, manners and passions of human beings. Looking at her in the large context of the Victorian novel, I am impressed anew by her freedom from simplification and caricature. The great social critics in nineteenth-century English fiction are Jane Austen, Dickens and Thackeray. Theirs is an art of complex fable, of bold and telling outline, of the conspicuous and critical embodiment of ideas in satiric forms. Mrs Gaskell is unusual as a social novelist in her avoidance of satire. Not that this avoidance is always a merit in her novels: at times she too is writing a kind of fable, most notably in her first novel, *Mary Barton*. Here the portrait of the manufacturing class and of trade unionism is the worst kind of caricature, crude, very simplified, stereotyped and lacking both the bite of humour and its frank admission of bias and exaggeration. But strengths and weaknesses are often closely associated and if we pay for this absence of satire by such embarrassing and implausible crudities, we also gain the particularly intimate, alert and live creations of her sympathy, which manage to stay well on this side of sentimentality. Pollard has said that Mrs Gaskell 'is never a propagandist; or if she is, she is only a propagandist for sympathy'. This seems to point to the heart of her individuality as a novelist, as well as showing the way to reconcile the praise of her sociological imagination with that of her psychological powers. If I had to fix a label to her special contribution to what we conveniently call 'The English novel', I would describe her as essentially a novelist of sensibility. It is a phrase which describes her changing powers throughout her career. Although she wrote only six important novels, one fine novella, *Cousin Phillis*, and one of the best Victorian biographies, *The Life of Charlotte Brontë*, (as well as many stories and sketches, some good but many undistinguished), her talent is a various one.

Mrs Gaskell did not say a great deal about her art but what she did say provides an excellent entry into the imagined world of her novels. That very phrase, 'imagined world', is a commonplace but useful critical formula, expressing the novel's inventiveness, unity, and double concern with the individual life and the portrayal of environment. But it seems rather inappropriately used of Mrs Gaskell. When she talks about her novels, she insists, rather as D. H. Lawrence did, on her own therapeutic relation to her creations. This comes out noticeably, for instance, when she compares her own writing with that of Charlotte Brontë, whom she knew and responded to sympathetically. She says in a letter of April 1853:

> The difference between Miss Brontë and me is that she puts all her naughtiness into her books, and I put all my goodness. I am sure that she works off a great deal that is morbid *into* her writing, and *out* of her life; and my books are so far better than I am that I often feel ashamed of having written them and as if I were a hypocrite. (*The Letters of Mrs Gaskell*, ed. J. A. V. Chapple and Arthur Pollard, Manchester University Press, Manchester, 1960, p. 228.)

In no way at odds with this comparison, is her suggestion that *Mary Barton* was a novel which perhaps suffered from working off too much that was morbid into the novel out of her life. It is well known that she undertook the novel, at her husband's suggestion, after the death of her ten-month-old son from scarlet fever, and she talks revealingly about its darkness and its origin in what she thinks might be 'a wrong motive for writing . . . sure only to produce a failure'. She saw the novel as an especially effective refuge and calm refreshment for women, but concluded, after a good deal of wounding criticism, not entirely of an aesthetic kind, that she was perhaps in error when she used the composition of the novel as a 'refuge to exclude the memory of painful scenes which would force themselves upon my remembrance'.

To begin then, with *Mary Barton*. Seeing it as a novel of sensibility is essential when we look at its origin in personal suffering, and when we look at her reactions to the criticism of the novel, so different from the confident resentment of insensitivity which can be found, for instance, in George Eliot. In Mrs Gaskell's self-doubting, honestly explanatory and searching comments on the response (not so much of literary critics as of people in Manchester of whom she knew) can be sensed a wounded nerve of feeling disappointed and frustrated in the very act of heartfelt

appeal. She has this to say about the possible imbalance or injustice
which certain readers felt in the novel:

> I can remember now that the prevailing thought in my mind at
> the time when the tale was silently forming itself and impressing
> me with the force of a reality, was the seeming injustice of the
> inequalities of fortune. Now, if they occasionally appeared
> unjust to the more fortunate, they must bewilder an ignorant
> man full of rude, illogical thought, and full also of sympathy for
> suffering which appealed to him through his senses. I fancied I
> saw how all this might lead to a course of action which might
> appear right for a time to the bewildered mind of such a one, but
> that this course of action, violating the eternal laws of God,
> would bring with it its own punishment of an avenging
> conscience far more difficult to bear than any worldly privation.
> Such thoughts I now believe, on looking back, to have been the
> origin of the book. 'John Barton' was the original title of the
> book. (*Letters* p. 74.)

Mary Barton, as it was eventually called, is a novel which cuts a
deep channel both for the personal bereavement and her sympathy
for the sufferings of the industrial poor. Those feelings are so
merged in their profound and fierce flow that I would make no
attempt to speculate about their causal relation: feelings for
children are conspicuous, and highly relevant in the book, but
coming invariably out of all such feelings, from every aspect of this
story of family unity, disintegration and pain, is a bewildered and
frustrated social questioning. Arthur Pollard quotes her attempt to
reason with a poor man about his bitter hostility to the rich, and his
answer, reasoned in tears, 'Aye, ma'am but have ye ever seen a child
clemmed to death.' *Mary Barton* begins with a revised version of
this question when John Barton asks what the 'gentlefolk' have ever
done for him:

> If my child lies dying (as poor Tom lay, with his white wan lips
> quivering, for want of better food than I could give him), does
> the rich man bring the wine or broth that might save his life?
> (Ch. 1)

The novel is punctuated by comments on child-death. Some are
very muted, and no less touching for that, as in the words 'the aged,

the feeble, the children, when they die, are scarcely noted by the world'. Some are more strikingly personal. Moreover, the novel insistently takes us back to the childhood even of the adult characters, and certainly two of the long digressions (sometimes criticised as instances of imperfect grasp of construction) seem to be justified by this insistence. Job Legh's story of how he and his friend brought their granddaughter Margaret, as a small and helpless baby, from London to Manchester, and Alice Wilson's tales of her childhood (to which she reverts in her happy deathbed) both give new colour to the primary feeling for children. Job's story has a comic, even grotesque, way of loving and pathetic appeal, Alice's has a radiant, innocent, pastoral joy. Not only is there this variety of emotional colour, and the much-needed relief from the horrors and desolations of the child-deaths, but also there is always Mrs Gaskell's characteristic social and psychological particularity. I would claim that it is this particularity that distinguishes her 'morbidity' from the strong general demands, sentimental and distastefully morbid, of Dickens's Nell and Tiny Tim. Her morbidity is excessive, in a strict aesthetic sense, taking us out of the novel in a way which is both painful and under-distanced, but which also makes it appropriately painful propaganda for the sympathies. It is revelatory fiction such as George Eliot was trying to write in *Scenes of Clerical Life*, but its materials have a horror, pity and passionate hysteria, which find no place in George Eliot.

This hysteria is in the materials. Mrs Gaskell dramatises the passions, but controls them and keeps them individual. At times she steps outside the story to reason and explain, to placate her gentle reader and beg a tolerance for the violence of these agitators and assassins, but then she says, 'Let us now return to individuals'. Her sensibility takes in and shows the full range of experience, to take us, as Zola does, from comfort to bleakness, from nourishment to starvation, from some small colour and ornament to bareness and squalor. The interestingness of the novel and its emotional appeal go together. She wants to show the fall from one state to a worse, like any tragedian. She wants also to show, in a sharply argumentative way, the working-class culture, its ceremony, sociability, hospitality, song and science. Thus she creates not only a realistic picture of the culture (in a way that Gissing, when he takes us inside the houses and habits of the poor, usually fails to do), but gives animation and richness to what is not just a fable, and shows not the being of two nations, but their becoming. If she simply contrasted the starvation and disease in the poor home with the breakfasting of the rich (as she does at one point in the novel) we would have an effective simplification but a less complete picture and, ultimately, a less potent appeal to the heart. Hers is, like George Eliot's, a conservative imagination, and these novels combine a realistic report with a modest demand, not for a radical redistribution, but for a minimal nourishment for body and soul.

A similar truthfulness comes out of her knowledge that her two nations are not all that separate in origins: she knows Mrs Carson, who was working-class, is particularly isolated and barren because she has no resources, and we appreciate also the importance of goods and money, in a novel about the material, not the hereditary, basis of class, about labour and capital, not about blood and rank. I stress this truthfulness because the novel's plotting, as too often in Mrs Gaskell is strained and even implausible. She said in the letter previously quoted on the subject that John Barton was her hero, the character round whom 'all the others formed themselves . . . *the* person with whom all my sympathies went, with whom I tried to identify myself at the time, because I believed from personal observation that such men were not uncommon', and his displacement is the novel's great failing. Her publishers apparently persuaded her to call the novel *Mary Barton*, but the chief cause for the change must be the shift in the emotional centre. With John's guilt comes his inevitable absence from the scene, and our lack of access to his inner life. Though the thread of Mary's feelings has from the beginning been woven in with his, it too thins out in the more heavily plotted final episodes, where the novel turns from sensitive social appeal and psychology to the sensational, highly active, and rather over-optimistic conclusion. It is perhaps because of the powers of feeling in the main body of the novel that the last third is so disappointing.

Like *Mary Barton*, the other novels, whatever their material and themes, have this potency and variety of feeling. Even the stagey villain, Harry Carson, his father, and Esther, the prostitute, lose a little of their staginess in being brought into the mainstream of feeling: we see them too as children and parents, not as divided from the rest of the action in melodramatic stereotype throughout. The only other novel which shares the partial staginess and the over-optimistic ending is *Ruth*, another social novel, separated from

Mary Barton by *Cranford*, and thus making it impossible for us to talk about Mrs Gaskell's sociological period.

Mary Barton's powerful topicality (as a novel about Chartism appearing less than ten years after the Charter had been rejected, and at a time of depression, insecurity and great want) made it a successful and much-discussed novel. *Ruth* had a similar success. It was very widely reviewed, receiving high praise for its truth and moral beauty, as well as hostility and disapproval. Mrs Gaskell was deeply hurt by the disapproval, but even though the book was banned by fathers of families and even burnt, she believed in its seriousness and fervour. There are perhaps two chief reasons for the antagonism it aroused: its subject, which was seduction and illegitimacy, and its theme, that of Hardy's *Tess*, the moral innocence of the seduced girl.

Ruth is in fact a narrowly didactic book, which deals with a more simple saintly woman than Tess, and which is a fable of atonement, by love and death. Ruth's nobility almost puts her beyond the typical social problem which she is intended to represent. The book has certain flaws: it begins by showing the seduction of a simple little girl, and eventually shows her as a much more intelligent and complex woman, rather startlingly enlarging her character and creating a resolution which to my mind makes for disunity and implausibility. We may very well understand how the flaw came about. Mrs Gaskell shows the inner life of Ruth sporadically, so that some of her reactions are available, some rather arbitrarily absent. The necessary sexual reticence of the Victorian novel, even in the eighteen forties, means that our knowledge of Ruth is incomplete, and though some aspects of her sensibility are finely presented—like her reactions to the natural scene and to people in Wales—some of the portraiture is rather external. In the later parts of the novel Ruth's fears and insecurity about her child, especially when her seducer comes back into her life, are movingly and persistently shown, as are the feelings and moral life of the Bensons and the Bradshaws. Live and sharp too is the more reticent but decorous treatment of the alienation and reserve of Leonard, the child, after he finds out that he is illegitimate, and the breaking of shame by eloquent pride in the moment when he finds that his mother is a beloved public heroine. But there are ellipses and dead patches in the novel, and the apotheosis by death seems at once inevitable and unadventurous. Unlike *Mary Barton* and *North and South*, the novel fails to give a complete enough rendering of its characters. What is meant to be another typical plea on behalf of social suffering becomes inappropriately idealised—why plead for saints like Ruth?—and over-simplified—how about the sympathy needed by more ordinary victims of the social traps? But it must be admitted that the idealised portrait has considerable beauty and if the novel is read as a study in saintliness rather than sin, its humanity and drama will be more impressive.

Mrs Gaskell's novels always have the interest of particularity. Ruth's idealisation never takes off from the solid earth to become stereotyped or lachrymose, like the portraits of Agnes Wickfield or Esther Summerson. In *Ruth* there is the solidity and vividness of the comic-serious relationships of the Bensons and the Bradshaws, the enacted and implied complexity of Jemima Bradshaw, and the unpatronising beauty and humour of the characterisation of the servant, Sally. In *North and South*, the best of the three social novels, there is this kind of solid and varied realism of character and a much freer treatment of the element of fable. Mrs Gaskell realises at this stage that fictions are created by people, necessarily but falsely, and that degree of simplification and crudity which escaped her control in *Mary Barton* and *Ruth* seems, in this remarkable novel, to have been assimilated, dramatised, and finally criticised. In *North and South*, it is the characters, not only the author, who construct fables. The novel shows the dangerous inadequacy of fables, and its characters are educated out of their fictions and face the complexity of loving, working, serving and leading. Having said this, I must add that the novel's ability to face complexity and do, as George Eliot said we must, 'without opiates', is in the end limited. Like most Victorian novels, it mends matters with authorial magic, and the problems of love and industrial failure are solved and dismissed by coincidence and that favourite device of the bourgeois novel, the unexpected legacy.

Mrs Gaskell shares these limitations with Dickens and George Eliot and Charlotte Brontë—with all the great Victorian novelists, perhaps, except the Thackeray of *Vanity Fair*'s great, sour, truthful satire. In spite of them, she writes a novel of penetrating psychology. In the previous novels we are moved by the poignancy of feeling, which makes the ever-interesting and effectively appealing narrative medium, but in *North and South* there is a new element, of surprisingly psychological content. We are moved and held not just by the dramatic liveliness, but by what it reveals of human nature.

This revealed depth of content is the fact of human fiction, the fabling about *North* and *South* which forms the central dream of the novel. It is a dream dreamt by the heroine, Margaret Hale and, like many human dreams, it is dreamt as a stabilising reaction to instability. Intuitively or deliberately, Mrs Gaskell shows Margaret on the eve of returning to the place and parents she has known only discontinuously during her adolescence. Her return brings her not the pastoral peace and family joy she expects and needs, after the disruptions and oppressive joys of London life, but a father who is about to resign his ministry, and indeed a father and a mother who lean on her, heavily and pathetically. This is the first stage in her waking and dreaming: the pastoral dream and the childhood idyll fail. When the Hales move to the North, the dream returns again in a protective and temporarily restorative fashion. She has been teased in London for the sort of pastoral idealised picture she has of Helstone, the village of her childhood, and in the grim Darkshire where they try the new life, the pastoral dream is first needed, then tried and, after a long, slow testing in complex experience and varied relations, found wanting.

It is not the only illusion in the novel. Matched with it, in strength, unity and partial plausibility, is Mr Thornton's unenlightened belief in autonomy, freedom and power of master over worker. This is a dream which, like Margaret's, is dreamt by someone sufficiently sensitive and intelligent to allow intransigent experience to shatter the dream. Both dreams are theoretic, and when Margaret learns what the urban North is like, and when Thornton learns the humanity and limited freedom of his workers, theory collapses before the largeness and complexity of life as it is. As Pollard is careful to point out, Thornton remains a benevolent master, putting his faith in workers' welfare and good communication. Moreover, he does not succeed in trade but fails. As in the earlier novels, what is impressive is not a confident radicalism but a tentative questioning of the present, not a grasp of economics but a grasp of the individual case. She takes a step beyond *Mary Barton* and *Ruth* in the very mutedness of *North and South*: the action is on a smaller, less heroic scale, and there is no trace of the stereotyped fable of *Mary Barton*.

The novel moves insistently from and between its two personal centres of feeling. At last her novel of sensibility is both balanced and complete. We oscillate between Margaret and Thornton, and their range of sensibility prominently includes pride, passion, anger, sensitive sympathy and moral admiration. These passions largely make up the characters and their affinity. They unify the action as well as the characters because they are dramatised most potently, in the intimate personal relationship of sexual and filial love, and in a series of reactions to society that cut across class divisions. This kind of emotional continuity and complexity is in its very nature inaccessible to illustration, especially in an essay, and I can only briefly refer to typically rich and mobile scenes like that of Thornton's first proposal of marriage to Margaret, the scene in which she first makes friends with Higgins and Bessy, and the scene where Thornton first goes to see Higgins in his home. You notice the way Mrs Gaskell always shows or tells—usually both—what the characters are feeling, and how she pushes on the emotional development and change variously and continuously. There are no *lacunae* where you do not know (and need to know) what the character is feeling, as in *Ruth*. You notice too how often the feelings are not specialised, not kept in separate compartments. Thornton's anger at Margaret's refusal resembles his anger at Higgins's egalitarian and rational honesty, and these strong characters can feel furious and respectful as their pride and anger fight, against each other's pride and anger, and against themselves. One of the admirably honourable qualities in the characters of Mrs Gaskell is the reasonable passion. If Jane Austen is the first English novelist to show and be aware of showing a reasonable sexual love, so Mrs Gaskell deserves praise for showing, with depth and delicacy, a reasonable pride, a reasonable anger, a reasonable despair. The characters are animated, distinguished, and, finally, unified by their feelings.

It is this dramatised sensibility, which takes us over the weak spots of the action, like the melodramatic and coincidental business of Frederick's return, Thornton's encounter with Margaret and her brother and the consequent misunderstanding. It is the display and analysis of passions and intelligence which makes such an effective medium for what I have called the theme of dreams and fables. Margaret is forced by reason, respect and sympathy to see that North is not wrong to South's right, and Thornton is forced by reason, respect and sympathy to see that communication between master and servant is not only possible but honourable, and that violence and despair have their reasons, as well as their madness.

The novel has many complex moments of feeling, and such complexities are present in the other novels which are less conspicuous in their social criticism. To go back to *Cranford*, her second novel, we find there not only the charm, pathos and humour for which it has always been celebrated, but a considerable complexity and subtlety in the presentation of feeling. It is a novel with a displaced personal centre, unlike the others. It is a deliberately handled, almost a Jamesian, displacement. The narrator is Mary Smith, whose sympathy and irony are both more sophisticated and more available than the sensibilities of any of the more involved characters, and with Mary we gradually accumulate a full view of the story. The true active centre is Miss Matty. We piece together, from retrospect, hint and expressive incident, her timidity, her courage, her spinster's loneliness, her lost love, her family feeling and her suffering. Ultimately, when all is pieced together, it becomes a story of unguessed-at integrity, loss, and oppression. The bits fit together: Miss Matty's pride, consistency and real dignity when she, unlike the other dear ladies, assumes that they will not accept Mrs Jamieson's afterthought invitation; her insistence on honouring the Town and County Bank note instead of buying the new dress; and her forbearance when Martha wants to have a follower: these illustrative incidents create the strong side of Miss Matty, whom we, like Mary, first see as a sweet, eccentric, not very bright, dependent old lady. We piece together the story too, first seeing the man she might have married, in the opaque humour of the visit, which allows no tremble of sentiment to get through, and later learning slowly what had happened, through odd bits of gossip, and then in the news of his death. The piecemeal method, like the indirect discovery, is natural, in this most natural-seeming chronicle where naturalness is decorous, and moving, as we accumulate impressions in a continuous process of slight shocks and revisions. Moreover, the rambling and anecdotal form picks up unity in this process. What looked at first like (and probably started as) a series of episodic sketches, turns out to have a very cunning continuity, quality, and power to move. What looked like insipidity or mere charm turns out to rebuke us for having jumped to interpret it as insipidity or mere charm. *Cranford* teaches us, by a dynamic process, not to be too easily charmed by quaintness, not to pity precipitately what we may have eventually also to admire. Without wishing to analyse its delicacy out of existence, I praise it for the kind of delicacy which reveals strength. It is an apparently unassuming novel, and its apparent charm and sweetness are as profound and as deceptive as Miss Matty's. It is a novel whose form is perfectly appropriate to its content, so that the two are not separable.

Cousin Phillis, *Sylvia's Lovers*, and *Wives and Daughters*, coming together, in that order, at the end of Mrs Gaskell's short life, all possess the perfection and subtlety of *Cranford* and add *new* profundities of vision and feeling. *Cousin Phillis*, her best piece of short fiction, has a displaced and detached narrator. Paul Manning is rather like Nelly Dean, in *Wuthering Heights*, not all that detached from the passions he observes and narrates. Again, by a slight delicate shift of a kind usually praised in Henry James, Mrs Gaskell makes a perfect movement from expectation to surprise. We learn to read Paul as narrator, but in the precipitating event of the story he becomes a responsible agent, and yet preserves the observer's role, which has encouraged his fault and determines the nature of his punishment. It is also, like *Wives and Daughters*, a perfect instance of control and reserve: its joys and griefs are largely inner and unspoken ones, its very action is contained in the mind and in the heart. It is also, like everything she wrote, full of psychological variety. Mrs Gaskell really has no minor characters, and both Holdsworth and Holman are as complete, complex, and surprising in their individuality as Phillis herself. The beautiful and bookish country girl, vulnerable, strong, romantic, realistic, loving and sharp, is a brilliant creation who might even, read at the wrong time, suggest a certain softness in Hardy's Tess.

Wives and Daughters, like *Cousin Phillis*, reveals almost unbearable sadness, and shows how human beings bear it. The intensity of grief and the reserve or resolve that makes heartbreak endurable or even mendable, is shown in Molly Gibson with a patience, pride and self-aware humour which belongs both to the presentation and to the character. The novel is remarkably modest, quiet and genial. Molly's passionate feelings are recognised and proffered in a complexity which cannot even be named—does she feel 'anger, dislike, indignation', her author asks, and takes refuge in the intensity and open suggestiveness of an image: 'It was as if the piece of solid ground on which she stood had broken from the shore, and she was drifting out into an infinite sea alone'. Molly's loss of her happy life with her father, then later, the loss of her lover, and later still, the temporary loss of her good name, are all fairly small and fairly private griefs, compared with the deaths and pangs and shames in *Mary Barton, Ruth,* or even *North and South,* but they are real, important, and fully expressive of the problems of moral and social growth and adjustment.

Molly and Sylvia of *Sylvia's Lovers,* in my opinion Mrs Gaskell's greatest novel, are interesting passive characters, whose lives, like those of many women in and out of fiction, are more manipulated than the lives of men. Their passiveness, however, is different. Sylvia's life is determined by social forces: her lover is carried off by the press-gang, her father hanged for violence against the gang, her mother's reason destroyed, and her marriage made by the isolation, desolation and economic dependence brought about by all these incidents. But her feelings, unlike Molly's, are not only strong but have to be expressed: and if she is acted upon, her vitality of feeling becomes an active force. It attacks and exiles her husband in its sheer ferocity. But her passions are complex, and if Philip had learnt to read them as we do, he would have seen her characteristic shift, brought about by sympathy and by reason, from rejection to forgiveness. In *Sylvia's Lovers* and *Wives and Daughters* Mrs Gaskell seems less interested in the development of sensibility, as in some of the earlier novels, than in its individual patterns and consequences. In a way anticipatory of Hardy, she shows the ironic clash between individual passions. Mrs Gaskell sets out the kind of vulnerability, innocence, pride and acceptance, which we will find typical of Molly's adult life, in the early scene where Molly is lost and neglected and let down by her future stepmother. In the varying crises of the novel, the same pattern of feeling and response is provoked, developed, and worked out. Similarly, Sylvia's passionateness, sensuousness, imaginative sympathy, and toughness are shown in the first scene when she goes to buy a cloak and stays to cheer and grieve with the crowd, and are repeated later, many times. The cycle returns most importantly when she refuses to forgive the man responsible for her father's death, but then recoils on her own hardness. This anticipates the revengeful unforgiving passion and recoil to love with which she meets the discovery of Philip's deception. Philip's track of feeling plays against and with hers, and they are two of the most moving, emotionally complex and morally tolerant studies of human strength and weakness in the English novel. Sylvia has a vitality and range of passions which is seldom shown in fiction apart from high intelligence. And the novel's ending, which brings us face to face with inevitable hurt, unnecessary hurt, spent life, new life, strong love, endurance, exhaustion, and the joining of reconciliation with parting, is one of the saddest experiences in the range of Mrs Gaskell's imaginative achievement.

First published in the *Sphere History of Literature in the English Language*, Vol. 6 (Sphere Books, London, 1969).

9. George Eliot: Patterns of Life and Fiction

Mrs Gaskell wrote to tell George Eliot how much she admired *Scenes of Clerical Life* and *Adam Bede*, and George Eliot replied saying that she had been aware that her attitude to Life and Art 'had some affinity with the feeling which . . . inspired "Cranford" and the earlier chapters of "Mary Barton" ', and that she had read *Cranford* while writing *Scenes*, and *Mary Barton* while writing *Adam Bede*. What she thought about the affinity is a matter for guessing. We know that she also liked *The Life of Charlotte Brontë* and *Sylvia's Lovers* but was critical of the 'dramatic effect' and 'love of sharp contrasts' which she said were obstacles to complete sympathy and typicality in *Ruth*. She rather liked such contrasts herself, though hers are endowed with subtlety and finesse. There is an affinity between her early work and Mrs Gaskell's attitude to life and art, in their sympathy, a quality of imagination not restricted to the creativity of art. It is interesting that George Eliot speaks of the affinity as felt in the early work. In *Scenes* there is not only the deliberate attempt to show ordinariness and average sensibility, but even the convention of a spectator's *persona*. There is also the half-critical but sympathetic reaction to quaintness and humour. But such novelistic affinity was not lasting. The sympathy that showed itself in analysis of average lives and ordinary sensibility created all Mrs Gaskell's novels, but none of George Eliot's, except for the three stories in *Scenes* and *Silas Marner*, all, significantly, short pieces. She began by wanting to reveal ordinary life to over-stimulated palates and sensational expectations, but soon moved from homely realism to what was truly her *métier*, the drama of intellect and sensibility in strong and unusual characters.

We should carefully distinguish the social and the psychological aims here. Both novelists set out, and succeeded, in showing lower-class sensibility and suffering, after the manner of Dutch painting, as George Eliot says in *Adam Bede*. But Mrs Gaskell is very much more socially and politically didactic, despite her conservatism, than George Eliot, and one might argue that she is more sharply sceptical and less complacent than George Eliot is in her treatment of labour-relations in *Adam Bede* or of political agitation in *Felix Holt*. George Eliot is much more confident of the rightness of Adam's attitude to his more frivolous fellow-workers, and of the evil of the mob violence than Mrs Gaskell's more troubled questioning ever allows her to be. George Eliot seldom goes into the psychology of the 'wrong' action as sympathetically as Mrs Gaskell. Indeed, one reason for the revival of interest in Mrs Gaskell may lie in her appealing lack of moral absolutism. George Eliot is closer to the unmodern Shavian character who is certain of the difference between right and wrong, both in political and personal morality. She is also more rationally in control of her moral system. When she criticised Mrs Gaskell for siding so simply with Branwell Brontë, we can see her rationality criticising the more impetuous sympathies of the older novelist. The comparison is ironic since it was Mrs Gaskell who wrote to admire the younger woman's novels *and* to wish that she was really Mrs Lewes. But even George Eliot's social deviation was moral and rational, perhaps a little doctrinaire.

What George Eliot swiftly moves on to do is to depict the social and personal dramas whose protagonist has considerable stature. Adam Bede, she says, is not an ordinary man. His rationality, his intelligence, and his creative competence make him the first of her line of extraordinary heroes and heroines. They are always embedded in a 'world' of Amos Bartons, Silas Marners, and Hetty Sorrels, but their mind always provides a complex and articulate stage for inner action. George Eliot's characters have a capacity for moral action and development which seems, pretty clearly, to derive from her own experience, transformed, varied, and inventively re-created though it was.

Mary Anne Evans, as she was born, led the kind of heavily plotted life of crisis we find in her novels. As a young woman, she was very sensitive to periodicity, discontinuity and development. What seems to have been a temperamentally cyclical responsiveness must have encouraged and in its turn been further provoked by larger crises. George Eliot is like Wordsworth in the way she seems to need and perhaps to create crises which force a formulation of identity. They shared an acute sense of continuity and discontinuity: of needing and losing a feeling of temporal unity in which past, present, and even future seemed to be linked, and of needing and losing a unity of sensibility, in which reason and the passions seemed to be linked. George Eliot can see life as divided into eras and epochs, as a series of gains and losses, as movements from 'the poetry of girlhood', 'the poetry of love and marriage', 'the poetry of maternity' and 'the very poetry of duty' into the world of 'naked prose'. This kind of pattern can be traced in most of her novels, as a process of illusion and vision which takes us from dream to dream until we are—at times by assertion rather than demonstration—'nearer reality'. Such process is a mid-Victorian evolutionary myth, itself an illusion persuasively grounded on an awareness of the psychological processes of deception, dream and drug.

In her personal life, however, we see a series of crises arranged in a less evolutionary sequence. There was the first crisis of identity and continuity when, in 1848, she stopped going to church, in an almost sacramental disclosure of her loss of Christian faith. There followed a troubling period of dislocation, uprootedness, and subsequently an attempt to restore good relations with her father, in the realisation that there was emotional continuity even if belief had been sharply broken. The second crisis, about which we know rather little, in terms of the chronicle of inner life, comes in 1854, when she went to Europe with George Henry Lewes. In her letters to some of her friends, to whom she can admit the truth about their unmarried 'marriage', and in a letter to her brother Isaac, in which she cannot tell the truth, the attempt to hang on the past and to the personal tradition of family unity, is plain. It is this need for a temporal and personal unity which explains her gratification when, on her marriage to John Cross, Isaac wrote to break the long silence and to forgive.

Her own life was no doubt even more eroded and discontinuous than we know, but these two conspicuous crises involved a break with the past, choice and conflict between emotional conservatism and intellectual and emotional courage, and provide a model for her art. Characteristic imagery in her novels always reminds us of the importance of a sense of unity: the image of the labyrinth, the snapped thread, the path, and the current, amongst others, all stand as emblems for the dramatic choices and conflicts to be found in her life as well as her books.

The content as well as the structure of personal experience creates art from life. Because she rejected Evangelicalism, (at some stages as narrowly puritanical as her aunt's and Dinah's Methodism) in favour of a life-devoted humanism, her novels persistently make a plea for social love, fellowship, duty to people. If the insistence on human relationship as a duty replaces the Christian ethic (in her case, as seen in some of her early gloomy letters, an especially uncreative and unattractive ethic) so the sense of collective creation took the place of the Christian immortality. The Positivist hymn, 'O let me join the choir invisible' shows this replacement, and so also does the emphasis placed in the novels on the contribution to society, like Adam Bede's and Caleb Garth's land-improvements, or—twisted ironically—Rosamond Vincy's deceptive legacy from a fine musician's dead touch.

There is the value, too, attached to moral self-determinism, as seen in all the novels but most plainly in the wrong moral choices of Tito Melema in *Romola*, set out as a pattern of deterioration, and the right moral choices of Maggie, set out as a more complex and unsteady pattern of growth. This gives to the novels something like the systematic, confident, and usually optimistic framework of the Christian Providence novels of Defoe or Charlotte Brontë. It is the kind of firm moral pattern and reference that is both typically Victorian in its humanist substitutions, and typical of George Eliot.

This kind of pattern is not the only moral interest to be found in the novels of George Eliot. Her imagination creates characters, events and relationships that have an individual colour and complexity that light up the system, make sense to us today, make a picture out of the diagram, *incarnate* (her word) the ideas.

Scenes of Clerical Life show how soon she could look sympathetically at the religious life, whether successful or unsuccessful, and they show too her interest, even within the span of fairly short stories (first serialised as two-part tales in *Blackwood's Edinburgh Magazine*) in the ethic of love. She dramatises lovingly both the great demands of human intimacy and need, and Wordsworth's 'little, nameless, unremembered acts/Of kindness and of love', with their warming or restorative powers. The *Scenes* show, too, her interest in human development, though in a simplified pattern, and sometimes rather said than shown to have happened. On the whole, the process of growth is not melodramatised but implied in the crucial moment, rather than set out at length. There is the awakening moment, as when Caterina strikes the piano, an incident which effectively dramatises and particularises the metaphor of 'striking a chord' and plausibly restores past feeling after breakdown. There is the temporary growth, which is *not* a final transformation, when Amos Barton throws himself on his wife's grave not only in grief but in the desperate effort to retain grief. Such events show George Eliot's emphasis on the continuity of feeling.

If there are these good moments, there are also the weak ones, such as the assumption or appearance of growth and conversion or change in Janet Dempster, Tryan or Gilfil, where difficulties are passed over and the resounding triumph over the victory of love is scarcely earned. But the *Scenes* have good moments of humour, and at their best an honest, almost Wordsworthian gaucheness.

George Eliot's psychological powers were no doubt inhibited by the chosen materials. Unlike Mrs Gaskell, she needed a highly complex intellectual and creative centre in character. When this is achieved, as in Adam, Maggie, Dorothea, Felix, Esther, Romola, Gwendolen, Deronda, Mordecai, she can produce marvellously live and sympathetic small studies of the simple soul. Hetty Sorrel's narrow little fantasy-life, with scarcely room in it for more than clothes and faces, is an animated and functional miniature, but the central characters of Adam and Arthur give George Eliot her proper scope. In them she takes time and space to show two very different types of moral character, both changing, both clearly conditioned by position, possessions and economic morality, both in a way self-regarding and narrow, even though one acts benevolently and the other selfishly. Perhaps we can see here why a novelist who so delighted in antithesis, both of character and event, should criticise the contrasts in Mrs Gaskell. George Eliot's formalism is always overlaid and qualified by a complex pattern of resemblance, difference and change. Her contrasts are mobile, so that when we think we are reading them accurately, we may be caught out, and suddenly forced to see Dinah's limitations of sympathy as well as Hetty's, or Adam's hardness as well as Arthur's.

The novels of George Eliot depend on a constant presence and movement of feeling, but the intellectualised subject makes for a cross-hatching of feeling and analysis. Mrs Gaskell is the kind of novelist whose inner action is filled to the brim by the passions and reflections of the characters. George Eliot's, despite her intellectually eloquent characters, has a space between the life of the created world and the world of author and reader. There was a time, when it was necessary to explain and justify the insistent presence and commentary of the omniscient author, in the novels of George Eliot, but criticism has shown the mobility, the varying function, and the dramatisation of the author's presence, both in language and imagery. It would be a mistake, however, to insist too strongly on George Eliot's dramatic merits. Henry James, happily and deservedly praising his own creation in the Preface to *The Portrait of a Lady*, said that he had tried to achieve—and believed he had achieved—scenes of inner action which had 'the vivacity of incident' and 'the economy of picture'. George Eliot's own commentary has the vivacity, but not the economy. It is an essential part of her individuality as a novelist that there should be a spread of reflection.

It is this authorial centre from which the feelings of the novel are directed, and I emphasise its sensibility, as well as its intellectual activity. It is very rare to find the author's voice commenting in order simply to explain or analyse: even where explanation and analysis is present, it is presented in the medium of feeling. Because George Eliot tends to have a fairly small spectrum of feeling 'for' and 'about' her characters, the light and shade is chiefly presented in the dramatised actions and language, and in each novel there is a movement to and from this drama and the personal centre. Her voice tends to speak compassionately, sometimes satirically, sometimes in a combination of irony and sympathy, sometimes affectionately, sometimes wryly. It speaks 'for' and 'about' the characters but it also speaks 'for' and 'about' a generalised human nature, using 'we' and 'you' and 'I' in a roughly similar inclusive fashion. When it pities, it pities 'all poor mortals'; when it caresses (which it sometimes does too heavily) it caresses a human object, which, like any human object, needs love; when it praises, it praises the common, not the rare, virtues. For although George Eliot puts in the centre of action characters who are powerful, energetic, creative, and intelligent, she keeps in the highroad of human powers, and even her exceptional characters are representative. Compared with the central characters of Mrs Gaskell, Thackeray and Dickens, her characters have considerable imagination, but in their relation to their environment, in their moral mixture and complexity, and in their passions, they are typical enough. This typicality is important to George Eliot, partly because she wants, like Wordsworth, to write an unspecialised literature of human beings speaking to human beings, *from* and *of* what she constantly calls the 'human lot', partly because it allows her to move naturally and freely from particularity of character and action to the generalisation that bridges the experience in the novel and the assumed experience of the reader.

In *Scenes* and from time to time in other places too, she miscalculates her tone, reaches too eagerly towards us, is too arch, too intense, too solicitous, too affectionate. In a sense it seems wrong to do what we generally do, and call these artistic faults. When I use the concept of miscalculation, it suggests a control of personality which is probably impossible, for the voice of George Eliot is usually offensive, not on aesthetic grounds, but distasteful as personality. And at times particularly distasteful, no doubt, because speaking in a voice of unfashionable feeling, vibrating richly and warmly where we like our voices to be cool, expansive where we like dry contraction and laconic understatement, uninhibited where we are inhibited.

In *The Mill on the Floss* George Eliot creates a picture of imaginative richness which has most plainly a reference back to her own experience. It is not indulgent, even in its portrayal of Maggie, in being, as Leavis suggests in *The Great Tradition*, insufficiently critical. It is, on the contrary, very carefully critical of Maggie, both in direct commentary and through the voice of Philip: it criticises Maggie's shift from one dream to another, it criticises her religiosity and her lack of self-knowledge. Where it is indulgent—and I think it is 'indulgent' and not 'self-indulgent'—it is in pitying while it criticises, in pouring over Maggie, or Mr Tulliver, or Philip, in a constant flowing of love, knowing and maternal. It is also indulgent in the resolution by plot, the restoration of the dream of childhood, relationship, and total understanding in the flood.

George Eliot is a deliberate artist who builds up the appropriate structure by imagery, casual-seeming *double entendre*—'She'll tumble in one day'—landscape, and folk tradition. But in spite of the aesthetic unity of the river imagery, in spite of the foreground and background of the great waters, their economic importance and their wild threat, there is no doubt that George Eliot provided Maggie and Tom with a special Providence which is more damaging than we can suggest by simply calling it unrealistic or melodramatic. It is neither: people are killed by storm and flood, and this flood is given plenty of substance. But it goes against the grain of the novel's sensibility and argument, which concern themselves with an evolutionary movement away from dream towards waking, from poetry to naked prose. In what seems to me George Eliot's richest and most particularised piece of characterisation, Maggie is presented, against her environment, family, education and religion, as struggling to know and not to escape or to delude herself. At each stage of shedding the dream or the drug, she moves into another, slightly less delusive, stage of dream or poetry. We should observe, by the way, that when George Eliot uses the idea of moving from poetry to prose, she is thinking in terms of Romantic poetry. Maggie uses Scott and Byron as escape, Esther Lyon and Mrs Transome, in *Felix Holt*, use Byron and Chateaubriand. Maggie first makes childish make-believe daydreams, simply cutting out unpleasant friction and shaping the experience anew, to her liking. Later, she finds literature an effective aid to this process, when her intelligence and experience cease to tolerate the cruder forms of wishful shape-making. Later still, when the golden gates of childhood close, and she and Tom go home to illness, loss and the frightening responsibility for the once-responsible parents, literature fails too. George Eliot is very good on the desolation which fills Maggie's life between illusions. Her portrayal of ennui, bewilderment, inactivity and misery, all joined together in a feeling defying the power of naming, is painful in its sharpness and truth. But humankind cannot live long without a dream, and Maggie is ripe for religious illusion. Again, George Eliot shows Maggie's conversion with truth and sympathy, observing without harshness, the element of self-indulgence and histrionics. What is perhaps even more remarkable an achievement for such a systematic moralist as George Eliot is the next stage in Maggie's process, which is not given the evolutionary treatment, but shown, quietly and unfussily, as sliding back into the pre-religious stage of self-gratification. At this stage various dreams merge: Maggie is scarcely carrying out her self-denying intention, but she does retain something of the Thomas à Kempis altruism. She reverts to Scott, and she is fed, too, by a new source of energising illusion, the companionship with Philip, an undemanding form of relationship, a kind of loving which can be refuge and repose. Finally, she is forced to discard all the illusions, after a crisis of moral choice and miserable renunciation which seems to reverse George Eliot's own moral choice, in going to live with Lewes, while bringing out plainly the nature of her personal ethic. Maggie refuses to betray an unofficial engagement, George Eliot committed adultery; Maggie renounces Stephen on the grounds of feeling and duty, to people, not laws, George Eliot committed herself to Lewes for similar reasons. In the most subtle way the novel disguises, socialises, but also defends George Eliot's social deviation. In another subtle way Maggie's extreme conversion to religious self-denial and subsequent partial return to her 'habitual self' reverses but uses George Eliot's conversion from Christianity. The novel is a thoroughly externalised but personal story. It is also rich, complex, and complete in its rendering of the processes of frustration, exhaustion and desire. Not only in the figure of Maggie, but also in the characters of Tom, Mr Tulliver and Philip, George Eliot's ability to show and to analyse reveals itself in moving and various human materials. With the powerful sensibility and imagination of Maggie placed in the centre, George Eliot's ability to substantiate the more average human stuff of Mr and Mrs Tulliver is given a subordinate but adequate place. When the wife persuades the husband to work for Wakem, or when Tulliver makes Tom write the vow for vengeance in the family Bible, George Eliot writes a wonderfully individualised version of the stuff of human crisis: the ties of marriage, for instance, are seen as powerfully binding and strangling, against the background of country and family ritual and tradition and in the words of folk-saying, proverb, and the Bible.

It is this kind of richness and honesty which seems to be falsified when George Eliot answers her heroine's final prayer, to spare her further pain and loss. In her other novels, which grow in scale and intellectual analysis, there is always a tension, never quite satisfactorily concluded, between a truthful rendering of people and the meliorist attempt to show the possibilities of love, content, harmony. It is a kind of tension not found in Mrs Gaskell or the Brontës, and it reveals, I think, the imaginative powers and ambitions of George Eliot's genius. She was, like Dickens, writing the kind of novel that asked all the questions, and was aware of a whole range of possible answers.

She asks about the environment: contemporary society, ideal society and society localised somewhere in history—usually in the early nineteenth century, except in *Romola* and the fully contemporary *Daniel Deronda*. So she handles three periods at once, combining the carefully researched past history (of say, a county town in the 1830s), the present time which is implied or symbolised through historical reference (as the Second Reform Bill is in the First Reform Bill), and the future, in implications for the progress of societies shown through criticism and ideals.

She handles, too, the moral questions of individual conduct: problems of earning a living, of marrying, of staying single, of finding marriage or your job good, bad, indifferent, bearable. She handles a great range of relationships, all typical and sharply individualised: relationships between brother and sister, brother and brother, sister and sister, parents and children, husband and wife, passionate lovers, romantically sexless lovers, friends, master and servant in a very role-limited relation, master and servant in a freer man-to-man relation, rivals, old people and young people, and so on, in a very long list indeed. The list's length must only be stressed at the same time as we insist on the individuality. All these relationships are dramatised so as to show the social and personal colours of, say, the Lammeter sisters in *Silas Marner*, or Fred Vincy and Rosamond, or Gwendolen Harleth and her mother, or the Princess Halm-Eberstein and her son, but they are also all sufficiently typical of social and psychological conditions and roles, to make their contribution to the total moral argument.

George Eliot is a very considerable artist, as we see when we shift from the human problems—the actualities and ideals which form the subject, the end of art—to the forms, methods, and style of the novelist. In the last four novels, *Romola, Felix Holt, Middlemarch* and *Daniel Deronda*, there is a constant experimentation with language and design. Sometimes it is a failure, as with the translated Italian no-language of *Romola* (see Hemingway's *For Whom the Bell Tolls* for another disastrous version of the same answer) or in the poetic style of Mordecai in *Daniel Deronda*, where the imagery and syntax are adapted from the Old Testament and the poetic style of Jehuda Halevy. Sometimes it is a subdued triumph of impersonation, as in the characteristic languages of *Middlemarch*, where no character lacks an appropriate style. There is always a discrimination, a realism, and an ordering in language. The language transcends character, and its irony, movement and unity rely on a cross-reference from image to image or phrase to phrase.

The characters in Middlemarch, one by one—Dorothea, Rosamond, Fred—all ask, 'What can I do?' in an almost operatic arrangement of words, timbres and pitch, though that effect is a muted one. The characters in *Middlemarch* are comparatively described in imagery of water, and the characters in *Daniel Deronda* in the imagery of horses, riders, chariots, control and submission.

The experiment in form is an experiment in humane analysis and argument. The shape of the novel is the shape of the moral vision. George Eliot's characteristic form, present early but fully developed and plain from *Romola* to *Daniel Deronda*, is that of the typical Victorian three-decker novel, the double or multiple action that we find in *Vanity Fair*, *Bleak House* and *Our Mutual Friend*. George Eliot was using a form typical of her time, shaped and conventionalised by reading habits, costs, serial publication and a demand for expansiveness. But she shapes the form for her purpose, and the form of *Felix Holt*, *Middlemarch* and *Daniel Deronda* is individual, each novel differing not only from a novel of multiple action by Dickens or Tolstoy, but from each other.

The double plot of *Romola* is the comparison of Romola and Savonarola, the contrast between problems and conflicts of duty and egoism, feeling and reason, in private and public life. The double plot of *Felix Holt*, (a novel too unified to be precisely described in this way) compares two Radicals, two kinds of political commitment and action, two classes. The act of contrast and comparison creates the form, but we also have to analyse it in terms of the relationships of the parts in final form, for the convergence comes about differently, and individually, in each novel. In *Felix Holt* the destinies and actions converge, and what has been ironically a relationship visible to the reader but not to the character, breaks the narrative irony to become junction and discovery. After the tension, the novel's final scenes dissolve the unity, and the double action is felt to diverge, startlingly converge, and diverge again. Each shift in relationship is expressive of the social and personal separations and joinings which form the subject of the novel. In *Daniel Deronda*, which has a more distinct double action, there is a similar narrative irony, though it is much more crucial and terrifying. Once more, there is a social division, though this time roughly between Gentile and Jewish ways of life. But the hero of *each* action is Daniel Deronda and the contrast and comparison made by the structure is made the more powerfully and ironically for this strong unifying bond, like the bloodstream yoking Siamese twins. That conceit is an appropriate one, for Daniel has to break the bond, and Gwendolen has to bear the pain of its undreamt-of breaking. The reader's double vision has given special context for reading both ways of life, as social and personal histories, and has created the felt knowledge of the final break. George Eliot's formal comparisons in these three novels embody stories which generalise and also show the tragic differences and dissociations of the human lot.

Her greatest novel, written between *Felix Holt* and *Daniel Deronda*, is *Middlemarch*. Here the form is one of quadruple action, though once we begin to count the parts we might well feel impelled to enumerate even more divisions. The same kind of social ironies and personal isolations are pointed out as in the other three novels, but there is no special irony of ignorance and junction and separateness, only a series of small ironies, such as Lydgate's thoughts of Dorothea and the reader's silent answering superior knowledge. The multiple form of this novel is perhaps most expressive of two other ideas: the idea of equality of interest and the idea of contingency. The form is the perfect one for proving that George Eliot's 'we' is truly meant, for it creates a rotation which makes us displace each prominent character and move on to another. It creates a model of that illusion of centrality and that fact of typicality which the novel explicitly discusses. 'Why always Dorothea?' asks the novel on one famous occasion. The perfect proof of the question's sincerity is made in a form which refuses to allow central figures to engross our attention. There is a limited number of central figures, true, but the form acts as a model, not a total imitation, and its point seems to be clearly made. The theme of contingency is discovered in the form. It is a novel which sadly but imaginatively sees not the fixity of destiny, which is so limiting and also so morally terrifying in the portrayal of Tito Melema, but its flux, its selection. How free? how determined? asks the novel and shows the variety of possibilities. The very shifts of action, the transformation of minor character in one plot to major character in another, the chanciness, the permutations which come out of contrast and comparison, the generalisation, the fast movement which seem at times to blur identity, all these aspects of the structure are expressive. It is a novel as astonishingly broad in social rendering as it is profound in inner analysis and drama. It impresses us passionately with the feeling that these highly differentiated people, these various moral commitments, these richly individualised styles, are made from the same humanity. They are all George Eliot.

George Eliot is perhaps the greatest psychologist in the English novel, so it is important to see her departures from psychological realism. She knows what she is doing when she simplifies character. The deviations from her richly various complex norm, like Dinah, Felix, Daniel, Mordecai, are made in the interests of that passionate vision of human societies and moral action which was more important than perfected substance, than writing the good novel. All these characters have a complex enough psyche, but they have a certain fixity, a certain monolithic quality. They are reassuring monumental instances of virtue, landmarks needed for George Eliot's hope and faith. Adam progresses from unimaginative rectitude to the pains of loving and knowing beyond himself, Daniel Deronda finds his roots, his identity, his role. They are not characters who are existentially open, who can show new facets, who can surprise themselves, the other characters or the reader, but characters who show, like the desperately wish-fulfilling endings, the author's need to idealise, to dream, and to transform. But her deviations from realism are not only seen in the form of such simplifications of the psychological units. The notion of the classic realist text is a myth: George Eliot's medium is one which constantly moves away from fiction, to argue and generalise in discursive language. Her worlds are consistent, but not structurally closed. Her endings open to uncertainties; her beginnings may be aware, and want us to be aware, of facts of art, and of facts beyond art.[1]

First published in the *Sphere History of Literature in the English Language*, Vol. 6 (Sphere Books, London, 1969)

Note

1.   For further discussion of the limits of George Eliot's realism, see Barbara Hardy, *Forms of Feeling in Victorian Fiction* (Peter Owen, London, 1984).

10. The Ending of *Middlemarch*

Middlemarch, like all effectively progressive works of art, begins to end when it begins, and constantly looks ahead to conclusion while it unfolds and develops. I shall discuss the very last stages of the novel, observing some features which are unique to *Middlemarch*, some which are unique to George Eliot, and some which are characteristic of Victorian fiction.

Like most Victorian novels, *Middlemarch* moves to closure. That closure is qualified. The novel not only brings its various stories to a clear narrative and thematic conclusion, but seems to undermine such conclusion by looking ahead into an imputed future, suggesting or creating new action and new characters in the projection, while confirming ethical conclusions. In this respect it resembles most of the novels of Dickens, and some of the novels of Charlotte Brontë and Thackeray. What is new is presented in order to resolve what is old, futurity confirming what has happened up to the ending. What is new is narrated briefly, foreshortening event, and sketching, rather than substantially inventing, new characters. As in Dickens, the new characters are the offspring of the old, rounding off love stories with procreation. There emerge the children of Dorothea and Will Ladislaw, the increase of Celia and Sir James Chettam, and the family of Fred and Mary Vincy. Summary and shadow are vivid with particularity. The children on the last pages are not, as they usually are in Dickens, mere items in a family tree, but are introduced through specific action and event.

The last chapter, called 'Finale', is set apart from the numbered chapters, to complete the frame half-made by the first unnumbered and named chapter, the 'Prelude'. The 'Finale' is first introduced with the narrator's customary emotional expectation of emotion, which pluralises, generalises, and breaks the fictional emotion: 'Who can quit young lives after being long in company with them, and not desire to know what befell them in their after-years?' This is a confident question, born of established community of feeling, delicately appropriate to an acknowledgment of fiction and a self-conscious pretence of reality. The growing family tree of the Garths and Vincys exfoliates in individual detail, not generality. The narrator introduces that growth through the new fact of Mary's book, 'Stories of Great Men, taken from Plutarch' written 'for her boys'. This cunningly-casual side-reference is extended in the same vein as we are told about Fred's stabilities and instabilities, 'it was remarkable that he submitted to be laughed at for cowardliness at the fences, seeming to see Mary and the boys sitting on the five-barred gate, or showing their curly heads between hedge and ditch.' Information is subtly seeded, and explicit details placed after the preparatory hints and glimpses. When they are formally related, it is through the variety and particularity of dialogue and direct speech, 'That would be too great a trial to your mother', and of images, one of the children being given a brief but substantial presence in 'a marvellous nicety of aim in playing at marbles, or in throwing stones to bring down the mellow pears', 'very much what her father must have been when he wore a round jacket'. In other words, the narration of new facts is presented in a medium which is active and visualised. This applies not only to the conventional glimpse into future generations, but to less conventional matter, like the unexpected facts of Fred and Mary's authorship, which cleverly gives the impression of new twists and turns, in keeping with the body of the fiction, but branching out in inventive directions.

The completion of the story of the Lydgates is even more inventively productive of new action. There is moral continuity. Expectation rather than surprise—Coleridge's phrase—takes us into Lydgate's failure and Rosamond's complacent victory. The particulars are startling, not simply fresh. Lydgate's death at fifty, his treatise on Gout, and Rosamond's second marriage, extend the events of the novel with remarkable proliferation. This narration, too, is retarded, elaborated and dramatised by significant speech and image, like Rosamond's brief but cogent words about happiness coming to her as 'a reward', and Lydgate's powerful completion of the fatal symbolism of flowers, as he ironically and allusively calls her his basil-plant. There is an idealistic streak in the stoutly realistic presentation of Rosamond's egoism: 'But it would be unjust not to tell, that she never uttered a word in depreciation of Dorothea, keeping in religious remembrance the generosity which had come to her aid in the sharpest crisis of her life'. This not only modifies the moral depreciation of Rosamond, but provides a tiny straw of evidence, handily close to the last judgements and praise, for Dorothea's 'incalculably diffusive' effect 'on those around her'.

It is Dorothea's finale which is prominent, and part of that prominence is the dynamic extension of her presentation, though not of her portrait. Her story was finally developed in the details of the marriage to Will, though particularised in this last section by such details as her contribution to Will's career in the First Reform Parliament: 'Dorothea could have liked nothing better, since wrongs existed, than that her husband should be in the thick of a struggle against them, and that she should give him wifely aid'. This feeling about her auxiliary function is strictly placed within her point of view, but the narrative commentary and analysis of the novel always shuttles subtly and consistently between one viewpoint and another, and the Finale is no exception. Story is finished, commentary goes on. Dorothea's character is fixed, but the narrator's commentary, guiding the reader's response, is not; it takes a longer view, and a less passive one, than that of mere sympathy for Dorothea's wifely compliance. Despite (or perhaps because of) her consciousness of history, Dorothea is embedded in her time, thirty years before the feminist movements and controversies of the eighteen-sixties, with which George Eliot was connected and acquainted through friends like Barbara Bodichon and Bessie Parkes. Unlike the characters, the narrator is endowed with a feminist consciousness appropriate to writing-time and reading-time, to go beyond Dorothea's acquiescence in her lot. After the assertion of the wife's content and help comes a vital sentence which extends the judgement and sensibility of narrator, reader and novel:

> Many who knew her, thought it a pity that so substantive and rare a creature should have been absorbed into the life of another, and be only known in a certain circle as a wife and mother. But no one ever stated exactly what else that was in her power she ought rather to have done—not even Sir James Chettam, who went no

further than the negative prescription that she ought not to have
married Will Ladislaw.

This speaks from the politicised feminist consciousness of the late
eighteen-sixties, though, tactfully kept within historic
appropriateness, it is deliberately vague. It is veiled by that 'what
else . . . she ought to have done', an allusion without specifically
feminist question here, but carrying larger resonances from its
formulation in the first paragraph of *Pilgrim's Progress*, where
Christian asks, with a lamentable cry, 'What shall I do?' It echoes
the early question about what Dorothea should 'do', and specific
pointers within the population of the novel. It brings out not only a
larger historical perspective, but also the deliberated limits of
Dorothea's lot. The novelist, through the sympathetic but
uncharacterised narrator, makes it plain that her ending is meant,
like *Vanity Fair*, to make us uncomfortable. It is taken up again, in
the last two paragraphs of the novel: 'certainly those determining
acts of her life were not ideally beautiful', and 'Her full nature . . .
spent itself in channels which had no great name on the earth'. This
is neither a pessimistic nor an optimistic conclusion, but a
melioristic one, admitting the historic limits and the diffuse
influence of Dorothea's aspirations and benevolence, in a way
which re-imagines Carlyle's insistence that history is composed of
innumerable biographies, 'for the growing good of the world is
partly dependent on unhistoric acts; and that things are not so ill
with you and me as they might have been, is half owing to the
number who lived faithfully a hidden life, and rest in unvisited
tombs'.[1]

An ending both scrupulous and moving, mingling admiration,
compassion, and hope, typical of the narrative voice in judgement
and passion. It was not an ending which George Eliot formulated
without effort. As with the ending of Dicken's *Great Expectations*,
revision brought about a softening of an original harshness. Gordon
Haight pointed out, in his Riverside edition of *Middlemarch* (1956),
that the first edition of the novel (1871–2) had a different ending,
with another emphasis. In the penultimate paragraph, after the
words 'the mixed result of young and noble impulse' and before the
words, in that same sentence, 'will often take the aspect of error'
there appeared nine important lines omitted from later editions
from 1874 onwards, reprinted by Haight:

. . . struggling under prosaic conditions. Among the many remarks passed on her mistakes, it was never said in the neighbourhood of Middlemarch that such mistakes could not have happened if the society into which she was born had not smiled on propositions of marriage from a sickly man to a girl less than half his own age—on modes of education which make a woman's knowledge another name for motley ignorance—on rules of conduct which are in flat contradiction with its own loudly-asserted beliefs. While this is the social air in which mortals begin to breathe, there will be collisions such as those in Dorothea's life, where great feelings . . .

The change is considerable, removing not only the emphasis on social responsibility but the facts of the Casaubon marriage. The first version utters a plainer feminist judgement than the revised ending admits, though one which has already been sounded, on many occasions, within the omniscient narrative commentary. George Eliot chose, however, to end on a less politically radical note.

There is an interesting omission from the Finale which makes it impossible to call it a conventional roll-call of all the characters. It begins with that warm assumption that the reader will want to know more, but we have already been told everything about one set of characters, the Bulstrodes. Their finale is separated from that of the other characters and destinies. This makes for an interesting asymmetry. Bulstrode's bitter history is completed in Chapter 85, which includes futurity, in Bulstrode's typically uncandid fantasy of dying, up to the moment when he may, but will probably not, make a full confession, and in its anticipation of the family's exile, 'going to end his stricken life in that sad refuge, the indifference of new faces'. The ironic portrayal of continued deception and evasion is the conclusion to this story, which receives a chapter to itself, leaving the Finale free for destinies which are not only more heterogeneous, but susceptible to more or less dynamic extension. We have only to think of the possibility of applying such techniques to Bulstrode's story, to applaud George Eliot's decision to apportion and separate the narration as she did.

A last word about these last words. Despite the extended particularities, and despite the fresh and emphatic summons to judgement, the Finale does not alter the narration of moral histories, completed in the last numbered chapter (86). The

Finale's first paragraph is cleverly deceptive, as it admits that
novelistic metonymy is fictitious, that 'the fragment of a life,
however typical, is not the sample of an even web: promises may not
be kept, and an ardent outset may be followed by declension; latent
powers may find their long-waited opportunity; a past error may
urge a grand retrieval'. This slurs over the distinction between life
and art, or fact and fiction, as it has done so often, insisting on the
fluidity of human destiny while making its own fixities inexorable
and exemplary. When presenting Casaubon's frigidity, the narrator
observes that we must not judge a man by style, even while making
use of the convention of expressive moral languages. When showing
the determining deeds of Dorothea, Ladislaw and Mary Garth, the
novel also admitted the unacted possibilities beyond the verge of
plotted acts and destinies. Here it makes the admission that a brief
historical coverage of a few years, such as the novel has presented,
does not guarantee an even development. But the Finale itself is to
make crystal-clear the evenness of a web which only art can weave.
The novel, so often called realistic, makes full use of the fiction of
exemplariness, as it uses forecast to show that every one of these
characters, for better or for worse, has (or had) a future which
simply formed a continuation of the past which the novel has
created and related up to the time of the Finale. Like the Prelude,
the Finale sounds and summarises dominant themes. The Prelude
dealt in exemplary characters who do not act in the novel, like those
of St Theresa and her male relations, and with nonce images, like
the exiled cygnet. The Finale deals only with the particulars of the
novel, except for the brief extension of the last sentence to include
'the number who lived faithfully a hidden life'. The Prelude dealt
with historic, the Finale with unhistoric, lives. The Finale lingers to
detain the fictitious characters a little longer, on the pretext of
historical truth. It does not dwell on the major characters, who
receive a larger valediction, but with metonymic effect, on Fred and
Mary:

> On inquiry it might possibly be found that Fred and Mary still
> inhabit Stone Court—that the creeping plants still cast the foam
> of their blossoms over the fine stone-walls into the field where the
> walnut-trees stand in a stately row—and that on sunny days the
> two lovers who were first engaged with the umbrella-ring may be
> seen in white-haired placidity at the open window from which

Mary Garth, in the days of old Peter Featherstone, had often been ordered to look out for Mr Lydgate.

The ending plays with the illusion of realism and the fact of fiction, and in so doing responds to the beginning, which admitted fact as it moved into fiction. The proportions are different, the balance shifts from history to fiction, but the constituents are repeated, completing a frame and achieving a balance, then shifting back to history, to break the closure. The conclusion makes that emphasis appropriate to *Middlemarch*, one of the first English novels to deal with the sense of history, and with the historical significance of unhistoric people. The last sentence breaks form and fuses fictionality with life outside fiction:

But the effect of her being on those around her was incalculably diffusive: for the growing good of the world is partly dependent on unhistoric acts; and that things are not so ill with you and me as they might have been, is half owing to the number who lived faithfully a hidden life, and rest in unvisited tombs.

To be published in Italian as *La conclusione di Middlemarch*, in *Middlemarch il romanzo*, ed. A. Weston and J. McRae (Loffredo, Naples).

Note

1. For a fuller discussion of this subject see Barbara Hardy, *Particularities: Readings in George Eliot* (Peter Owen, London, 1982), Ch. 6.

11. *Daniel Deronda*

Daniel Deronda is the last of George Eliot's novels, and while it is always naturally tempting to make the most of the final achievement in a great career, this really is a last novel which can be called a remarkable conclusion. Of course it has many connections with her earlier novels, and it explores and develops subjects and techniques which go right back to the beginnings of her writing, but it also marks some striking new departures, new not only for her but for the English novel.

Like nearly all her novels, it is a love-story, a psychological study in human relationships and individual growth, a challenging moral argument, and an analysis of contemporary Victorian society. The new departures can be seen everywhere. This is a love-story of a subtle and original cast, dealing not only in problems of sexual relationship rarely touched in contemporary fiction, but laying bare kinds of feeling and impulse which the common run of Victorian love-stories did not recognise. It is a story about a woman who marries for power, not love, but in doing so meets her match in a man of greater and more perverted power. It is also the story of a man in love with two women, though the necessary phrase, 'in love', begs too many questions to be an adequate description of Daniel Deronda's relations with Mirah Cohen and Gwendolen Harleth. Its moral fable shows a pattern familiar to readers of George Eliot or Dickens or Jane Austen: a moral rescue, a story of potent influence and redemption carried out by one human being for another. George Eliot moved away from the convenient coincidence which she and others had exploited, the coincidence of love and moral rescue, and showed a difficult and embarrassing clash of different kinds of need, dependence and attraction. In showing Daniel's double commitment, to Mirah and to Gwendolen, she was led into a subtle discrimination of the difficulties of moral rescue and of the variations of human love. It is a discrimination which marks an advance in honesty and complexity, an advance even on *Middlemarch*. In showing the difficulties of loving and helping, George Eliot is indeed doing what she described as conducting 'a set of experiments in life'. The novel is experimental in form because its materials are complicatedly and truthfully close to realities: the good, clever, handsome hero and the less good and less clever, beautiful heroine do not find that the course of true love runs roughly only to be smoothed out in a happy-ever-after. Love is shown as difficult and painful, settling some things but disturbing others. And the novel breaks away not only from simplified human relationships but from the simplified happy ending. It experiments with the novelist's conventional use of time in order to handle its human materials. Its technical originality and its experiments in life go together, for, like all great works of art, it makes no separation of vision and technique.

Its vision goes beyond what I have been describing as a more complex and honest view of human relationships. Its concern is with societies as well as individuals, and the career of Daniel Deronda is one of considerable social and political interest, for he is a study of a Jew, and a leader. George Eliot is attempting to include new aspects of life, both social and psychological, which she had only touched on in her earlier 'experiments in life'.

As an experimental novel, *Daniel Deronda* is a work of peculiar excitements and difficulties. It pushes beyond the achievement of its predecessors, and the very nature of its push makes it less easy and less entertaining than these predecessors. We have to look at it as a remarkable instance of T. S. Eliot's definition of artistic development as a series of 'wholly new attempts' and 'new kinds of failure'. *Daniel Deronda* is trying to do many things, and not always succeeding. It is one of those works of art whose greatness is inextricably bound up with imperfection. It touches the limits of Victorian fiction, and its imaginative courage (covering both art and vision) results in a certain strain and tension.

It suffered in its own day and perhaps in ours too by the inevitable comparison with its immediate predecessor, *Middlemarch*. *Middlemarch* is, in everyone's opinion, George Eliot's greatest novel. Its complex drama has extraordinary breadth and depth and, in addition, it has the strong and immediate appeal of a novel about family life and local politics. It is a more balanced and concrete novel than *Daniel Deronda*, and an easier and more attractive book to read, clothing its ideas in lively flesh and blood and inviting us to move in a world where we can at once get our bearings. It is the great novel of the here and now, of the everyday, and its world is the world of our own familiar experiences, ordered, explained, questioned, made vivid, comprehensible and moving. *Daniel Deronda* begins by presenting the everyday world, but beyond the first stages lie more remote and less accessible ranges. The world it takes us into is exotic and often uncomfortable. And this discomfort takes several forms: it is a world of alien sensibility, and this sensibility remains in places abstract and disembodied. It is a novel which reveals or betrays the large effort of imagination which has gone to make it.

I realise that this last sentence sounds vague and grandiose, but I mean it to be a precise description. *Daniel Deronda* is not a novel like *Middlemarch*, a novel which has consumed its creative fires, whose finished life shows very little trace of the struggles and researches that lie behind it. It is a novel which shows the effort in effects not totally achieved, ideas not perfectly embodied in character, language not having a firm impact. And it is an effort to move into bigger areas—of the mind, of the world, of the art of fiction. Its successes and its failures illuminate the meaning of 'imagination' as do the successes and failures of other great but uneven writers like Wordsworth or D. H. Lawrence.

I do not want to exaggerate the failures. George Eliot is a skilled and crafty worker, and she takes us into the unfamiliar and difficult territory by first leading us through a known and familiar landscape. The first sentence, the first page, the first chapter, and the first book are arresting and brilliantly attractive, and the novel draws us slowly into its depths and breadths before we know exactly what is happening. Because the author does not, in the opinion of most critics, remain in complete control of the material or of the reader, it is an advantage to know a little about the range and purpose of the novel at the outset. If it is helpful to know something about the aims of the novelist and the conditions in which it was written, it may also be helpful to see it in relation to our own time. The modern reader is in some ways better equipped than the Victorian reader, for reasons both sociological and aesthetic, to give the book the sympathy and comprehension which it demands. In spite of the fact that it is a Victorian four-decker, lavish, detailed, slow-moving, written in the formal and highly-finished prose of its time and using certain conventions which have more or less disappeared from the novel of today, it has many features of form and of feeling which are very familiar. Because it pushed ahead of most contemporary fiction it has much in common with the best novels of our century.

Some of its first readers criticised the novel on grounds that were at once aesthetic and sociological, objecting not only to the presence of 'the Jewish problem' but to the way in which that problem was presented, to a kind of writing which was more conspicuously ideological and symbolic than anything George Eliot had done before. Nearly a century later, we are now perfectly familiar with the ideological novel in its extreme form in the work of Huxley or Orwell, a form of fiction which uses argument, caricature, and fantasy in the interests of satire or polemic, and which often makes no attempt at psychological realism. I am not suggesting that *Daniel Deronda* is a kind of Victorian version of *Island*: George Eliot may be writing a novel in which character is simplified in order that values should be clearly stated, but the simplification only works in some of her characters, just as her use of something approaching fantasy only shows in some parts of the action. Simplification and fantasy are embedded in a richly and in some ways realistically psychological novel. It is perhaps useful to call to mind the writings of less schematic but violently polemic novelists like D. H. Lawrence and James Baldwin, whose novels are very different from the fables of Orwell, much closer to the movement and complexity of life, and who constantly appear to sacrifice repose and unity to their impassioned concern with life. Their passion for humanity shows itself in a more than literary love and hatred which disrupt old forms and old feelings. Like Huxley and Orwell, though in different ways, they are typically twentieth-century in their hortatory and didactic art, their naked involvement with anguish, horror, pity and uncertainty. It may seem a far cry from George Eliot to Baldwin, but for all its grand style, *Daniel Deronda* has much in common with his underdistanced art. One can of course go too far in finding modern equivalents. I make these comparisons only in order to suggest that readers who are moved by the imbalance and injustice of Baldwin's plea for justice, who can see why Lawrence makes Sir Clifford Chatterley impotent, and who are capable of appreciating the difference between novels aspiring to fable and those attempting a realistic imitation of human action, may find the difficulties of *Daniel Deronda* congenial and understandable.

At the beginning of 1874, three years after *Middlemarch*, we find the first hints of the new novel in George Henry Lewes's letters to John Blackwood, George Eliot's publisher. Lewes tells Blackwood about her 'simmering'—the word she used for early broodings over a novel—and urges him to write to her encouragingly, to give her confidence in the depression and despair that returned with each new composition. Blackwood was a model of intelligent tact and sympathy and he warmed to the hint, wrote to ask how the new work was taking form, and elicited wry and pessimistic response. But the simmering went on, the talk became more definite, and by September Lewes is saying that he believes the new book will be a 'glorious' one. By the end of the year the novel has its name, and a good part of the first volume has been written, and has passed beyond the simmering process 'into the irrevocable'. From the correspondence with Blackwood, with Frederic Harrison (whom she consulted about points of law) and Leslie Stephen (whom she asked about Cambridge and academic life), we can see the slow building up of the novel, her depression, illness, lack of confidence, plans and difficulties. We have a significant impression of Blackwood's first reading and reactions. He read manuscript and proofs as they came in, and as the novel went to the printer's before George Eliot had finished it, his position was that of the serial reader, wondering (in the most enthralled and the most practical way) what was going to happen next.

Blackwood and his family, all devout admirers, plunged into the story of Gwendolen Harleth, responding to the fascination and charm of the 'witch', exclaiming 'splendid', 'glorious', 'stupendous', and praising the novel for its life and for the art that rendered the life. After reading the first 256 pages, the verdict of the Blackwood family was that she was outdoing *Middlemarch*. But as they read on, there comes a change in the tone. Blackwood was involved in the destiny of Gwendolen, and hoped that she would ultimately be saved, but he also had his eye on the reading public, and we find him suggesting that it might be useful to let loose a little gossip about the novel since the title, *Daniel Deronda*, did not really suggest that it was to be a picture of English life. Lewes's business sense was at least equal to Blackwood's and he suggested that the advertisements should emphasise the subject of English life, life of 'our own day', and also say that it moved 'for the most part in a higher sphere of Society'. Then begin the doubts, mostly exchanged behind the author's back or emerging softly between the lines of Blackwood's letters. When Blackwood admires the early scenes of ordinary Jewish life in the Cohen family, Lewes admits that he has sometimes shared the author's doubts about the Jewish parts, and George Eliot herself writes anxiously about comparisons with *Middlemarch* and irritably about the 'incalculableness' of the public. She was ill and usually depressed about each book but the doubts about this one are clear and specific. Will the public respond to a novel which is partly about English life of high society and partly about the Jews?

It is worth noticing that when, in February 1876, the first of its eight books came out, the publisher had read no more than the first four. He first read Books Five and Six (which take us into the Jewish section) in February, and there is an interesting little gap in the correspondence, followed by Blackwood's explanation that he has not written sooner because he has been puzzling over the new phase, and feels that it would still be 'presumptuous' to speak of Mordecai until he has read more. The author replies instantly with the nervous sensitive hope that he will see the bearings of Mordecai later, and the comment that she thought he might feel doubtful about this new material. She explains what she is trying to do: to aim at strength and complexity of character, and a 'higher strain of ideas'. She says despondently that giving 'new elements' in sufficiently vivid forms is the most difficult thing in art. Her letter is followed by one from Lewes regretting that Mordecai has not impressed Blackwood more, and warning him that his reactions have had a dampening effect on George Eliot, confirming her gloomy feeling that the presentation of the Jewish ideal would call out only imperfect sympathy. Blackwood takes his cue and hastens to write placatingly (though just a shade evasively and generally, for one who usually went into great detail) that 'there is no doubt about the marvellous Mordecai and oh that Cohen family', but her journal notes that the Jewish element is likely to please no one. Blackwood later commented, as the novel came out in its eight monthly parts from February to September, that she was holding the public even in her transitions, and that the 'Anti-Jews grumbled but went on'.

She writes to Harriet Beecher Stowe, author of *Uncle Tom's Cabin*, that she had always expected the Jewish element to create resistance and repulsion, 'But precisely because I felt that the usual attitude of Christians towards Jews is—I hardly know whether to say more impious or more stupid when viewed in the light of their professed principles, I therefore felt urged to treat Jews with such sympathy and understanding as my nature and knowledge could attain to' and she goes on to speak of anti-Semitism as merely one branch of the typical English superiority 'towards all oriental peoples . . . a spirit of arrogance and contemptuous dictatorialness' which she called a national disgrace. After she and Lewes returned from the long holiday they always took after the completion of each book, she writes that she has now become aware of the hostility and repugnance felt towards the Jewish parts. Lewes later writes to Dowden, admirer and critic, that she has been pained to find friends and devoted readers 'utterly dead' to all the Jewish part. I must stress again the mixture of social and aesthetic response in such deadness: many of her readers objected to being forced into a Jewish environment, but such comments as 'Who can believe in such a prig as Deronda', and 'Mordecai is a Shadow' are not necessarily anti-Semitic objections. But it is in fact a book where social and aesthetic response are inextricably mingled, where the form and the dramatic psychology of the novel show the clear pressure of her social feelings. Amongst the unequivocally social responses, however, may be included *The Tablet*'s lament that 'the author commits a literary error when she makes Deronda abandon on learning the fact of his Jewish birth all that a modern English education weaves of Christianity and the results of Christianity into an English gentleman's life'.

Reviewers objected to the ideal portrayal, sometimes on the grounds that it was false, sometimes on the grounds that the characters were implausible or schematic. But one section of the reading public did appreciate the Jewish parts, and these were the Jewish readers. Their response was not only an appreciation of sympathy but also strong words of praise for George Eliot's learning, and she had some compensation for the hostility of English readers in the appreciation of Jewish critics. One learned Jew, David Kaufmann, who wrote a short book on the novel which was translated from German into English, went so far as to say that only the Jewish reader could appreciate the novel. This was scarcely the point and scarcely a compliment, though its grain of truth is incontestable.

The Jewish element was likely to cause hostility for many reasons, apart from social and racial prejudice. The psychology and style of the Jewish characters, notably Mirah, Daniel and Mordecai, is simplified and idealised. The language of Mordecai is inflated and visionary, and the style of Mirah in every way sentimental. Daniel is a very interesting result of imaginative effort straining and almost, but not quite, succeeding. These ideal creatures are representative of a Semitic world placed in contrast to an English genteel and Gentile society. There are imperfect Jews in *Daniel Deronda*— Lapidoth, Mirah's father, is one, and a splendid creation he is. But there are more imperfect Gentiles. More to the point, the portrayal of Jewish society is almost entirely approving, whether of family life in the East End of London or of the aspirations of learned Jews for a Jewish community where separateness and communication could be maintained, whereas all the social portraiture of English life is highly critical. The county society of a corner of Wessex, presented and represented entirely through its gentry—their houses and pastimes—is satirically drawn. The scenes of high society are no mere renunciations of the fashionable 'silver fork' novels of Disraeli and Bulwer Lytton which she had criticised in her early writings but strong satires of superficial culture, insincerity, mercenariness, triviality and marriage-trading. Even a complex and sympathetic character like Gwendolen's uncle, Mr Gascoigne, represents all these defects, as well as desire to gild unpleasant worldliness with a glow of feeling and virtue. The rich and influential Arrowpoints are brilliantly coupled in satire, she with her apparent cultivation and bourgeois greed, he with his good cigar and 'This will never do, Cath', which is so articulate. And central to both story and satiric intent is Grandcourt, created by imagery of sadistic oppression, shown with his dogs and his horses, made narrow-minded, superior, bored and contemptuous. He has a sense of style instead of a sense of value, and would, the author observes quietly, have made an excellent governor of a colony.

Gwendolen, like Dorothea in *Middlemarch*, is seen as the product of a certain education, a certain breeding, a certain set of narrow and dangerous expectations about life, class and money. Concepts of blood, breeding and gambling are nailed down in explicit symbols like the house of Grapnell, whose fall carries the Harleth fortune with it, and in many a biting and flashing piece of local dialogue. Mrs Arrowpoint's Godwinlike disharmony of theory and practice comes out excellently in the fun of her exchanges with Gwendolen and with her own daughter; and Mr Bult, the politician, is comically and offensively pinned down, like the butterfly he is, in one exchange with Klesmer, who represents real culture as against bourgeois shams and superiority, and European (and Semitic) imagination as against political dullness. All the Englishmen (and some of the Englishwomen) in this novel give themselves away by being patronising, and this piece of dialogue, for instance, shows George Eliot's criticism at its most satiric:

'I had no idea before that you were a political man.'

Klesmer's only answer was to fold his arms, put out his nether lip, and stare at Mr Bult.

'You must have been used to public speaking. You speak uncommonly well, though I don't agree with you. From what you said about sentiment, I fancy you are a Panslavist.'

'No; my name is Elijah. I am the Wandering Jew,' said Klesmer, flashing a smile at Miss Arrowpoint, and suddenly making a mysterious wind-like rush backwards and forwards on the piano. Mr Bult felt this buffoonery rather offensive and Polish, but—Miss Arrowpoint being there—did not like to move away.

Mr Bult is one of a whole hierarchy—artistic, not social—of critical portraits of the English. He shows up Grandcourt's total lack of energy in at least being political (Gwendolen is almost amused at the pointlessness of a suggestion that Grandcourt should stand for Parliament) and in being slightly more decorous and delicate (Grandcourt really does just move away in the middle of conversations he finds irritating or tedious). The English are in varying degrees the objects of satire, and the European, especially the Jew, is in varying degrees, the object of praise. The bias is unmistakable. It is in favour of the Jews and of the Jewish community, however dispersed and fragmentary this may be. Readers of James Baldwin will see the point of my earlier comparison. When George Eliot shows a favourable image of English family life, for instance in the rather over-cosy scenes at the Meyrick fireside, it is worth noticing that the Meyrick family is made half-French. This allows them some genuine culture. The

English (including Gwendolen) bear a strong resemblance to Matthew Arnold's Philistines. Few Victorian readers were likely to be easily won by this anti-English bias into a sympathy with the Jewish winners of her satiric competition. In her first stories, *Scenes of Clerical Life* and *Adam Bede*, she had canvassed for sympathy with dull, small, ordinary people, ungrammatical curates, broken-nailed carpenters, and unattractive Methodists, but without manipulating them blatantly and exaggeratedly as models to be contrasted with the reader's own class and type. She had sometimes idealised them but often simply asked that we feel compassion for dull people, for limited virtue and null imagination, shown in convincing individual shape. In *Daniel Deronda* the handling of satire and sympathy is understandable but undiplomatically blatant. What George Eliot produced was neither a distanced work of art nor a coolly contrived piece of diplomatic persuasion.

Such reasons for contemporary hostility are unlikely to have any effect on the modern reader. Now that the ideological dust has settled, the central criticism of the novel is a literary one. Critics from Leslie Stephen to F. R. Leavis continued what George Eliot resentfully called the 'cutting-up' of the novel, and their preference for one part of the story over the other, shared by many common readers, has been a preference for the characters who are felt to be 'realised' as against those who are simplified and conceptual. Mordecai and Daniel are not intended to be narrowly typical of Jews: they are explicitly broad-minded and unorthodox in dogma, and fairly complex in psychological presentation. But the feeling shared by many readers is that they are wooden, static, and unreal. It is, by the way, misleading to talk about the two 'halves' of the book, especially when discussing Mordecai: his character, for better or for worse, depends on about three scenes of visionary or political speech: two with Daniel and one in a working-man's club at the *Hand and Banner*. Daniel is a different matter, and indeed fills more than one 'half' of the novel which is named after him. But his actions and reactions bridge the Gentile and Jewish worlds.

It is possible to list various qualities in Daniel's make-up which show that George Eliot was trying to make him complicated, moving, changing, aware of the problems of being a model and a 'hero'. His jealousy of Hans, his resentment at the wrong kind of admiration, his mixed feelings about lower-class Jews, his susceptiblity to the feelings and causes of others and his personal

excess of empathy and open-mindedness—all these are interesting
and complex features of the character, and are, moreover, shown to
some extent in the process of growing. Like Goethe's Wilhelm
Meister, he serves an apprenticeship and searches for relationships
and a vocation. An interesting and unaccountably neglected aspect
of the character, to my mind, is the trap which his altruism sets for
him by providing him with two beautiful women in need of his
rescue and support: George Eliot may be accused of a certain lack of
development here, especially in her muted mentions of Daniel's
feelings for Gwendolen, which would almost certainly have to come
out as more sexual in a modern novel, and push difficulties even
further, but she does create and face the issue, and Daniel suffers
from Gwendolen's assumptions and needs as from his final need to
free her from her last illusions. He is the kind of character one can
make sound very interesting by giving an account of his qualities
and problems, but who is less interesting than he ought to be. There
is, within the same novel, the challenging presence of Grandcourt,
as monolithic and simple a character as we can find in the Victorian
novel, but a horrifyingly real presence. It is not just a matter of
quantity, of the sheer number of features possessed by a character,
but more a matter of effectively varied viewpoints. We see
Grandcourt from many points of view—from Gwendolen's, Lydia
Glasher's, his lackey's, his children's, his dogs', Daniel Deronda's
and, very briefly, from his author's sparing analysis. We slowly
accumulate our impressions, touring the incredible monolith which
comes to strike us as solidly alive. Views of Grandcourt are
impressed, wary, intimately horrified, ambitious, cowed, right,
wrong, serious, frivolous, dismissive, contemptuous, and deeply
critical. We see him on some occasions almost as a caricature, on
others as a felt power. Daniel Deronda is a character we are told all
about in one long breath of exposition. The novel never quite
recovers from its method of introduction, and tends to continue a
single presentation from an unvarying point of view.

A round character is a character we can see round. Instead of
seeing round Daniel Deronda, we see through him, and very
rapidly. He is never opaque, almost transparent. He, Mordecai, and
Mirah are always being wheeled into different positions, like Dr
Coppelius's doll, but with little effect. It is not, I think, that we
object to noble characters (though we do tire a little of all the very
wise and sound sayings that Daniel produces from what is limited

and protected experience) but rather that we object to an absence of personality. The question of personality in literature is not an easy one, but I think it depends on an impression of vital responsiveness in characters who change according to the company they keep. Even Pecksniff varies from situation to situation, and is created through a multitude of viewpoints. Not so Daniel Deronda. When there is an apparent shift in the point of view from which we see him, as when we move from the idealised views held by Hans and his sisters to the inner feelings of Daniel, the difference is a slight and predictable one. He is not really seen from any but an admiring point of view. When he is criticised it is for noble faults, like excessive sympathy and altruism. He is never, like Dorothea Brooke, subjected to irony or even mild satire, even though his psychological content and situation might lend themselves to wry commentary. Neither his tendency to rescue maidens nor the subsequent leaning on the part of the maidens to prolong the rescue produces a situation totally uninviting to humour or irony. It is significantly impossible to imagine Daniel being laughed at, criticised ironically, or—alas— acting out of humour or irony himself. He is the kind of character his author cannot be deeply critical of, or ironical about. This exemption is a sign of lifelessness. Take Dorothea Brooke, or Adam Bede—you may want to call them prigs, but so does the author. If you could smile at Daniel, and be ironical about him, it would be in defiance of the author. Sir Hugo smiles but he's flighty.

How can we account for this? Why do we see through him and not round him? I suggest that George Eliot created an individual in a way we may understand by looking at our feelings for a whole class of people. Her sympathy and admiration worked out aesthetically in just the way our sympathy for classes works. We all know in ourselves and others the automatic sympathy for 'the poor' or 'the old' or 'little children' or Blacks or Jews. Such sympathy is indeed necessary and appropriate for classes of people who are in need of it, who are unprotected, vulnerable, or persecuted. But it can, in life as well as literature, deflect our attention from individual members of the class and produce that automatic and insensitive response to individuals which is one of the things we mean by sentimentality. In literature, this class-response can produce brilliant satire, funny minor characters, and dead heroes. And the hero's deadness in this novel is shown up by the heroine's vitality. Gwendolen's tantalising iridescence makes her alive and opaque in a vivid way which shows up the lack of individual personality in some of her fellow-characters. The dislike or coldness that may be felt for Mirah or Mordecai or Daniel is understandable, even in a modern reader who may be, like nineteenth-century Jews, on the side of George Eliot's own bias. George Eliot's feeling is understandable too. She is attempting to correct prejudice, and prejudice is the response to classes rather than individuals. The contemporary Jewish reader was in the same position as the author, in responding to the class rather than to the individual. In the same way some readers will warm to the categorised sympathies of James Baldwin, while others may shy away from aesthetic criticism through a fear of sounding prejudiced. George Eliot's feelings for her character, and her conception of his qualities, his actions and his destiny are determined by her view of him as a Jew, and by her need to represent that view in a polemical context. She put pure class-feeling into the major Jewish characters, simplifying and reducing them, and injecting them with pure approval, admiration and compassion. The result is a lack of balance, understandable and praiseworthy, once we recognise that the artist has failed to keep her head in her art because she has lost her heart in a good cause. It is no use pretending that the feeling for the cause has produced perfect art.

Up to now, my analysis has also been in danger of cutting the novel into two parts, because I have discussed only one aspect of the relationships between the 'English' and Jewish parts, and that an ideological one. We know that George Eliot, though accused by Henry James of giving a 'diagram' rather than a 'picture', was aware of the need to embody or 'incarnate' or ideas in the life of individual characters and action. Though there are failures in *Daniel Deronda*, there is an abundance of felt life. The ideas are, moreover, embodied in the feeling of life. It is not a novel in which we can skip the ideas and simply enjoy certain aspects of the story and the psychological analysis. The most important source of the novel's unity is not the contrast between two societies and sets of values that I have just been mentioning, but the social contrast as it impinges on the life of individual people. In *Middlemarch* there is a celebrated excursus by the narrator in which 'she' laments that readers and writers so often expect novels to be only love-stories. In most of her novels she gives us a love-story, but a love-story with a difference. The story of *Daniel Deronda* is not only his story, but also that of

Gwendolen Harleth. George Eliot has made an original and ironical link between a man of destiny, concerned with political life, problems of leadership and social order and value, and an ordinary woman whose immaturity and egoism show themselves in her total isolation, both in experience and in imagination, from the world of great causes. In Chapter 11 George Eliot makes this comment about Gwendolen's relation to the great world:

> Could there be a slenderer, more insignificant thread in human history than this consciousness of a girl, busy with her small inferences of the way in which she could make her life pleasant?—in a time, too, when ideas were with fresh vigour making armies of themselves, and the universal kinship was declaring itself fiercely: when women on the other side of the world would not mourn for the husbands and sons who died bravely in a common cause, and men stinted of bread on our side of the world heard of that willing loss and were patient: a time when the soul of man was waking to pulses which had for centuries been beating in him unheard, until their full sum made a new life of terror or of joy.

The historical reference was topical: in 1862–3 the Lancashire mill-workers suffered because the Northern blockade of Southern ports in the American Civil War made cotton exports impossible. Slavery, poverty, and freedom are words that mean nothing to Gwendolen in political terms; she lacks the imagination, the knowledge, and even the necessary environment, for she is presented as typically sheltered and ignorant, a woman brought up like most upper-middle-class women of her time. The slave-owner mentality and problems of poverty and freedom mean a great deal to her. Moreover, she is eventually to be brought into staggering contact with the real world of large events, when she finally turns to assume that Daniel Deronda will love and protect her only to find that he has roles and destinies in a world of which she knows nothing. The very qualities that equip him for leadership—understanding, altruism, empathy—make him influence, protect, change, and finally leave Gwendolen. From the beginning of the novel George Eliot is creating a heroine whose character and development are bound up with Daniel's very different life.

It is a novel where we have to talk about character and structure at the same time. There are three especially brilliant features of the form of the novel: a use of retrospect and flashback, which presents us with a significantly formed beginning and middle; a subtle and original use of double plot; and a conclusion which is extraordinary in its force and in its realism. But we cannot talk about these things as mere formal devices. They result from a special conception of character and action.

To take the flashback first. We start *in medias res* with the mysterious impact of Daniel Deronda's first encounter with Gwendolen, but the strong attraction which they both feel is placed in a context of other commitments: Gwendolen has met and is running away from Grandcourt, Daniel has met and is moving towards Mirah. There is no question of an obviously romantic love-story. More important, we are able to move backwards in a double flashback, which covers the action before the book begins for Gwendolen and for Daniel. In its compressed drama and reflective analysis this retrospect brings out the marked differences between these two people and their environments. We see Gwendolen as 'the princess in exile'. She is wilful, ignorant, powerful but limited, rootless and frustrated. We see Daniel as an exile too, not knowing his parentage, also rootless, but moving always towards other people in a selflessness which is admired and also gently criticised for a certain passiveness and lack of definition. The things that the characters have in common—isolation, lack of real work, striking personal charm—serve only to bring out the strong contrast between them. She lives entirely for self, and cannot conceive other people living from their separate centres of consciousness. He lives at the extreme of altruism, and his centre of self exists chiefly as a mirror for other lives. Here it must be noticed that successful psychology consists not merely in content but also in expression: a compressed account of the two characters can make them both sound interesting and complex, but Daniel's character is chiefly put forward, in this flashback, in undramatic exposition, whereas the omniscient author's commentary on Gwendolen moves along with the lively play of immediate and particular scene and dialogue. The function of the flashback is plain: we begin with the encounter between the two, so that the beginning of the novel makes conspicuous and pointed what would have been lost or blurred in a story which was told in chronological order. George Eliot was experimenting in controlling the reader's response to people and ideas. It is an experiment in form which should be placed beside similar experiments in time and narrative in *Tristram Shandy*, *Wuthering Heights* and *Ulysses*.

The beginning of the novel advertises the existence and importance of the double plot. Form is the form of the artist's vision, and the dual action of *Daniel Deronda* has to be considered as a special and appropriate way of telling *this* story, not merely as typical of the multiple actions we find in so many nineteenth-century novels in England and in Russia, novels which Henry James called 'fluid puddings' or 'large loose baggy monsters'. There is usually a function of contrast in the novel with a double plot. In *Can You Forgive Her?* Trollope shows us a serious case of emotional vacillation in one plot, and a comic case of merry widow's flirtatious choices in another. Thackeray shows us Amelia's marriage, loves, maternity and poverty in one half of *Vanity Fair* while we contrast it with the parallel adventures and sufferings of Becky Sharp in the other. Tolstoy in *Anna Karenina* shows us the contrasted destinies of Anna and Levin, and in *War and Peace* shows us the large events of the Napoleonic Wars set beside the individual destinies which are shaped by war and peace. In *Daniel Deronda* George Eliot is doing something which can be compared with Tolstoy's achievement in *War and Peace* and it is worth remembering that Tolstoy too has been criticised for showing history in an over-theoretical and inartistic fashion. Both *War and Peace* and *Daniel Deronda* show the difficulties of combining philosophical and general writing with the vividness and movement of psychological realism. Both juxtapose a marvellously rendered drama of individuals with a dryer and more schematic generalisation.

The double plot draws attention not merely to the intended contrast of two worlds but to the unintentional contrast between a successful and a less successful piece of characterisation. But we have to recognise that in drawing the memorably vivid character of her heroine, George Eliot was free from the need to express and develop general ideas about leadership and vocation. The point about Gwendolen is that she is a typical *individual*, and she can be all picture, without the hard outlines of diagram. She is one of those great characters in fiction whose vitality comes off the page like a blast of life. Her author had a long experience of creating heroines who grew, suffered, loved, changed, were guilty and were redeemed, but none of them, not even Maggie Tulliver, has the dimension and vitality and growth of Gwendolen. The flickering features of what George Eliot calls Gwendolen's 'iridescence' are not merely moral (ruthless demands for gratification, sense of power unrelated to reality, mercenariness, put beside imagination, love, compassion, sense of powerlessness) but extend also to the play of her personality. Personality is something easy to spot in a novel and easy to miss when it does not come off (as in Daniel Deronda himself) but, as I have already suggested, it is less easy to analyse. It is one of the great virtues of this novel that we see not only moral change and intellectual development in Gwendolen's painful education by suffering and disillusion, but also the light and shade of her personality. Her vacillation, her innocence, her consciously manipulated charm, her physical energy, and her exuberance are all strongly shown in wit and humour and exhilarated speech. We have the few striking incidents where her nervous susceptibility is shown too. A panel flies open showing the picture of a dead man's face, and she is terrified. Klesmer opens her vision to broad horizons where her boasted musical proficiency is as trivial as small-talk, and she feels awe, rebuke, embarrassment and resentment. Less unusual is her violent retreat from the love-making of her cousin Rex for whom she feels affection but no attraction. There is also a significant anecdote about the canary she strangled as a child, which makes its sinister contribution to her complicated character and personality. It makes its contribution to the plot, too, which involves a murder story in which the murder is nearly but not actually committed. The handling of Gwendolen's terrible marriage to Grandcourt shows the novel's advantage over the narrative poem. The novelist shows a change very like the subduing of Browning's 'last Duchess' but unfolded in slow and terrifying action. Gwendolen's wit, which was the bubbling of exuberance, confidence and personal gaiety, dries away to nothing, except for the odd forced flash when she tries to keep up appearances. Her controlled and brilliant acting turns to a passive and fearful questioning of life. She is never shown in physical exertion but restricted in movement as on the yacht. Only her pride and style remain. The susceptibility to nervous dread grows, in nightmares of both sleep and waking life.

As she changes she continues in ignorance of that great world in which Daniel is moving and discovering his race, his identity and his vocation. For marriage isolates her and imprisons her far more than her unmarried girlhood did, and there is the added irony that she married for power and freedom. The novel tells the story of her marriage with a compelling handling of both action and psychology, and since it is one of those Victorian stories where climax and surprise do genuinely astonish, I refrain from telling too much. For this novel does tell a good story. Its action of mystery, discovery and fears, of fate, death and guilt, places it with a group of Victorian novels of the eighteen-sixties called 'sensation novels'. We usually associate Wilkie Collins rather than George Eliot with this genre, but it was one which had some influence on writers whose talents and sensibility might be thought to lie right outside it—writers such as Trollope, Charlotte Yonge and George Eliot. *Felix Holt* is the purest example of George Eliot's contribution to the sensation novel, but there are many features of *Daniel Deronda* which make it 'sensational' too. What I want to draw attention to is not the tangled and intricate intrigue, the lost fathers and unknown mothers, the melodramatic confrontations, the mysterious past passions, the illegitimate children, and such skeletons in cupboards, but rather the actual psychology of sensation, the *frisson* missing from many Victorian examples as from many of their descendants, the modern thrillers. The tension, mystery, dread and strangeness of *Daniel Deronda* are not just manipulated to terrify the reader, but are part of the psychological experiences of the characters. Gwendolen differs from all the earlier heroines, whom she resembles so much in moral development, in her nervous equipment. She is afraid of being alone, she is afraid of being loved, she is afraid of certain changes in the light, she is afraid of large open spaces, she has dreams and nightmares. These feelings are sometimes symbolic of her values. Her fear of breadth is contrasted with the large visions of Daniel and Mordecai, and acts as a metaphor for her narrowness and smallness of life and experience. But we feel it as sensation first, and as symbol second. The fear of the picture of the dead face haunts her nightmares and eventually attaches itself in a horrifying way to the feelings of hatred and guilt aroused in her marriage. Nor is she the only character to have dreams and visions. Mordecai must also be seen as a visionary figure given an appropriate mind and nervous system and the study of his imagination should be looked at in connection with Gwendolen's. There are many subtle contrasts and cross-connections in this elaborate and finely formed novel.

The realistic psychology must be seen in relation to the structure of the novel. Gwendolen's sensations and hopes and ignorance are created in a context of something resembling dramatic irony, for as we follow her movement through a narrow world which to her is the whole world, we also follow the separate movement of Deronda in the world of new ideas and sympathies. For her, he is a character in her private drama, a support, a mentor and, at the end, a pillar of strength. For the reader, she is visibly only a small part of his life, and the part he plays in her story is far removed from his relationship with Mirah, Mordecai, his mother, and the destiny of the Jewish people. We do more than wisely observe her errors and illusions. We also follow the conflicting tensions of her dependence on Daniel and his separate and incompatible plans and discoveries. It is with something approaching nervous anxiety and apprehension as well as with superior knowledge that we follow the pattern of her feelings, and experience the final encounter between hero and heroine. It is one of the most moving and acutely rendered moments in the novel. The double plot has shown us two worlds. It has also moved in a form of counterpoint and tension which is a brilliant example of significant form—form giving significance to the matter it forms.

The double plot is sharply brought to a single conclusion. Gwendolen's fear of space and vision is justified and completed in a traumatic climax, the nature of which the reader has foreseen, the detail of which is rendered in a terrifyingly concrete and unpredictable immediacy. The conclusion to the novel is also something unusual in Victorian fiction. One should not make hasty generalisations about the neat and highly-finished endings in which we are told 'everything that will happen to everyone in the novel'. *Middlemarch* is like this, but the endings of *Tancred*, *Villette* and *The Newcomes* are certainly not tidy and easy. Nevertheless, *Daniel Deronda*'s conclusion has a special toughness and fluidity. Gwendolen is not like Maggie Tulliver, whose problems are solved by death, or like the preceding heroines, Esther Lyon in *Felix Holt* or Dorothea in *Middlemarch*, whose problems are solved by marriage. She stands alone at the end of the novel, facing the question-mark of the future. The ending is not completely open. The reader feels assured that Gwendolen is 'saved' as John Blackwood had hoped when he first began her story. There are hints and possibilities which seem to point ahead, but they are indefinite. The ending is not a 'slice of life' ending; it does not resemble the arbitrary chopping short of a life in the middle of the story. On the contrary, there is discovery and vision. But Gwendolen is not only alone, propped up neither by death, nor by marriage, but has to start on a new set of expectations. She has found that what seemed like a possible happy-ever-after was in fact a new and painful beginning in which many of the things she had learnt would be lost, re-tested and rediscovered. We are left with a new refusal to simplify the nature of moral development, as well as with a new kind of ending to a novel. It is an ending which leaves us with a sense of life's difficulties.

Daniel is also poised on the edge of a future deliberately left 'vague and grand', as Blackwood put it. This vagueness is necessary and tactful, like the similar vagueness at the end of T. S. Eliot's *Family Reunion*. Both Harry and Daniel are set free for a special destiny and then left conveniently in mid-career. George Eliot was concerned to show the qualities of political leadership—or what she saw as these qualities—but the nature of the political career itself she was scarcely competent to handle. Although there is some truth in the suggestion that the Jewish theme was simply a symbol of a larger humane interest, it seems evident that she was defining in Daniel the specific qualities of a Zionist leader, a new Messiah who was appreciative of the chosen people but felt the need for communication as well as for Jewish separateness. Her Daniel 'come to judgment' is taken to the brink, and wisely left there. Even in *Middlemarch* she had steered clear of showing Will Ladislaw in his actual political career, and in *Daniel Deronda* the Zionist materials would have taken her beyond the rendering of politics into the rendering of prophecy. She was held back by the real obscurity of the Jewish future, by her habitual avoidance of showing politics in action, and by her guarded meliorist vision. *Daniel Deronda* is a novel which I have called experimental, and I can do no better here than to quote George Eliot's own use of the word. It brings out very clearly the restrained, truthful and tentative imaginative exploration she is making in this novel, an exploration which pushes so far, but no further. George Eliot wrote this in a letter to Joseph Payne, on 25 January 1876, a few days before the first part of *Daniel Deronda* was published, and it is a statement both ambitious and honestly limited:

But my writing is simply a set of experiments in life—an endeavour to see what our thought and emotion may be capable of—what stores of motive, actual or hinted as possible, give promise of a better after which we may strive—what gains from past revelations and discipline we must strive to keep hold of as something more sure than shifting theory.

First published as the Introduction to The Penguin English Library edition of *Daniel Deronda* (Harmondsworth, 1967).

12. *Under the Greenwood Tree*: a Concern with Imagination

Although Thomas Hardy's novels show his interest in crafts and arts, religious, secular and military music, verse, architecture, landscape painting, and story-telling on the public platform (in *The Hand of Ethelberta*), they do not directly reveal his interest in the art of fiction. He does not write artist-novels, but all his characters are active in the narrative forms of fantasy and memory. His most profoundly argumentative novels, *The Mayor of Casterbridge*, *The Return of the Native*, *Tess of the d'Urbervilles* and *Jude the Obscure*, show an interest in imagination too wide to be confined to the nature and situation of the artist. Jude, Sue, Eustachia and Tess are examples of imaginative power. They all share a poor chance of survival, for their mental energy finds it impossible to conform to the restrictive and conventional demands of nature and society. To imagine is to imagine a better world, and in the Hardy world, to imagine a better world is to be subversive, and to be subversive is to be destroyed. Only one of his imaginative people, Elizabeth-Jane Farfrae in *The Mayor of Casterbridge*, comes to terms with life, and modestly but sensitively survives. However, she refuses to be 'demonstratively thankful', as Hardy says, for 'the doubtful honour of a brief transit through a sorry world'. She believes, and encourages others to believe, that life may be made endurable through 'those minute forms of satisfaction that offer themselves to everyone not in positive pain'. Even such mild anodynes are rare in Hardy.

Tess is more representative of his thinking characters. Her intelligence and imagination are articulated as finely as Elizabeth-Jane's, though she has less opportunity for intellectual self-improvement. Though at times inclined to speak with her author's voice, as when she compares our planet to a blighted apple, she meditates for the most part in a personal style. Her individual eloquence shows a profound, passionate, and properly generalised sense of her situation, as in her retort to Angel Clare's typically Victorian offer to help her take up some 'course of study—history for example?':

> '. . . what's the use of learning that I am one of a long row only—finding out that there is set down in some old book somebody just like me, and to know that I shall only act her part; making me sad, that's all. The best is not to remember that your nature and your past doings have been just like thousands' and thousands', and that your coming life and doings'll be like thousands' and thousands'.' (Ch. xix)

I am less concerned with the content of what Elizabeth-Jane or Tess say, with their attitudes of pessimism or meliorism, than with their ability to ponder and perceive, and their experience. They are endowed with an imaginative capacity sufficiently sophisticated and eloquent to act as a vehicle for Hardy to utter his ideas. But the vehicle is shaped, coloured and fully characterised. He creates characters who meditate and formulate in terms that serve the dual purpose of the particularities of fiction and the larger lines of his own argument.

Like most writers, Hardy uses mouthpieces as well as examples. Of course, imaginative literature tends to be about imaginative people—Odysseus, Antigone, Lear, Hamlet, Henry Esmond, Dorothea Brooke, Marcel, Stephen Dedalus. But the imaginative artist's interest in imagination and creation of imaginative character may show itself less conspicuously and heroically. *Under the Greenwood Tree* takes its place with *The Woodlanders*, *Far from the Madding Crowd*, and *The Trumpet-Major*, all novels which speak of and through the superficially limited minds and styles of characters who are rarely permitted to generalise, but stay and speak from their allotted empirical experience. It seems inaccurate to call them naive or even simple characters, because their apparent simplicity is not incompatible with intimations of imaginative grasp. The novels stand with other works of literature whose authors have decided to exclude their own close kin, those characters who can act as examples of expressive, bold, far-seeing, and inventive imagination. Among writings which take such a self-denying ordinance are Wordsworth's *Lyrical Ballads*. George Eliot's *Scenes of Clerical Life*, and Joyce's *Dubliners*. These poems and stories exclude characters directly and broadly representative of their author's powers, and attempt instead to work through less expressive and refined intelligences of people for whom the world of general ideas barely exists, or seems not to exist at all, whose concerns are with their day-to-day existence, their immediate environment, the place and society in which they find themselves, their families, work, pastimes, pleasures, births, loves, marriages and deaths. The last-named major events in the human cycle immediately signal the occasion for analysis, speculation and debate, and the works I am concerned with often avail themselves of the enlarged experiences of social and religious ritual. But even on such occasions, the cyclical or major events of human experience are usually presented and discussed empirically, and many of Hardy's actors are not strongly sceptical, subversive, or solemn in their attitudes to their own mortality, and are never unconcerned with immediate and particular action.

Under the Greenwood Tree can scarcely be said to have themes in the usual sense understood by literary critics. Its double plot joins the love-story of Dick Dewy and Fancy Day with a vital and fatal chapter in the history of the Mellstock Quire. It can be pressed into thematic conformity with Hardy's other novels through its concern with time and history, but although it certainly suggests or proposes views on change, conformity, continuity, tradition and modernity, such suggestions do not amount to an informing and conspicuous theme. To insist on such generalisation as dominant would, I believe, reduce or abstract much of the book's vitality and particularity. But I am not so much concerned to examine all the concerns of this novel, as to suggest the way in which one of them emerges. The emergence is subtle, natural, and unusually implicit.

The novel presents the novelist's interest in imagination entirely through its accretion of particulars. In *Under the Greenwood Tree* the characters, actions and environment, show the human mind sensitively, benignly and creatively at work. Such work, however humble, is characteristic of what we commonly call imagination. It synthesises and particularises, like Coleridge's favourite image of the shooting star which vividly condenses complex experience in Shakespeare's *Venus and Adonis*. The imagination shows itself in *Under the Greenwood Tree* as founded on knowledge, sympathy, sensuous response and synthetic force.

Under the Greenwood Tree is a narrative unity which invites an orthodox analysis. It joins the obstacles and triumphs of the love-story with the dismissal of the Mellstock musicians, and its synthesis is made through parallels and contrasts. Fancy Day is the new organist who replaces the old choir, and her two unsuccessful lovers, the churchwarden and the parson, bring about the local change as a testimony to their feeling for her. The lovers are young and must hurry, the musicians middle-aged and old, and must give way. Attitudes to love, youth, ageing and age are shown in fine blends and contrasts. The lovers are rapturous and blind, the middle-aged and elderly are calmly disenchanted. A sharply and fully realised natural environment creates Hardy's honest version of pastoral, neither wholly ideal nor wholly undesirable, in which the bitter-sweet human experiences are all chronicled.

The pastoral exerts its binding power. Each part of the novel is what Coleridge would call an organ to the whole, beginning with the resonant title's quotation from that earlier pastoral, *As You Like It*. Sentences are resonant, suggesting the motion of nature's rhythms: 'And winter, which modifies the note of such trees as shed their leaves, does not destroy its individuality' (in Chapter 1), or perfect harmony, 'a couple . . . so exactly in tune with one another as Dick and she' (in Chapter 2), or fruition and colour, in the description of grandfather William: 'an ardent vitality still preserved a warm and roughened bloom upon his face, which reminded gardeners of the sunny side of a ripe ribstone-pippin' (in Chapter 3).

The image of William's face marks one of Hardy's favourite methods of describing his characters. He is closely attentive not only to appearances, but to the sensibility and sympathy which they register, and which register them. He likes to show his characters through the variable responses of other people:

William Dewy—otherwise grandfather William—was now about seventy; yet an ardent vitality still preserved a warm and roughened bloom upon his face, which reminded gardeners of the sunny side of a ripe ribstone-pippin; though a narrow strip of forehead, that was protected from the weather by lying above the line of his hat-brim, seemed to belong to some town man, so gentlemanly was its whiteness. His was a humorous and kindly nature, not unmixed with a frequent melancholy; and he had a firm religious faith. But to his neighbours he had no character in particular. If they saw him pass by their windows when they had been bottling off old mead, or when they had just been called long-headed men who might do anything in the world if they chose, they thought concerning him, 'Ah, there's that good-hearted man—open as a child!' If they saw him just after losing a shilling or half-a-crown, or accidentally letting fall a piece of crockery, they thought. 'There's that poor weak-minded man Dewy again! Ah, he's never done much in the world either!' If he passed when fortune neither smiled nor frowned on them, they merely thought him old William Dewy.(Pt. 1, Ch. iii)

This joint attention to a man and to the shifting external viewpoint which regards, interprets and judges him, is characteristic of Hardy's medium of presentation in this novel. He is not altogether giving up the descriptive authority of the author, but inclines to share it provisionally with his characters, while reserving his own larger knowledge. He does not preserve this superior knowledge in order to create an ironical contrast between wisdom and ignorance, as George Eliot or Henry James often do, but suggests and ultimately proves that good judgement and vision are native to Mellstock. Hardy speaks about his people, through them, and for them. To present a character is for him to present a variable, not a constant, so as to recognise a local truth, and to create a community of linked and separated people. He may be omniscient, but masks the omniscience out of regard for the minds and responses of his people, who have their own rights and powers. If he is attentive to nature, so are they; and his description of the natural world, like his description of people, uses his people's eyes and ears.

The novelist's familiar knowledge, and his appreciation of individual human and natural life, is drawn from his characters and is delegated to them. This is not a critical conceit. One might well suggest that Hardy learnt to see, hear and know by observing the originals of his characters, the creation of art being a circular process rather than an imitation of nature.

We learn then from Hardy's people how imagery and imagination function. The novel's first sentence reports that dwellers in a wood can tell trees apart by voice as well as feature; then Dick Dewy makes his entry, while his author observes that the plantation 'whispered thus distinctively to his intelligence'. The author's sensibility is interwoven with the character's. Hardy immediately proceeds to delineate Dick's nature, confining himself to Dick's confining darkness. Dick is first sensed and presented through the sounds he makes: 'All the evidences of his nature were those afforded by the spirit of his footsteps, which succeeded each other lightly and quickly, and by the liveliness of his voice as he sang in a rural cadence . . .'. These evidences of his nature, which are allowed to speak for themselves, carry great weight through being unendorsed yet unmistakable. Many of the novel's people meditate, observe, and respond to the world outside through their 'intelligence', a word Hardy used rather broadly to include mind, feeling, senses. Reuben Dewy, the tranter, for instance, is first seen as his friends and neighbours arrive at his house, knowing 'by their footsteps that they were the expected old comrades' and so not bothering to look up from the hogshead he is about to broach. His son Charley is contemplating his own face in a small looking-glass, 'to learn how the human countenance appeared when engaged in crying, which survey led him to pause at various points in each wail that were more than ordinarily striking, for a thorough appreciation of the general effect'. His daughter Bessy is comparing the faded and unfaded pattern of her plaid dress, his wife testing the temperature of flitches of bacon which seem to be in possible danger from the festive fire's great heat. Hardy likes to show people engaged in fervent, absorbed, and curious attention to the things around them, including themselves. The child Charley is worth all the children in the novels of George Eliot put together, for that look in the glass, as he cries, and for his marvellous question about the inside of the cider cask, 'Idd it cold inthide te hole?' Hardy's grown men and women, as well as his children, are engaged in this barefaced and unmonitored response to life. Old William loves two things best, splitting apple-wood and playing the bass-viol. At one time Hardy intended to call the novel, *The Mellstock Quire*, and the whole choir is ruled by a musical passion, delighting in performance, discussing the merits and history of their instruments, and forcing music upon Farmer Shiner who can't stand their Christmas carols. This quality of fervour is a necessary aspect of imagination and sensibility, as Hardy conceives them. Fervour joins intellectual curiosity with physical and emotional response, to create the exhilarated and creative eating, drinking, singing, dancing and working of *Under the Greenwood Tree*.

The fullest instance of fervour is the music, a fervent labour and a fervent joy. But professional appreciation is also there in Fancy's expected 'sharp remark' which was expected of 'the village sharpener', in the villagers' disinterested praise of 'inventive sellers' like old Sam Lawson, and in the tranter's history of his cider and its barrel. Reuben Dewy discourses on the subject of his cider, the apples of which it is made, their names (where known), and the places where they grew, the hoops and tap of the barrel, once used for port wine and dishonestly sold by Sam Lawson, in an articulate history. Professional fervour involves a way of organising and ordering experience, not exclusively or distortingly, like a humour, but affording an entry to experience and a means of organising it. It depends on knowledge of people, objects and history. It is attentive to life, as Dick Dewy is when he attends to the swarm of bees even though it makes him slightly late for his wedding. It is presented through praise and delight. This knowledgeable fervour is more than a feeling for community and nature, for through its specialisation Hardy's people establish and order their lives and values. Mr Penny not only knows about shoes and feet, but tells his shoemaker's anecdotes to reveal an implicit feeling for family, neighbourhood and individual people. Ruling passions can blind or blinker vision, but Hardy makes his people benevolent and sympathetic in the exercise and defence of their jobs. For Penny, the foot is a creative synecdoche:

'Well,' said the shoemaker, seeming to perceive that the interest the object had excited was greater than he had anticipated, and warranted the last's being taken up again and exhibited; 'now, whose foot do ye suppose this last was made for? It was made for Geoffrey Day's father, over at Yalbury Wood. Ah, many's the pair o' boots he've had off the last! Well, when 'a died, I used the last for Geoffrey, and have ever since, though a little doctoring was wanted to make it do. Yes, a very queer natured last it is now, 'a b'lieve', he continued, turning it over caressingly. 'Now, you notice that there' (pointing to a lump of leather bradded to the toe), 'that's a very bad bunion that he've had ever since 'a was a boy. Now, this remarkable large piece' (pointing to a patch nailed to the side), 'shows a' accident he received by the tread of a horse, that squashed his foot a'most to a pomace. The horse-shoe came full-butt on this point, you see. And so I've just been over to Geoffrey's, to know if he wanted his bunion altered or made bigger in the new pair I'm making.' (Pt. I, Ch. iii)

and

> 'You used to know Johnson the dairyman, William?'
> 'Ay, sure; I did.'
> 'Well, 'twasn't opposite his house, but a little lower down—by his paddock, in front o' Parkmaze Pool. I was a-bearing across towards Bloom's End, and lo and behold, there was a man just brought out o' the Pool, dead; he had un'rayed for a dip, but not being able to pitch it just there had gone in flop over his head. Men looked at en; women looked at en; children looked at en; nobody knowed en. He was covered wi' a sheet; but I catched sight of his voot, just showing out as they carried en along. "I don't care what name that man went by," I said, in my way, "but he's John Woodward's brother; I can swear to the family voot." At that very moment up comes John Woodward, weeping and teaving, "I've lost my brother! I've lost my brother!" ' (Pt. I, Ch. iii)

In such professional humours experience is incised, remembered, and narrated. The anecdotes have their guiding theme or motif, whether it is shoes, music, drink, or Mrs Penny's harping on her marriage to her 'little small man'. As Penny talks to the group outside his shop window, he goes on stitching, and punctuates or emphasises remarks with the strong pulls of needle through leather. His special shoemaker's concern makes his responses sharply self-interested, and informed, and so keeps sympathy from spilling over into grandiose or sentimental effusions. Grandfather William's passion for strings allows him to remember warmly and acutely:

> 'Well, as to father in the corner there,' the tranter said, pointing to old William, who was in the act of filling his mouth; 'he'd starve to death for music's sake now, as much as when he was a boy-chap of fifteen.'
> 'Truly, now,' said Michael Mail, clearing the corner of his throat in the manner of a man who meant to be convincing; 'there's a friendly tie of some sort between music and eating.' He lifted the cup to his mouth, and drank himself gradually backwards from a perpendicular position to a slanting one,

during which time his looks performed a circuit from the wall opposite him to the ceiling overhead. Then clearing the other corner of his throat: 'Once I was a-setting in the little kitchen of the Dree Mariners at Casterbridge, having a bit of dinner, and a brass band struck up in the street. Such a beautiful band as that were! I was setting eating fried liver and lights, I well can mind— ah, I was! and to save my life, I couldn't help chawing to the tune. Band played six-eight time; six-eight chaws I, willynilly. Band plays common; common time went my teeth among the liver and lights as true as a hair. Beautiful 'twere! Ah, I shall never forget that there band!'

'That's as tuneful a thing as ever I heard of,' said grandfather James, with the absent gaze which accompanies profound criticism. (Pt. 1, Ch. viii)

These ruling passions are not despotic, and often divide their rule. Penny plays the fiddle as well as making shoes, grandfather William cleaves the apple-wood and knows how it will burn. Mr and Mrs Dewy and Mr and Mrs Penny relate a chequered but not cynical experience of married life. The passions chime together. Grandfather William's thought of singing to Fancy Day follows Mr Penny's story of the drowned man's foot, but takes place with natural and easy enthusiasm, not jockeying for position. There is room for stories about strings, cider, shoes, and marriage, told by many storytellers. Hardy's are not like Ben Jonson's satirical humours. No one 'peculiar quality' diverts and distorts the 'affects and powers' of his people, making them 'in their confluction all to flow one way'. The bias gives shape to imagination. These people have a solid and special ground, from which to regard their own and each other's lives. They usually know it is not exclusive.

Despite the great praise of strings, the choir can put aside their special interest with tolerance and generosity. When their deputation marches off to see the parson, it is not to give it to him 'hot and strong' as local intelligence expects, but to accept the decision and ask modestly for a proper season for their going. William's mild detachment refuses to be insulting or unjust to their enemy the parson:

'Still, for my part,' said old William, 'though he's arrayed against us, I like the hearty borus-snorus ways of the new pa'son.'

'You, ready to die for the quire,' said Bowman reproachfully, 'to stick up for the quire's enemy, William!'

'Nobody will feel the loss of our church-work so much as I,' said the old man firmly: 'that you d'all know. I've a-been in the quire man and boy ever since I was a chiel of eleven. But for all that 'tisn't in me to call the man a bad man, because I truly and sincerely believe en to be a good young feller.'

Some of the youthful sparkle that used to reside there animated William's eye as he uttered the words, and a certain nobility of aspect was also imparted to him by the setting sun, which gave him a Titanic shadow at least thirty feet in length, stretching away to the east in outlines of imposing magnitude, his head finally terminating upon the trunk of a grand old oak-tree. (Pt. 2, Ch. ii)

So Hardy evinces his approval of William's character and remarks. He and his companions are not sentimental, as their collective biography of the former parson makes clear:

'Ah, Mr. Grinham was the man!' said Bowman. 'Why, he never troubled us wi' a visit from year's end to year's end. You might go anywhere, do anything: you'd be sure never to see him.'

and

'And 'a was a very jinerous gentleman about choosing the psalms and hymns o' Sundays. "Confound ye," says he, "blare and scrape what ye will, but don't bother me!" ' (Pt. 2, Ch. ii)

The quality of the Mellstock imagination is well-wishing but not soft, self-respecting but not egotistical, specialist but not warped. These moral and intellectual qualities are invariably conveyed in those narratives that are the prevailing genre within the novel. Music may be a collective enterprise, but so is storytelling, ritualised in village feasts and gatherings, part of the ordinary social flow of reminiscence, gossip, praise, criticism, entertainment, hopes, fears, jokes and ruminations, and seemingly extended naturally to form Hardy's art.

A remarkable feature of his storytellers is their cooperation in narrative. The community is brought to life in its daily activities and its properties. Every object and every event tells many stories, and the stories are generous, but the actual harmony and community of the telling testifies and ministers to the benevolence. The tellers quote and build on other stories. Hardy's storytellers— like James Joyce's Leopold Bloom—are good men, and their sprightly and potent characters, with their ironic but tolerant acceptances, are expressed and implied in their stories. Perhaps the social psychology and morality of Hardy's narratives achieves its most complex response in the last sight we get of the community in *Under the Greenwood Tree*. In the last chapter Hardy shows us the communal act of imagination, practised by the onlookers at the nuptial dance:

> Here the gaffers and gammers whose dancing days were over told stories of great impressiveness, and at intervals surveyed the advancing and retiring couples from the same retreat, as people on shore might be supposed to survey a naval engagement in the bay beyond; returning again to their tales when the pause was over. Those of the whirling throng, who during the rests between each figure, turned their eyes in the direction of these seated ones, were only able to discover, on account of the music and bustle, that a very striking circumstance was in course of narration—denoted by an emphatic sweep of the hand, snapping of the fingers, close of the lips, and fixed look into the centre of the listener's eye for the space of a quarter of a minute, which raised in that listener such a reciprocating working of face as to sometimes make the distant dancers half wish to know what such an interesting tale could refer to. (Pt. 5, Ch. ii)

Those whose dancing days are over remember festivities past, and loves and marriages are summoned up unromantically to testify to the binding power of social ritual. The feeblest member of the Mellstock Quire is Thomas Leaf, who turns up, as so often, to take his place among his superiors. Like a good guest he makes his contribution to the ritual storytelling under the beech tree. Thomas Leaf's story is scarcely an imaginative creation, but takes its place in the common ritual.[1]

It is a feeble story, its rhetoric and form making it a model of how not to do it. His tale is one told by a warm-hearted simpleton, flat and unstructured, but signifying generous intent.

'Once,' said the delighted Leaf, in an uncertain voice, 'there was a man who lived in a house! Well, this man went thinking and thinking night and day. At last, he said to himself, as I might, "If I had only ten pounds, I'd make a fortune." At last by hook or by crook, he got the ten pounds!'

'Only think of that!' said Nat Callcome satirically.

'Silence!' said the tranter.

'Well, now comes the interesting part of the story! In a little time he had made that ten pounds twenty. Then a little time after that he doubled it, and made it forty. Well, he went on, and a good while after that he made it eighty, and on to a hundred. Well, by-and-by he made it two hundred! Well, you'd never believe it, but—he went on and made it four hundred! He went on, and what did he do? Why, he made it eight hundred! Yes, he did,' continued Leaf in the highest pitch of excitement, bringing down his fist upon his knee with such force that he quivered with the pain; 'yes, and he went on and made it A THOUSAND!'

'Hear, hear!' said the tranter. 'Better than the history of England, my sonnies!'

'Thank you for your story, Thomas Leaf,' said grandfather William; and then Leaf gradually sank into nothingness again. (Pt. 5, Ch. ii)

The tranter and his father, two of the best tellers in this novel full of telling, move their generous vote of thanks. In *Under the Greenwood Tree* the chorus often ceases to be choric, to take its prominent place in the centre of our attention. It holds such a place through its imaginative appreciation of the past, well-preserved and alive, but naturally conservative and conserving. The middle-aged and the old men are constantly telling the comic story of courtship and marriage, wryly, drily, but not chillingly or cyncially. The two lovers are naturally forward-looking. Hardy's appreciation of their amorous creations is beautifully balanced against the old stories. Dick's vision is a vision, delicately appreciated in its intensity and fervour, comedy insisting on its inventiveness and force. His exuberant ideality is contrasted with the acquired common sense of the choir, whose unromantic and unvisionary look at love amazes the young lover. The choir's imagination dwells on the reliable pleasures of music, song, food and drink and festivity, but they sigh over Dick tolerantly, their breath scarcely dimming the brilliant reflecting glass of creative love.

Dick Dewy sees visions. Fancy Day's imagination has been busy with a more complicated vision of future possibilities than Dick Dewy's. She follows Thomas Leaf's unimaginative simple tale with her carefully kept secret and her white lie. She has made up her plain tale of love and marriage with Dick, but into this realistic construction has strayed the less palpable vision of higher things, thoughts of marriage with Parson Maybold. This is a vision entertained but not followed through. She chooses the plain tale, though Hardy makes it truthfully apparent that her imaginative endeavours, in their selective and creative efforts, are painfully struggling, as Coleridge says of poets, to idealise and unify. The choir's creativity taken an understated form, right for its stoicism and sense of proportion. Fancy's imaginative infidelity is also understated, remaining a straying of the mind which reminds us, like the novel's title, that idylls are fictions. The personal autobiography we are all engaged in constructing as we look before and after depends on visions and revisions.

First published in *The Novels of Thomas Hardy*, ed. A. Smith (Vision Press, London, 1979).

Note

1.   I have discussed Leaf's story in *Tellers and Listeners* (Athlone Press, London, 1975).

13. George Meredith's *Evan Harrington*

Evan Harrington, published in 1861, is a novel which offers various delights. Like everything George Meredith wrote, it is the individual expression of an idiosyncratic intelligence and temperament, irreplaceable and inimitable. It is one of the most entertaining comic books in English literature, to be placed with the novels of Sterne for exuberant language and hilarious farce, with those of Fielding for good humour, commonsense, and affectionate ridicule. It looks ahead to the work of Ivy Compton-Burnett and Ronald Firbank in its elegance, acidity and startling comic invention. It stands significantly apart from the fervours and solemnities of the great Victorians. The only nineteenth-century writer who may have influenced Meredith is his father-in-law, Thomas Love Peacock, another peculiar genius, though the subtlety and cunning of Meredith's social criticism can remind us of Thackeray, the only other Victorian novelist who can be earnest without sounding earnest.

Artistic personality is hard to define. It resides in style, and Meredith's style is strongly present, as a self-conscious source of pleasure and as a test of intelligence. It draws attention to its own quality, teeming with images, aphorisms, epigrams and pictures. *Evan Harrington* is not a novel in which an omniscient narrator is always telling us what to think and where to look, but it is imbued with a sense of the companionable author, aware that his reader is there to be amused and provoked. This is not a novel in which we hasten on to conclusions, but one in which the experience of reading must be savoured. It is not for fast readers, concerned only with reaching the end, but with appreciative readers, who can enjoy a journey. Scenes and words sometimes need to be tasted slowly, sometimes to be sensed and then analysed, read and re-read. The reader must not be in a hurry, and must not be lazy. Meredith said that comedy flourished in a civilised society where the sexes were equal, and one of the civilised pleasures he provides for his reader is that of a constant appeal to the intelligence. It is true that the tone of Meredith's direct address to the reader in this novel tends to be more intimate and confidential than in his other fiction, because of the requirements—or what the author saw as the requirements—of its serialisation in the magazine, *Once a Week*, but the play of intelligence is not warm or cosy. This novel is not populated by highly intelligent characters, and some of those who have wits (like Evan himself) don't use them, or are slowed down or over-excited by passion or appetite. Many of the characters are fools, sometimes inarticulate and slow-minded, like Harry Jocelyn, sometimes eloquent and crafty, like the Countess. Meredith gives us the spectacle of a feast of fools, like that in Shakespeare's *As You Like It*, but the reader must discriminate and look out for traps and trip-wires. This is a novel rather like *Tom Jones*, where the most intelligent character is the author, who imputes appropriate intelligence to his reader. The novel depends on a communion of superior spirits, over the heads of the besotted or beguiled or bewildered characters. This isn't a complete picture, because it leaves out a certain appeal to sympathy, though this appeal is cool and critically alienated.

This detachment of Meredith is part of our sense of the author. So also is his geniality and warmth, not towards characters or reader, but towards the social and phenomenal world in general. All works of art are suffused with their author's tastes but what is striking in Meredith is the contrast between a comic coolness and distance, and a warmth and intimacy of the senses and feelings. This contrast is also a happy combination. If the reader is forced to be alert and strenuously engaged with words and meanings which do not yield to superficial response, she is also allowed to be relaxed and gratified. If she is teased and tested by implication and indirection, she is entertained by direct and simple scenes and sensations—a game of cricket, a dinner in an old-fashioned inn at which two brothers drink an improbable quantity of good port, a country picnic, a gossip after the funeral. The conversation scenes are sometimes exchanges of gossipy narrative, and even dialogues of elegant cut-and-thrust are frequently grounded in the sensuousness of everyday things, like food, drink, clothes, weather. George Eliot wrote nostalgically in *Middlemarch* about the good old leisured days of Fielding, when the author could expatiate and digress, and the reader find time to listen. To most modern readers, George Eliot's own pace seems leisurely, but her narrative texture is concentrated and purposive when compared with Meredith's. His narrative medium is sometimes episodic and anecdotal, varying in pace, at times slowing down to savour and provide holiday pleasures. Meredith's wit and narrative fertility are of course often pressed into the service of moral argument and psychological portrayal, but at times they seem to be off duty. Conversation and anecdote can loom large in their own right. Take, for example, the scene after the Great Mel is buried, when the Countess de Saldar has to adapt her conversational powers to the low-life demands of her rejected environment. Like all of us, she sometimes has to behave herself and be nice to the family, and it is entirely characteristic of Meredith's comedy of character that he should ground such grandiose and ridiculous humours in familiar moral experience. His comic characters, including Richmond Roy in *Harry Richmond* and Sir Willoughby Patterne in *The Egoist*, are never monsters, but speak to us, uncomfortably, as near neighbours. The Countess has several styles of eloquence, of which narrative is only one. It has its consistent tones and forms: her storytelling, like all her styles, is class-aggrandising, and here she characteristically shifts the scene and raises the class of the anecdotal material. The reader has the doubled pleasure of enjoying both the story and the story of the story, but while we place the characteristics of style, manner and purpose, the telling itself is both amusing and—here—part of the comic-macabre colour of the wake:

> For instance, there was the Portuguese Marquis de Col. He had married a Spanish wife, whose end was mysterious. Undressing, on the night of the anniversary of her death, and on the point of getting into bed, he beheld the dead woman lying on her back before him. All night long he had to sleep with this freezing phantom! Regularly, every fresh anniversary, he had to endure the same penance, no matter where he might be, or in what strange bed. (Ch. II)

Meredith throws in the extra joke of Mrs Fiske's re-translation of the story into English lower life, where the Marquis de Col, as imaginary a Marquis as the Great Mel, is metamorphosed into Peter Smithers, an old flame of the Countess, once Louisa Harrington, the tailor's daughter.

The Countess de Saldar is a splendid comic character, and Meredith feels free to make her entirely comic, with no affective appeal or complexity. She is a much more single-minded creation than Pickwick or Micawber. Meredith makes of her an entirely solipsistic and impenetrable character, never eroded by a sense of the world outside self, bent on expunging the past, indefatigable in social intrigue and performance, aided by lies, inventions, boasts, solicitations, and liable to error. She is given the glorious accessory of a husband, the Count de Saldar, who never speaks and scarcely appears. (He doesn't need to after his head-and-shoulders-only appearance above a dinner table.) She has the important structural function of representing the Great Mel, her dead father, of whom she is at once intensely ashamed and intensely proud.

Perhaps Meredith's most original feat in the making of comic character is the Great Mel himself, evoked through decease and absence. Like *Tom Jones, Joseph Andrews, Roderick Random*, and some Victorian novels in the same form and vein, *David Copperfield* and *Pendennis*, the novel blends the making of a hero with the coming of age of a young man. The young man is explicitly described and dramatised as having no character—he is, as the narrator reminds us, like Pope's characterless women. He is also like most of the other young heroes in the books just mentioned in having an initial shapelessness and immaturity, gradually taking shape and acquiring some measure of vocation, self-knowledge and identity. Unlike the heroes in these earlier books he has a dead father whose prominent presence has to be acknowledged and exorcised. Mel's ghost haunts the novel with its gargantuan comic presence. From the first page, which announces his death in words which echo Dickens's emphatic declaration of Marley's death in *A Christmas Carol*, 'that he was dead there could be no doubt', Mel is intensely alive as a character. His corpse is animated, by the significant sartorial detail of his military costume, ill-fitting and with a burst seam. His ghost, like the women's ghosts in the stories of the Countess and Mrs Fiske, refuses to be laid. Its haunting is thematically insistent: his children try, in one way or another, to cut themselves off from their father, his class, and his trade. The irony lies in their inheritance of his own grandiose way of life. He refused to tell, or even act, lies about his tailoring trade, but his Regency style, his looks, his air, his 'gallantry', his brief military career, his refusal either to charge his debtors or pay his creditors, makes him a dangerous and irresistible role-model for his children. His ghost refuses to be laid in another sense too: his name keeps coming up, his fame will not die. His children are frequently present when his past glories burst into the present: compulsive and embarrassing reminiscence ensures his comic presence for characters and reader, from the first post-mortem conversation of the creditors to the many disclosures in polite society. And for Evan, there is another haunting. As his mother says, in one of several strong recognition scenes, Evan's destiny is to become a tailor, to pay his father's debts, and so make his father a (posthumously) honest man. By a fine stroke, Evan's own way to honesty is through accepting his parentage, taking on the tailor's stigmatised trade and telling the truth. The comic conjuring of the Great Mel, through the stories within the story, is brilliantly done. The novel sets up a pattern of comic expectation, tension and revelation, and the anecdotes about the dead man who won't lie down are presented as ironically two-faced. They are usually told innocently, and heard guiltily and fearfully. The skeleton in the cupboard, that stock-in-trade of so many Victorian plots, has seldom been more amusingly manipulated than in this story.

For modern readers, there is an additional irony created by scholarship. We now know that Meredith was making comedy out of his own story. Melchisedic Harrington is based on Melchizedeck Meredith, Meredith's grandfather, and Evan bears some resemblance to Meredith's father, and some to Meredith himself. The portrayal of the family's attempts to rise above the tailoring trade, by performance, lies, affectation, education and social success, was recognised during Meredith's lifetime and after, and formed the impulse for the bitter biography, *George Meredith* (1920) by S. M. Ellis, a descendant of one of Meredith's aunts (the source for Caroline Strike). What is remarkable is Meredith's confrontation with his own sense of shame. There is some evidence that he was evasive, if not deceitful, about his origins and this is an instance of fiction being used for revealing the very secret which the novelist, as a man, tried to keep. The novel turns truths into fiction. The novelist is skating on thin ice, in a way both flagrant and daring. He keeps close to life, even giving the comic ghost the actual name of his prototype, so that readers who knew the story would—and did—recognise its source. Some of the other characters, like Rose Jocelyn and Lady Jocelyn, based on the Duff Gordons, also have real-life origins. Ellis's complaints about the unfair treatment of his grandfather, the origin of the obnoxious Strike, who 'looks as if he were all angles and sections, and were taken to pieces every night and put together in the morning' is evidently a bad case of showing that the cap fits through wearing it. The novel, like its predecessor, *Richard Feverel*, draws freely on autobiographical materials, but it is a novel, not an autobiography. Though Meredith's portrayal of the lovers, Evan and Rose, may have been fuelled by the novelist's affection for Janet Duff Gordon, he uses fiction in order not to expose reality but to toy with hopeful fantasy. Like Thackeray in *Pendennis*, and Dickens in *David Copperfield*, Meredith is mingling fact and fiction to license and criticise romantic fantasy by presenting it in a comic medium. Evan Harrington, like Pendennis, is a comic hero who is mocked and treated seriously. Through the dazzling and brittle mock-heroic language and farce, the hero's feelings are indulged, analysed, respected, educated, and ridiculed.

The novel is a comic epic in prose, in the ancient tradition of Cervantes. It is significant that Evan, like Thackeray's Henry Esmond, is nicknamed Don Doloroso. His adventures take a Quixotic form. (In *Harry Richmond* [1871] Meredith was to use Homer's *Odyssey* and Fénelon's *Télémaque* as models and metaphors for a son's attempt to lose and find a father.) Like Odysseus, Telemachus and Don Quixote, Evan Harrington travels, and the journeys are geographical, anthropological and personal. Like Odysseus, Evan fights battles, defeats the suitors and is ensnared by enchantresses. Like Molly Bloom, the Countess is both Circe and Calypso. Like Telemachus, Evan loses and finds a father. Like Don Quixote, he rides and rescues, is serious and comic, honest and deluded. Meredith is writing comic epic to insist on the unheroic nature of his hero and his story. If we fail to recognise this comic tradition, we fall into the trap of taking the novel's social criticism in too solemn and simple a way.

Much critical energy has been expended both by critics who have wanted the novel to be more radical in its social attack than it really is, and by critics who have wanted it to be more conservative than it really is. Meredith gives us neither a subversive nor a reactionary story. Evan's adventures show compromise, not collision, and his author not only extricates him from the realities of work at a 'degrading' trade but never really forces him to earn a living. The world of high society is criticised, especially in the brilliantly gross presentations of the two callous and stupid young gentlemen, Laxley and Harry Jocelyn, but no one is made so blatantly a comic butt as the low-life aspirant, the Countess de Saldar, and one of the most generously humane portraits in the novel is that of Rose's mother, the blue-stocking, Lady Jocelyn. Though Meredith reveals social and economic pressures which distort human truths and freedoms, his is not a revolutionary satire, but an amusing story with a wish-fulfilment conclusion, in which social criticism, as well as the characters, ends in compromise.

However, the hero is subjected to ordeals and humiliations. The path of education, ambition and true love is narrow and stony, even though it is eventually broadened and smoothed. Meredith very clearly—through plan or intuition or both—makes the Countess the scapegoat and rescues and rewards Evan Harrington. *Evan Harrington* is difficult for the modern reader who is probably inclined to expect a more lucid social analysis from works which offer some measure of satire and criticism. (Meredith's later fiction became stronger and more coherent in its criticism of rank, class, wealth and privilege.) Here Meredith's own compromises and conformity soften and evade the criticism of society. His playfulness creates puzzles, and offers pleasures. Its style is an unfailing delight, both in a subtle appeal to the moral sense, and in its comic insistence that we cannot always take life seriously. Like the characters, the reader is presented with what Jane Austen, in *Mansfield Park*, calls life '*à la mortal*, finely-chequered'. Meredith's rendering of sorrows, injustice and cruelty, is as profound as Jane Austen's, but his comic complexity must not be underestimated. Readers who feel that the sense of humour is frivolous, permissive, or even cynical, can always go from *Evan Harrington* to *The Egoist*, *Diana of the Crossways* and *The Amazing Marriage*, novels which take comedy to the verge of tragedy, and offer a more radical criticism of our patriarchal and acquisitive capitalism.

In this novel, we are invited to play. Sometimes the play is serious, as when the narrator enjoys the creativity of the Countess who, like Odysseus and Pallas Athene, is a fertile liar: 'The poetry of our Countess's achievements waxes rich in manifold colours: I see her by the light of her own pleas to providence'. In *Harry Richmond*

Meredith is to turn the Providence novel, the norm in eighteenth-century and much Victorian fiction, on its head, and in *Evan Harrington* the Countess's religion and religiosity is significantly stressed. The novelist-poet presents the Countess as a poet, and the recognition is both grandiose and admiring. Her language moves through Protean time-shifts; one moment she speaks, even to her brother, in terms and tones which are extravagant, blatant, conventional and effective:

> You have your father's frown. You surpass him, for your delivery is more correct, and equally fluent. And if a woman is momentarily melted by softness in a man, she is for ever subdued by boldness and bravery of mien. (Ch. IX)

Evan is significantly moved by this rubbish, but while his 'wounded pride' bleeds 'through his eyes' she changes 'to another voice, and an English accent'. This moves him to a great sob, after which, 'marking the impression she had produced on him, and having worn off that which he had produced on her, the Countess resumed the art in her style of speech, easier to her than nature'. Meredith is able to do several things at the same time, to place and develop his characters, to perform tricks of language, and to link the arts and crafts of his fictitious people to his own arts and crafts. The novel has a comic reflexiveness. When Evan (like an epic hero) is laid low, the narrator assures us that 'Heroes don't die, you know'. We are constantly reminded that the art of fiction, like that of tailoring, is the art of making costumes and disguises.

It is also, like tailoring, a decorative art. Meredith's wit makes images that develop his social and moral arguments, but also surprise and delight:

> Lady Roseley was an exquisitely silken dame, in whose face a winning smile was cut, and she was still sufficiently youthful not to be accused of wearing a flower too artificial. (Ch. II)

> . . . tell a woman to put back, when she is once clearly launched! Timid as she may be, her light bark bounds to meet the tempest. I speak of women who do launch: they are not numerous, but, to the wise, the minorities are the representatives. (Ch. XIII)

Some might have thought that those fair large blue eyes of hers wandered now and then in pleasant unambitious walks behind the curtain, and toyed with little flowers of palest memory. (Ch. V)

Rare as epic song is the man who is thorough in what he does. And happily so; for in life he subjugates us, and he makes us bondsmen to his ashes. It was in the order of things that the great Mel should be borne to his final resting place by a troop of creditors. You have seen (since the occasion demands a pompous simile) clouds that all day cling about the sun, and, in seeking to obscure him, are compelled to blaze in his livery: at fall of night they break from him illumined, hang mournfully above him, and wear his natural glories long after he is gone. (Ch. VII)

The dramatic proportions to which ale will exalt the sentiments within us, and our delivery of them, are apt to dwindle and shrink even below the natural elevation when we look back on them from the hither shore of the river of sleep—in other words, wake in the morning. (Ch. XIII)

That last example might come from the talk of Micawber, in its swelling circumlocution, lofty archaism, and final translation into commonplace and matter of fact. It is carefully tuned to subject and sentiment; Meredith embroiders his prose to provide sophisticated pleasures. We enjoy the image, receive the meaning, appreciate decorum, and admire the process which is flourished for our edification and amusement. These instances, chosen at random, are examples of Meredith's rich, cunning, and comic prose, the appropriate medium for a rich, cunning, and comic story of manners and morals. We are required to take language, character and story seriously, but comically too.

First published as the Introduction to *Evan Harrington* (The Boydell Press, Woodbridge, Suffolk, 1983).

14. George Meredith's *Lord Ormont and his Aminta* and *The Amazing Marriage*

I want to look at these two late novels together, at the risk of doing less than justice to *Lord Ormont and his Aminta*, because their chronological neighbourhood and affinities of story and theme throw their difference in fictional quality into strong relief.

Meredith's critics are often too repelled to say much of interest or too won over and absorbed in his mannerism to see anything wrong in it. The polarity of hostility and admiration tends to be self-perpetuating: the more rudely Meredith is excluded from the Great Tradition without much in the way of argument, the more passionately his admirers protest. The protest is understandable. To read even one of his novels properly (with the exception of the accessible *Harry Richmond*) involves considerable investment of time and mental energy. And as with other cases of mannerism, the slow and patient reading that his obscure narrative and clotted prose demand may over-acclimatise us to idiosyncrasy. This can happen with Henry James, George Moore or Ronald Firbank, but in Meredith it is almost guaranteed by the combination of artificiality with difficulty, and in a fairly even spread throughout the novels. With James, for instance, the habituation to mannerism can happen gradually, as the novels grow more mannered and difficult, as they do, in a gradual curve, steepening towards the end. Or it can simply break off, with the late novels, so that much hostility to James is hostility to late James. Meredith's mannerism and obscurity are present from the beginning, and though I would not want to suggest that they do not vary from novel to novel, in form and degree, there is no slow development which habituates us gradually or alienates us at certain points. Meredith criticism does tend to fall apart into all-or-nothing judgements. I think this is a pity, not because I am interested in the sport of submitting literature to competitive and graded examinations, but because I am interested in the imagination and values of Meredith, and believe that his admirers can afford (and need) to become tougher with their author and themselves.

Lord Ormont and his Aminta is a more readable and simple version of 'the Meredith novel' than *The Amazing Marriage*, but it is also a novel which shows him at his most sentimental, and where artificiality serves the interests of sentimentality. *The Amazing Marriage* has that particularity and continuity which *Lord Ormont* lacks, and explores the same ideas and values with complexity and completeness, justifying the mannerism which postures so vapidly in *Lord Ormont*.

Perhaps one reason why Meredith appeals so strongly to some is his apparent worldliness, his refreshing difference, in candour and toughness about love, marriage, egoism, women, religion—so many of the mid-Victorian sacred cows. In worldly awareness and dislike of contemporary cant, Thackeray was before him, but Thackeray has a marvellous capacity for acknowledging the walls of convention and propriety he cannot respect, leaving them standing, effective resonators for his irony and satire. Meredith comes late enough to break down these walls, and we tend to find his sheer extension of subject and lack of moral and religious cant refreshing and exciting.

We also like Meredith not just because he is less sentimental about faith and ethics and social convention than Dickens and George Eliot, but because he is sentimental about different things. He is the sentimentality of the eighteen-nineties, which still has a certain appealing, if diminishing, affinity with our own time: it tends to be strongly affirmative about youth, about sex rather than love, about the good relationship rather than the perfect marriage, about nature rather than God, feminism rather than womanliness, discovery of identity rather than moral change of heart. We might want to say that Meredith's beliefs are progressive, or *avant-garde* in the double sense that implies both courage and progress, but his ninetyish *avant-garde* sentimentality is still sentimentality. He can become as ludicrously ecstatic, soft and blurred on the subjects of feminism, England and co-education as Dickens could be on the subjects of womanly virtue, religion and child-death. It is this sentimentality which marks Meredith at his worst, and whose triumphant absence marks him at his best. It has also, I suggest, an interesting relation to his mannerism and his obscurity. When Meredith is flaccidly and pompously directing our sympathies, his artificial style and elliptical manner can work in the interests of evasion and open invitation to the feelings. But artificiality and obscurity are still present when his values and ideas are more thoroughly and toughly analysed. There is no simple one-to-one relation.

Lord Ormont and his Aminta was published in 1894, *The Amazing Marriage* in 1895. The chronological relation was more complicated than these dates suggest, for he had been working on *The Amazing Marriage*, on and off, since finishing *The Egoist* in 1879. He was in fact writing both the last novels at once, so their twinship is as difficult to sort out as that of Esau and Jacob. It is misleading to make too much of their similarity, convenient as it is for my purposes. It is sometimes said that novelists are always writing or trying to write or trying not to write the same one novel, and a proper examination of Meredith's treatment of the amazing and unsatisfactory nature of marriage would have to take in *Diana of the Crossways* and *The Egoist*, and some novels not directly concerned with marriage, such as *The Tragic Comedians* and *One of Our Conquerors*. Amazing marriage—and few of the implications of that phrase are irrelevant—is one of Meredith's obsessive themes, but as I am concerned with his last two novels, I say merely that their relationship is a fairly common one, since novelists frequently write novels in the conscious or unconscious attempt to recast or revise or rewrite the novels they have already written.

There is no simple and straightforward relation between his own broken marriage and his discussion in the novels. 'Modern Love' retold his story with the painful eloquence and valuable reticence of poetry, and may have freed him for more impartial (or effectively disguised) contemplation of the difficulties and disadvantages of this bourgeois institution. In many of his novels he attacks marriage as a typically possessive and proprietorial relation, and I believe that his last novel, *The Amazing Marriage*, is the most effective mythological attack and the best novel. Perhaps it is no accident that its title comes closest to a generalised proclamation of theme, and that the framework of the novel is an argument and a struggle between a modern realistic novelist and a myth-making Dame Gossip. It has the kind of complex success that suggests that the qualities of good myth and good psychological fiction are not, after all, in opposition to each other.

The married woman was for Meredith as blatant a case of social oppression and unfair possession as the child was for Dickens or the working man for Mrs Gaskell. Let me quote a letter in which he makes this plain. He wrote it to Lady Ulrica Duncombe in April 1902:

I give my sympathy to the stumbling human instrument of a possible progression—Have you read the Letters of Lady Sarah Lennox? Her history is instructive, you will know it. The wife of an ardent fox-hunter, she quits him for an amorous lord, and after a year retires to a penitential solitude, out of which she is drawn at last by a worthy man, to become the mother of the three Napiers. I follow her and am with her throughout. . . . By and by the world will smile on women who cut their own way out of a bad early marriage, or it will correct the present rough Marriage system. No young woman knows what she gives her hand to; she will never be wiser until boys and girls are brought up and educated together. Let me add, until English girls have wiser mothers. Such donkeys are those dames in all our classes! It is true that the upper need not to give so much instruction where knowledge is in the atmosphere—Apropos of Lady Sarah's story, an old Cornish lady told me of one ending differently. A hunting squire of her neighbourhood had a very handsome wife, whom he valued at less than the fox's tail. One of the Vivians eyed her, admired, condoled, desired, and carried her off. Some days after, she was taken with compunction, or compassion, and about midnight the forsaken squire sitting in his library heard three knocks at the window. That's Bess, he said, and let her in. She was for weeping and protesting repentence . . . but he kissed her, taking the blame on himself, rightly, and the house was quiet. Old Lady Vivian, like many old ladies, had outgrown her notions of masculine sentiment in these matters; she said to my friend: 'What are the man's family making such a fuss about! My son only had her a fortnight!' Even young women have but a confused idea of this masculine sentiment of the complete possession, down to absorption. . . . I have tried in my time to enlighten them and humanize their males. (*Letters of George Meredith*, ed. C. L. Cline, Clarendon Press, Oxford, 1970, Vol. III, pp. 1438-9).

The historical sources for most of Meredith's attempts to write novels which shall 'enlighten and humanize' only make even plainer the need for the enlightenment. Whatever his personal discontent, the amazing marriage was a social fact. And it is as a social fact that Meredith treats it, not attacking its permanence, its fragility, or its relation to other ties, but bringing out, in particularly plain cases of marriage between aristocrat and commoner, wealth and poverty, the acquisitive typicality of the institution. He brings this out—very noticeably in comparison with Dickens and George Eliot—not by describing or stereotyping the extremes of marital suffering in incompatibility but with increasing emphasis, in the ties and torments of reasonable, decent, complex and compatible human beings. If we trace the subject through, especially from *The Egoist* to *The Amazing Marriage*, this kind of candour, completeness and complexity seems to grow. The squire who said, 'That's Bess', and the old lady who said, 'My son only had her a fortnight!' can usefully stay with us as models for Meredith's honest worldliness—the right kind of worldliness which is strongly opposed to cant, grandiose moralising, and all kinds of lies, and believes like Ajax in fighting in broad daylight.

Lord Ormont and Lord Fleetwood are both immensely rich aristocrats. Their wives, Aminta and Carinthia, are commoners and very poor. In each novel it is as if Meredith wants to emphasise the psychic and sexual oppressiveness he analysed in *The Egoist* with a much clearer and fiercer attack on the social institution. *The Egoist* and *Diana* were implicit attacks on bourgeois marriage, but their central and explicit concerns were broader. In his last novels Meredith narrows down his action and his theme. He narrows it excessively in *Lord Ormont*, and he finds the right form in *The Amazing Marriage*. In both novels he uses fiction to sort out what he thinks about men and women getting married, getting unmarried, and finding alternatives to marriage, but the sorting out involved sentimental loss of control and distortion in the one, and effective control in the other.

There are several ways in which both novels show an advance in identifying the subject. First, Meredith needs to show the difficulty even in a marriage of strong attachment. We never really see Diana's first marriage, but are shown its motivation, the rude assaults and assumptions surrounding a single woman: the marriage is simply written in as a hasty solution to economic need and isolation. We are told—and lengthily—that Clara has believed herself attached to Sir Willoughby Patterne, but what is dramatised is the slow and difficult process of disentanglement. In the last two novels

Meredith seems to be realising that hard cases make bad myths: the January and May story, found in other Victorian novelists like Dickens, George Eliot and George Gissing, must not be told too allegorically or it will lack the particularity of a novel (obviously) and the typicality of the myth (perhaps a little less obviously). 'I have tried in my time to enlighten them and humanize their males': the attempt will be more didactically eloquent if it concerns the likely ordinary case, not the terrible error of Dorothea's missionary enterprise in marrying Casaubon, or Sue's physical ill-matching with Phillotson or Connie Chatterley's bad luck with her husband's war-wound. Although Carinthia's is an amazing marriage, it is, in extravagant form, the common story of affinity, passion and loss. Although there is too much ellipsis in *Lord Ormont*, we are shown and told enough of Aminta's hero-worshipping and her aunt's mercenary and snobbish social climbing. Meredith is looking at the social and economic reasons for marriage and at the power-structure even of marriages of feeling. It is self-evident that loveless and incompatible marriages are wrong, but all we can learn from the stories of total incompatibility or abject impotence is that bourgeois society can make marriages, despite an absolute lack of relationship. Meredith also wants to say that bourgeois marriage, even based on feeling and compatibility, is a difficult and dangerous enterprise. He is making an analysis that is social and psychological. And he is making a more fundamental criticism of the institution of marriage in terms of power.

Both husbands marry 'beneath' them. Meredith's emphasis on Lord Ormont's disgust with his class and his country, and Lord Fleetwood's more intuitive version of the same feeling, excellently shifts the emphasis from the lower-class wives who marry high rank and great wealth. It is important not just that the women should marry out of strong feeling (though in each case there is an economic motive, most delicately handled) but that they should be seen as victims. Meredith emphasises the purchasing-power of Ormont and Fleetwood, but he wants us to be less impressed by the actual purchase of the woman than by the power both rank and money exercise after the marriage. Aminta is deprived of social reputation; Carinthia of reputation, freedom, and security. The eventual release has great momentum, especially in *The Amazing Marriage*, where the relationships are more intricate and held in greater suspense, and where the woman is subjected to much more, and much less justified, restriction and pain. Both novels are feminist novels, and at the point of release or rescue Meredith makes this clear by forcing a large breach of convention. Lady Ormont not only leaves her 'tyrant' but goes off to live with an unconventional schoolmaster who has refused the obvious professions in favour of starting an international co-educational school. (The point is weakened when Lord Ormont dies and leaves the free lovers free to marry.) Carinthia not only leaves Fleetwood, but is willing to leave her child and to go off to the wars in Spain with her brother. (The point is weakened when this plan is frustrated and when Meredith marries her off to Owain Woodseer.) He takes each action to the point of dismissing marriage as the vocation for woman, but can't quite make it. But they are brave acts for their time.

To criticise is to expect too much of the liberalism of the eighteen-nineties, in public and moral art. But the woman is also presented in pastoral terms. As Empson would say, she is the swain of Meredith's fiction. Here we find the first instance of the superiority of *The Amazing Marriage*. In *Lord Ormont* the pastoral theme is only slightly present, and made rather arch, hearty, and slightly ridiculous by associations with athletics, fresh air and hygiene. Women are shown debarred from the free and healthy life, unable to play cricket or join in snowball fights. Aminta turns passionately to the hero-worship of a great general. Later a small girl rescues another child from drowning, helped from the rear by her elder brother. Later still the declaration of love between Matey Weyburn and Brownie (Lady Ormont) is expressed and ritualised in the famous swimming scene. Last we see the free and healthy life in the progressive school in Switzerland. There is nothing wrong with these values: it was hard on girls to wear long skirts and not throw snowballs, a sea scene has great erotic potential, and there is nothing wrong with co-educational schools in healthy spots, with open windows and good food. (As is evident in the letter to Lady Ulrica, co-education was one of Meredith's designs for humanising marriage.) But Meredith makes his pastoral small and rather ridiculous in such symbols, and, moreover, gushes over their value. I will quote some instances of his archness, and his dangerous and jovial assumption of sympathy in *Lord Ormont and His Aminta*.

Forth from the school-house burst a dozen shouting lads, as wasps from the hole of their nest from a charge of powder. Out

they poured whizzing; and the frog he leaped, and pussy ran and
doubled before the hounds, and hockey-sticks waved, and away
went a ball. Cracks at the ball anyhow, was the game for the
twenty-five minutes breather before dinner.

'French day!' said Calliani, hearing their cries.

Then he bellowed 'Matthew! Giulio!'

A lusty inversion of the order of the names and an Oberland
jödel returned his hail. The school retreating caught up the
Alpine cry in the distance. Here were lungs! Here were sprites!
(Ch. xxx)

Ah, friend Matey! And that was right and good on land; but
rightness and goodness flung earth's shadow across her
brilliancy here, and any stress on 'this once' withdrew her liberty
to revel in it, putting an end to perfect holiday; and silence, too,
might hint at fatigue. She began to think her muteness lost her
the bloom of the enchantment, robbing her of her heavenly frolic
lead, since friend Matey resolved to be as eminently good in salt
water as on land. Was he unaware that they were boy and girl
again?—she washed pure of the intervening years, new born, by
blessing of the sea; worthy of him here!—that is, a swimmer
worthy of him, his comrade in salt water. (Ch. xxvii)

. . . she had been privileged to cast away sex with the push from
earth, as few men will believe that women, beautiful women, ever
wish to do; and often and ardently during the run ahead they
yearn for Nature to grant them their one short holiday truce.
(Ch. xxviii)

The open-air cult is understandable enough, both as an educational
value and as a glance at the restricted female life—'the thought of
the difference between themselves and the boys must have been
something like the tight band—call it corset—over the chest'—but
its expression tends to be arch and humourlessly domestic—the
white ducks, 'The Jolly Cricketers', the heroine's love of long
walks. It is a Surrey nature cult which has suffered even further
from week-ends and country tramps and food fads—all excellent
enough in their way, but not grand enough for real pastoral.
Brownie anticipates Betjeman's athletic girls.

There is nothing of the week-end pastoral about *The Amazing
Marriage*. Something of the fad may cling to Carinthia's ideas about
child-rearing—weaning at nine months, breathing through the

nose, and sleeping in the open air. But the central symbols have a ring of grandeur, from the beginning in the German mountains, with the brother and sister going out to call the dawn and walk through the forests:

> The armies of the young sunrise in mountain-lands neighbouring the plains, vast shadows, were marching over woods and meads, black against the edge of golden; and great heights were cut with them, and bounding waters took the leap in a silvery radiance to gloom; the bright and dark-banded valleys were like night and morning taking hands down the sweep of their rivers. Immense was the range of vision scudding the peaks and over the illimitable Eastward plains flat to the very East and sources of the sun. (Ch. iv)

> The phantom ring of mist enclosing for miles the invariable low-sweeping dark spruce-fir kept her thoughts on them as close as the shroud. She walked fast, but scarcely felt that she was moving. Near midday the haunted circle widened; rocks were loosely folded in it, and heads of trees, whose round intervolving roots grasped the yellow roadside soil; the mists shook like a curtain, and partly opened and displayed a tapestry-landscape, roughly worked, of woollen crag and castle and suggested glen, threaded waters, very prominent foreground, Autumn flowers on banks; a predominant atmosphere greyness. (Ch. v)

Selection can be so misleading that I can only refer readers to each novel, and suggest that *The Amazing Marriage* establishes a real pastoral, as Wordsworth does in *The Prelude*, by building up, particularly, actively and variously, the landscape of the novel, especially of Germany and Wales, by creating the characters' relation with nature, through their sensuous and symbol-making reactions and by extending and developing the symbols in metaphor. In *Lord Ormont* the pastoral is stagey or sentimental because Meredith has not established the natural environment; it exists only in a few shorthand versions and stimuli, which will not do. In *The Amazing Marriage* we feel that Carinthia is swain or earth goddess, because she is seen as growing with nature, breathing in its air, climbing its rocks, having some affinity with the austerity and grandeur which justifies her Gorgon image. In comparison, Brownie seem simply hearty, especially when she is watching the cricket or going for a swim. The potentially ridiculous side of

Carinthia—the child-rearing fads and love of walks—is neutralised
by the sensuous particularity which *Lord Ormont* lacks. Meredith
had a real pagan feeling for nature, but it got into one novel
adequately and into the other in a tame, and domesticated form. In
The Amazing Marriage there is also the distancing effect of the two
cultists, the Old Buccaneer who has taught his children how to jump
with knees bent, and so on, and Gower Woodseer, the pastoral and
Stevensonian figure, who, as Gillian Beer points out, is no less
effective for being slightly ludicrous.[1] There is no such awareness in
Lord Ormont that there was anything ridiculous in making such a
business of the open-air-life, long tramps and outdoor girls.

Nature is sensuously realised, but it is also poeticised. This
happens in *Lord Ormont*, too: the cricket is symbolised, largely
through the episode at the country inn, 'The Jolly Cricketers',
where Meredith uses the inn-sign as a metaphor for spirit, health
and more specialised application to the chase and rescue in the
action; and the swimming metaphors, as in *Beauchamp's Career* and
Harry Richmond, are pervasive. They are neatly used, conspicuous
because having no real matrix in solidly particularised nature,
simply and diagrammatically traced. *The Amazing Marriage* has
more imaginative and less schematic image-patterns, which
perhaps may have come from its longer history in Meredith's mind:
its characteristic motion is that of transfer from the literal to the
metaphorical, to be found elsewhere particularly in *Harry
Richmond*. Here, as in the earlier novel, it gives us rich and casual
effects, though the clarity remains. When Carinthia is described in
terms of height, air, hardness, rock, we have seen all this in action.
These are earned and substantial images, looked at one way,
exhibiting the process of image-making, looked at in another.
Meredith often shares his authorial images with his characters. He
does this with the image he uses for Fleetwood, 'prisoner' of wishes,
which he allows Henrietta to use 'independently' in a letter. The
image of the Gorgon, the mad dog, and the fire also shift in this way,
and sometimes the metaphor precedes the symbolic or the literal
action.

It is the integrity rather than the blurring of the symbols I want to
stress. Fleetwood is a prisoner of his will, and the image of
imprisonment is a pervasive one, belonging to the pastoral
treatment of marriage. In the central case and all others, it is a
significantly urban restriction, a bond and pattern imposed by

civilisation on nature. In *Lord Ormont* the pastoral values are assumed; in *The Amazing Marriage* Meredith defines the pastoral nature of action and character more precisely and profoundly, and the second novel has profundities to be defined which the first lacks. Carinthia's actual imprisonments become more prominent than the pastoral habitat and cut across its symbolism; the mean, stifling and dirty street in Whitechapel, which began as a terrible restriction for her, ends by being the city pastoralised, like the London scenes of *The Prelude*, by the values of 'natural' (spontaneous, generous, uncommercial, unsnobbish, class-free) human love.

The rescue into freedom and love is marked by nature imagery and felt as the return to nature after constraint. But this is not confined to Carinthia's imprisonment and release. The criticism of society involves a complex contrast between the pastoral outsider, Carinthia, and the urban hero, Fleetwood. This is a less schematic and more complex version of the diagram of *Lord Ormont*, though Lord Ormont is also seen as an outsider. What he is 'outside' is an establishment attacked less for power and corruption than for giving him and his military schemes insufficient recognition and placing England in a weak position. Neither husband-figure represents the establishment in the simple and direct way that Casaubon or Sir Clifford Chatterley represent authority, money, intellectual and cultural sterility, impotence, the old order in Church and State. The complexity of Lord Ormont is muddled: we are likely to sympathise with him up to a point, and then sympathy should be deflected by his military values and his capitulation. The complexity of Fleetwood strikes me as entirely successful.

Here it is necessary to stress the common properties, not the differences, of the novels. In showing the husband-authority figures more complexly, Meredith is not just making the novel more 'realistic', as we say, making assumptions about complex verisimilitude, but is making a more devastating and profound criticism of Victorian England. Lord Ormont and Lord Fleetwood have something of the pastoral outsider in their make-up which reveals the destructive power of money and rank. The difference is that between simple and complex antithesis. The simple antithesis between George Eliot's Casaubon and Ladislaw, or between Lawrence's Sir Clifford Chatterley and Mellors, dramatises and presents a conflict of values. The complex antithesis, like that between Fleetwood and Carinthia, or Lawrence's Gerald and

Birkin, refuses to mythologise by abstracting qualities and mythologises the more effectively for showing the processes of social conditioning at work within the 'complete' individual. The destructive power of rank and money and all the unnatural sports of the sweet life which they command are not defined as 'that which is in opposition to nature', removed from the life of instinct and entirely role-determined, but as 'that which can tame, corrupt and constrict even the impulsive and imaginative man'. This corruption is analysed in both novels, enlarging the themes of marriage and feminism, but it only gets fully, persuasively and toughly into action, language and character in *The Amazing Marriage*. *Lord Ormont*'s sentimentality, ellipsis and confusion help us to see more clearly that Meredith is doing something of importance to all novelists—getting his political ideas clear and in the process increasing, not diminishing, the psychological interest.

In *Lord Ormont* we have the ageing general married to the young and beautiful woman who hero-worshipped him. Betrayed by the country he has served, he is obsessed by its military weakness and his own sense of outraged honour. He is both of, and not of, the establishment values, an authority figure, deeply traditional and conventional, but driven to deny his strongest allegiances, refusing to move in respectable society, refusing to live in his family seat, refusing to have his wife presented at court. Most of these refusals make admirable plot levers, and make his motives crystal-clear. But this clarity damages the presentation of his Aminta. It is not plain why she fails to see what the reader sees, possessing as she does the double advantage of long, intimate knowledge and a strong sympathy for her husband's unpopular position. Part of the obscurity may come from Meredith's reticence about the sexual history of the marriage. Aminta seems to look back to a passionate honeymoon, but it is not clear whether a developing coolness and separateness is cause or effect of her resentment at her social position. The implications seem to be those of the January and May pattern, with some deviation. Meredith adds the sinister and fascinating touch about the possibility—a rare one—of inflicting sexual refusal on a husband who is not completely impotent, but not demanding. If this part of the history were clearer, Aminta might be more thoroughly placed. As it is, we are left wondering why she plays with fire with Morsfield, why she attaches such importance to living at Steignton and being presented at court, since she is carefully shown as spirited, natural and drawn to Matey's pastoral virtues. It may be that Meredith is compressing some suggestion of change here: the second stage of her acquaintance with Matey disabuses her of some conventional notions about a gentleman's career, and she develops in 'naturalness'—if this is possible—throughout the novel. Even so, Carinthia would plainly snap her fingers at the presentation at court, so it isn't a matter of the novel having dated. Perhaps Meredith contracted Carinthia's changes in drawing Aminta. Carinthia is shown as spontaneous, unschooled, and ignorant, and such qualities are important in the novel's scheme of values as well as in the motivation of her amazing marriage. She is shown, subtly, as growing in all the externals of civilisation—speech, manners, deportment—and much of this change is drawn by the language which Meredith shows naturally and pointedly as a growth in the accomplished knowledge and use of English. But she does not grow an inch in the disapproved 'internals' of civilisation. I cannot quite accept Gillian Beer's view of Carinthia as 'uncivilized, instinctive' if this means primitive and under-rational. Carinthia acquires the analytic mode without losing instinctive strength. By the time she comes to refuse her bed—'I guard my rooms'—to Fleetwood, she has learnt not to react instinctively and spontaneously, but to analyse, judge and defend herself by a sophisticated intelligence. I do not see her as a large simple nature, but as very like Fleetwood, only on the right—the other—side of civilisation.

It is characteristic of the novel that it avoids antithesis where *Lord Ormont* is drawn towards it. *The Amazing Marriage* invites us to dismiss the tension we often set up between ideological clarity and complex realism; in it Meredith's fundamental social insight about the possessive marriage is inseparable from his profound rendering of the human hearts.

The novelist shows in great detail the pains of marriage for Carinthia and for Fleetwood—in his imprisonment by his word, in her imprisonment in ignorance, in his and her love, in her pregnancy caused by rape, in his gradual realisation of the meaning of the furtive memory and its enlargement in his consciousness. (This so-called instance of Meredith's obscurity seems to be an instance of inattentiveness on the part of his readers). He shows them both driven by outside forces—in the form of the unscrupulous Henrietta and Chillon and the miserly Lord

Levellier, as well as by the brilliantly interiorised instance of the *droit de seigneur*—passion, imagination, energy, courage, and generosity warped by power. Fleetwood's affinity with Carinthia and Woodseer (the name-overlap is important and links them all with Carinthia's forests) is important. Meredith shows the terrible conditioning power of money and possession, with the roles and relations they determine. His paradigm, Fleetwood, is a creature of heart. His pride, passion and imagination are ironically betrayed by the natural man—drawn to the beautiful Gorgon in the rocks—but betrayed more destructively by civilised society. He feels wildness, impulse, solitude, integrity, courage, and unconventionality, and the stroke that makes this a great love-story is his deep and long-denied recognition that all these are to be found in Carinthia.

What is right as social fable and as human observation is his inability to forget the jealous desire to buy Henrietta: he is kept goadingly reminded of her and her husband through Carinthia, so that what should take him away from the old love keeps it painfully in his mind, what should free him from money-determined acts makes him insist on them. If he can't buy Henrietta, or if he hasn't been able to buy her yet, he will keep money away from Chillon by denying it to Carinthia. Gillian Beer is right when she says that Meredith's revision was an improvement in this respect. In the original version, there is a more elaborate and 'plausible' rendering of Fleetwood's proposal to Carinthia, which comes as a rebound impulse after he has proposed to Henrietta and been refused: 'It is with this scene dominant in our minds that we hear of his proposal to Carinthia at the ball.' Gillian Beer argues that the cutting of the proposal to Henrietta makes Fleetwood's motivation more, not less profound, since it shows 'that acts of impulse come not from the surface of personality but from its depths', while the first version showed the amazing marriage coming out of 'the pique of the moment rather than from some deep but imperfectly acknowledged need in his nature'.

It is this need in nature that I emphasise. He needs those values expressed by and in Carinthia, Woodseer (in a more doctrinaire, and Stevensonian fashion) and in the forests and mountains of Wales and Germany. The scenes and characters which present the pastoral make a deep appeal—not wholly unacknowledged, even early on—to Fleetwood. He shares Woodseer's desire for solitude, freedom, hardness and grandeur, and has a contempt for what he knows and is and follows: the depths below the heights, the fouler air, money, gambling, sexual sport, fashion, a culture which is bought and sold. His unattractive contempt for his parasites and Livia, as well as his feeling for Catholicism, must be understood in terms of this need. The tragic aspect of the novel lies in the missed affinities. Fleetwood's case is put in reverse, for elucidation and stress: Woodseer's purity is tested and fails when he succumbs to Livia and gives her the letter that might help Carinthia, and he too gambles, and even buys new clothes out of social shame. The only one who does not succumb is Carinthia, and the hardness which is both her protection and her guarantee of integrity has to turn against Fleetwood at the end. He is right after all to see the Gorgon quality at the beginning, or to seize on it in Woodseer's vision. Their relationship is shown in fine and consistent detail. It is there in the rape, which she comes only slowly to understand for what it is, as she comes to understand the wild ride and the prize-fight. The rape becomes for him the cherished sexual evidence of that charm he had first felt, the proof of the body's wisdom. The quality of their love is revealed too in his defined passion for Henrietta, which combines desire, contempt, self-contempt, and a jealous desire to have her and be done with her. The sexual detail which is cloudy in *Lord Ormont* is significantly clear in *The Amazing Marriage*. Its presentation is apt: a shameful furtive act, hardly mentioned, shown and recalled in hurried glimpses and eventually given more space in his reverie as he comes to dwell on it in shame and new desire.

Meredith likes teasing things slowly out. The joke here is that it is not Dame Gossip, but the psychological novelist dwelling on the inner life, who creates the greatest puzzle and surprise. The second sexual attempt is a different kind of teasing. We can see Meredith using a stiff and elegant dialogue, dramatically implicit and then frankly explicit, with an eye always on character, past and present:

> 'Do you come in, my lord?'
> 'The house is yours, my lady.'
> 'I cannot feel it mine.'
> 'You are the mistress to invite or exclude'.
> 'I am ready to go in a few hours for a small income of money, for my child and me.'
> 'Our child.'
> 'Yes.'

'It is our child.'

'It is.' (*The Amazing Marriage*, Ch. xxxvii)

Meredith not only shows the use of words and refusal to use words here, but shows Fleetwood speaking familiarly, trying to break down 'the rebuke of her grandeur of stature', trying to induce 'her to deliver her mind, that the mountain girl's feebleness in speech might reinstate him'. She forces the dialogue back into staccato sentences, superficially like the brief, simple ones she had once to speak out of 'feebleness', but now manipulating brevity and simplicity, as he says, 'thrusting and parrying behind masked language':

'Ah! You must be feeling the cold North-wind here.'

'I do not. You may feel the cold, my lord. Will you enter the house?'

'Do you invite me?'

'The house is your own.'

'Will the mistress of the house honour me so far?'

'I am not the mistress of the house, my lord.'

'You refuse, Carinthia?'

'I would keep from using those words. I have no right to refuse the entry of the house to you.'

'If I come in?'

'I guard my rooms.' (Ch. xxxvii)

Meredith shows the girl, who, as Henrietta patronisingly assured Chillon, learned quickly to mince her step in the dance. She chooses the weapon of brief and formal dialogue, innuendo, a stylized question and answer which forces him to make the running and in the end to say what he means, and ask her, for what she refuses. Readers with good memories go back to the time when her brief sentences on the wedding journey made him suppose 'he would have to hear her spelling her words out next'. It does not do to see Carinthia as too instinctive and untutored. Like the heroine of James's *Washington Square*, she learns, from masters. The artifical style in this novel serves the interests of particularity, not of generalisation.

Meredith creates a major feminist triumph, which has its sadness. The fable is made possible by the fine analysis which the Novelist in the novel has to keep defending. He shows the importance of exhaustion and timing in the sex war: Carinthia is not unforgiving, and might have forgiven, but the last revelation of Fleetwood's attempt to seduce Henrietta comes at the wrong moment. It is no use 'coming round' or 'being converted' because, unfortunately but definitely, people come round at different stages, and Fleetwood's repentance is badly timed. Carinthia's capacity to endure is limited. What she cannot finally accept happened in the past, is only one more thing, smaller than others, but her feeling has worn out. When George Eliot's Dorothea finds that it is really love that she feels for Ladislaw, there he is waiting for her—there is a slight suggestion that it was almost too late, for George Eliot did know about these things—but the novel resolutely curves back into the conventional moral pattern. In *The Amazing Marriage* Carinthia is nearly but not quite a patient Griselda. It is a book where creative and strongly affined people tear each other to bits, commit rape, reject, are deeply revengeful, give up. An elective affinity is demonstrated and shown not as strong but fragile, subject to change, wars, desperate men, role, class, status and possessions. One man blows his brains out, another dies, and the fable and psychic history reinforce each other's clarity and power. This is why the Novelist and Dame Gossip struggle. Their conflict makes a good joke, just the kind of joke Meredith loved, at once boastful and self-deprecatory. Their joint presence insists that *The Amazing Marriage* is both realistic and fabulous.

First published in *Meredith Now*, ed. I. Fletcher (Routledge & Kegan Paul, London, 1971).

Note

1.   '*The Amazing Marriage*: a study in Contraries', *Review of English Literature*, Vol. 7, No. 1 (January 1966).

15. Women in D. H. Lawrence's Novels and Poetry

The only question to ask today, about man or woman
is: Has she chipped the shell of her own ego?
Has he chipped the shell of his own ego?

'The Egoists'

It is easy to see Lawrence as the enemy. He is hard on women. He creates saints and monsters as he sheds and fails to shed his Oedipal sicknesses, admitting, denying, and re-admitting his mother's stranglehold, asking her to free him by dying, then succumbing to the seductiveness of that last sacrifice. He criticises and harangues women for coming too close, being too personal, wanting to be loved, having too much mind, having too much cunt. He disapproves what he himself invents, Miriam's intensities, Pussum's mindlessness, Hermione's will, Helena's dreaming, Gudrun's life-denying and aggressive libertinism. He approves what he himself invents, Ursula's life-affirming sexual freedoms, Kate's exalted relinquishing of her orgasm, Connie Chatterley's gratitude for hers, the immolation of the Woman who Rode Away. He yearns after touch and tenderness in male friendships but finds lesbianism repulsive. He allows Ursula and Harriet to criticise his *Salvator Mundi* touch, but always gives himself the last word.

His praise of women is sometimes hard to take. There is a letter written to Henry Savage in 1913 when Lawrence and Frieda were in Lerici, in which Lawrence says some startling things in the course of attacking Richard Middleton, whose fears and sentimentality about women had been roused by the suffragettes:

I think myself he was stupid about women. It seems to me silly to rage against woman—as Sphinx, or Sphinx without a secret, or cunning artist in living—or in herself. It seems to me that the chief thing about a woman—who is much of a woman is that in the long run she is not to be had. A man may bring her his laurel wreaths & songs & what not, but if that man doesn't satisfy her, in some undeniable physical fashion—then in one way or other she takes him in her mouth and shakes him like a cat a mouse, and throws him away.

He is using the figure of the woman as artist in an offensive way, the very comparison preserving art's province for men. Jessie Chambers and Helen Corke agreed that it was hard for him to accept mind in women, and there is plenty of crude anti-female and anti-feminist anger, spite, fear, and pity in his poems. He can be silly, as in 'These Clever Women':

> Now stop carping at me! Do you want me to hate you?
>   Am I a kaleidoscope
> For you to shake and shake, and it won't come right?
> Am I doomed in a long coition of words to mate you?
>   Unsatisfied! Is there no hope
> Between your thighs, far, far from your peering sight?

He can be more consciously amusing on the same subject, in 'Purple Anemones' where the idea of the anemones as 'husband-splendid, serpent heads' getting after Persephone and Ceres, 'those two enfranchised women', shows him exuberantly, cheaply and not uncharacteristically teetering on the verge of wit. There are some places where he even seems to appreciate feminism for its energy and passion, as in a series of verses in *Pansies* which shift from the rueful hope that a properly redirected male energy might cure the 'modern Circe-dom', to a grudging recognition that women are the Lord's favourite vessels of wrath, helpfully and alarmingly collecting foreskins for Him. Occasionally he hits the right tone, amused, wary, mocking but not unappreciative:

> What has happened in the world?
> the women are like little volcanoes
> all more or less in eruption.
> It is very unnerving, moving in a world of smouldering
>   volcanoes.

It is rather agitating, sleeping with a little Vesuvius.
And exhausting, penetrating the lava-crater of a tiny
                                      Ixtaccihautl
and never knowing when you'll provoke an earthquake.
                                      ('Volcanic Venus')

Later in the letter to Savage, Lawrence has this to say: 'I don't agree
with you about our separation from women. The only thing that is
very separate—our bodies—is the via media for union again, if we
would have it so.' His phrases for such union in *Women in Love* are
familiar: it is a 'freedom together' and 'two single equal stars
balanced in conjunction'. When Birkin despairs of explaining his
images to Ursula, he decides that talking is no good, 'it must happen
beyond the sound of words. . . . This was a paradisal bird that could
never be netted, it must fly by itself to the heart.' His poetry is closer
to this soundlessness than his novels, more sustainedly sensuous as
it traces the particulars of feeling without debate and analysis.
Though it is not only in the poetry that Lawrence denies the
separation of men and women, it is easier to begin with it. His early
poems, *Look! We Have Come Through!*, and the late collection,
More Pansies, are not just to be negatively praised for admitting that
men and women are alike, but valued for their knowledge of sexual
feeling.

Some of the poems in *More Pansies* shift from man to woman
within poems or groups of poems. One pair of poems, 'The Gods!
The Gods!' and 'Name the Gods!' balances the image of a god in a
woman's body and a man's, the woman showing 'the glimmer of the
presence of the gods . . . like lilies' as she washes, the mower
revealing the god not in his own body but in the 'falling flatness' of
the wheat, 'the pale-gold flesh of Priapus dropping asleep'. This
turning from man to woman or woman to man is a marked two-beat
rhythm. Many of these poems show an insistent self-consciousness
about the well-known deficiency in our language, its lack of an
equivalent of the German *Mensch*, which avoids the ambiguity and
condescension of *Man* and the flatness of *person*. Particularly in the
late poems, Lawrence uses 'person' as he uses 'creatures' or
'individuals' or 'people'. He often uses 'Man' all-embracingly, but
its condescensions are obliterated, if we read the poems as they flow
and grow into each other, a rhythm which turns from the man to the
woman, separating in order to join in common experience: 'man or

woman', 'man and woman', 'most men, most women', 'no man knows, no woman knows', 'a fellow-man or fellow-woman' 'men and women', 'when most men die, today/when most women die', 'living women and men', 'it is no woman, it is no man'.

In 'The Cross' he remakes that image which was ironically and aggressively phallic in 'Last Words to Miriam', proclaiming the frailty of the sexual distinction, and merging it in that 'man' which must be urgently distinguished from the robot:

> Behold your Cross, Christians!
> With the upright division into sex
> men on this side, women on that side
> without any division into inferiority and superiority
> only differences,
> divided in the mystic, tangible and intangible difference.
>
> And then, truth much more bitter to accept,
> the horizontal division of mankind
> into that which is below the level, and that which is above. . . .
>
> That which is truly man, and that which is robot,
> the ego-bound.

The lustrous noon in 'Andraitx-Pomegranate Flowers' reveals 'a man, a woman there'. The pulsing content of 'The Heart of Man' is shut off from both sexes, 'no man knows, no woman knows'. The naked 'I' of 'Moral Clothing' approaches a 'fellow-man or a fellow-woman' who must be naked too. When Lawrence attacked and decided to give up what he called 'image-making love' it was because he had spent his life fixing and then unfixing sexual images. But certain natural and social truths forced him to see men and women as persons and not as men and women. The second letter to Savage declares that 'Sex is the fountain head, where life bubbles up into the person from the unknown . . .'. The word 'person' is a vital one.

Never trust the artist, trust the tale. And since tales create certain fixities of ego and action that poetry can avoid, never trust the tale, trust the poem. Amongst the persuasive and not quite persuasive indictments of Eliseo Vivas's *D. H. Lawrence: the failure and triumph of art* (Northwestern University Press, Evanston, 1960), is the suggestion that Lawrence's concern was with *eros*, and the loss of self through sex, as distinct from *agape*, and its loss of self in generous outgoing. Vivas is confident that Lawrence admits the reflexiveness of *eros*, and quotes an example from Ursula and Skrebensky's love-making in *The Rainbow*, which leaves each lover with the sense of maximal vitality, from which he concludes that self-knowledge is all Lawrence thought we gained from *eros*. There is a danger in relying on the far from beneficent relation of these lovers, created for mutual destruction, to suggest the limits and threats of pure self-possession through sex, in a demonstration made again through Gudrun and Gerald in *Women in Love*. But it is difficult to argue briefly about the novels, and all I can do here is to suggest that Vivas could not have come to this conclusion so easily had he been working with the poems. It is knowledge that bubbles through the unknown, in sex: the poetry of *Look! We Have Come Through!* seems to invoke a more companionable *eros* than that of Ursula or Skrebensky, a loving which is a mode of other-knowledge as well as self-knowledge, if rather less heroic than *agape*.

Look! We Have Come Through! has a title which announces the theme of sexual and moral triumph. Its 'We' is the 'We' of lovers sufficiently freed by love from anxiety, fear and bewilderment, to make a passionate analysis of passionate love. (Lawrence shied away from the word 'love', but it seems simplest to stick to it.) One convention of love-poetry and love which he questions in these poems is the lover's praise of the beloved's beauty, and this radical questioning is made as part of his argument about liberation for man and woman. Birkin's declared lack of interest in Ursula's good looks in *Women in Love* is part of the general redefinition of love argued there, but the protest against aesthetic appreciation in sex is most sensitively and lucidly found in the poems. 'She Said As Well To Me' begins with the woman's praise of the man's body, and sets against it the man's protest against her appreciation. He objects not just because aesthetic celebration is shallow (as of course it often is) but because her compliments hold sinister suggestions of instrumentality, thanks for services excellently rendered to her ego. She argues, in a way which manages to be both superficial and overpoweringly rapturous, that lovers should be free to gaze, admire, and show each other their naked beauty, but as she tries to talk him out of what she calls the typical male timidity, she dwells on function. It is not surprising that the man begins 'to wonder', and decides that what she says doesn't make him free but 'trammelled and hurt'. His defence is made through images of animal freedom like those in *Birds, Beasts and Flowers*, the poems which try to do for animals what he wants her to do for him, to honour the individuality of others, and hesitate before its strength and privacy. But such respect depends on some knowledge of the other, and is not reflexive. The *noli me tangere* felt but given up in *The Man Who Died* is not shown as a matter of male feeling only. The woman in the poem generalises, matronisingly—'Men are the shyest creatures, they never will come out of their covers'—but the images that answer and defy her are both male and female:

> Now I say to her: 'No tool, no instrument, no God!
> Don't touch and appreciate me.
> It is an infamy.
> You would think twice before you touched a weasel on a fence
> as it lifts its straight white throat.
> Your hand would not be so flig and easy.
> Nor the adder we saw asleep with her head on her shoulder,
> curled up in the sunshine like a princess;
> when she lifted her head in delicate, startled wonder
> you did not stretch forward to caress her
> though she looked rarely beautiful
> and a miracle as she glided delicately away, with such dignity.
> And the young bull in the field, with his wrinkled, sad face,
> you are afraid if he rises to his feet. . . .'

It is easy to argue that Lawrence's rejection of intimate praise and fondness comes from his Oedipal wound and produces his dangerous fascination with violence. It is easy to see the retreat from Miriam's intensities, as Jessie Chambers herself saw it, as a fiction made in order to strengthen his mother's image. I think it is also necessary to see that such rejection of praise and appreciation beats a wise retreat from that instrumentality familiar to lovers and artists. It was not only a response which Lawrence had to the intrusiveness of loving women, but a temptation he must have felt as an artist, if not as a friend and lover. It was certainly one which he sometimes did and sometimes didn't resist.

The rejections and appreciations in *The White Peacock* and *Sons and Lovers* are clearly made in the interests of defining the man; they help to show and analyse George Saxton's degeneration and Paul Morel's coming of age. Helen Corke, always unstridently alert to Lawrence's use of women, says as much in her brief essay on *The White Peacock*: 'These women are fully drawn, but Lawrence is not interested in them as individuals. He sees them only in relation to their men. "Take," he would seem to say to his reader, "a male creature! We shall now study its reactions to these various forms of feminine stimuli." '[1] Her essay ends with the image of Erda, whose single concern is with the race, who cuts away the psyche 'so that the reproductive physical self cannot develop individually, and the woman, in motherhood, is absorbed into the lives of her children . . . sister to the servant of the One Talent'. Helen Corke seemed to Lawrence to be the defiantly dreaming and thinking woman who could resist him, and in what she calls the 'deferred conversation' in *Lawrence's Apocalypse*, she accuses him of too simply and crudely separating masculine and feminine extremities of what she saw as a spectrum of sexuality. There are occasions in both letters and fiction when Lawrence seems to reduce the individual woman to an outline, type, or complex convenience, but it is essential to recognise that such reductions are not confined to his portraits of women.

There is the denigration of his father in *Sons and Lovers*, of Bertrand Russell and Middleton Murry in *Women in Love*, not to mention the reductions of Sir Clifford Chatterley. Even where Lawrence's women present tendentious types or images, their needs and passions often derive from his own intimate experience and fantasies. Although in 'The Woman Who Rode Away' Lawrence chose a woman as an appropriate victim of *ennui*, wildness and masochistic sacrifice, there is no doubt that the feelings and values of his immolated heroine lay within his own experience. In his finest volume, 'The Ship of Death', the poems most fluidly and shiftingly create their repetitions, modulations and permutations on the themes of death and rebirth, and we see that the crude lines of the brutal little fable have an intimate connection with Lawrence's imaginative experience of dying, dying away from deadly society, from human attachments, from a sick body. Where he seems most chauvinistic he is probably most personal. Anyone who can see 'The Woman Who Rode Away' simply as a man's sadistic immolation of woman cannot have looked properly at 'The

Ship of Death' or compared Lawrence with de Sade.

Lawrence has lapses into crudity, and does not always work with sufficient imaginative energy and thought. The allegorical modes and moments in his fiction are often reductions of human complexity which place male and female in opposition to each other instead of showing them as human beings engaged in similar struggles with class, sex, education, work, art and mortality. But Lawrence's allegory is sometimes subtler than it appears, and we should always be wary of accepting his characters' instant interpretations. In the 'Mino' chapter in *Women in Love*, for instance, Birkin takes Ursula through his revised syllabus of love by using the demonstration-model of male and female cats. As the female cat waits submissively, cuffed and longing, Ursula tells the cat that he is 'a bully like all males', an observation which seems especially abstract and unfair if we remember her beaked passion and hostility at the end of *The Rainbow*. (The abstraction and unfairness is not hers but her author's.) The Ursula of *Women in Love* has more Frieda and less Lawrence in her than the Ursula of *The Rainbow*, and so needs the lecture:

> 'No,' said Birkin, 'he is justified. He is not a bully. He is only insisting to the poor stray that she shall acknowledge him as a sort of fate, her own fate: because you can see she is fluffy and promiscuous as the wind. I am with him entirely. He wants superfine stability.'
> 'Yes, I know!' cried Ursula. 'He wants his own way—I know what your fine words work down to—bossiness, I call it, bossiness.'
> The young cat again glanced at Birkin in disdain of the noisy woman.
> 'I quite agree with you, Miciotto,' said Birkin to the cat. 'Keep your male dignity, and your higher understanding.' (Ch. XII)

And he goes on provoking Ursula's fury about 'this assumption of male superiority'. It is worth observing, however, that Birkin, despite his ironical looks and laughs, is not talking about male superiority and female inferiority but about stability, strays, and wildness. Ursula's impetuous attack seems to be created by superiority, whether it had its origin in Frieda Lawrence's jeers, as seems likely, or not. (The cat, drawing on proverbial tradition, looks at Birkin with a look of 'pure superiority'.) Birkin insists that what the cats represent is not Gerald's bullying of the mare, the 'Wille zur Macht', but 'The desire to bring this female cat into a pure stable equilibrium, a transcendent and abiding *rapport* with the single male' because without him 'she is a mere stray, a fluffy sporadic bit of chaos'. The she-cat is an unrelated stray, though I wouldn't suggest that Lawrence presents the debate very ingratiatingly, for women readers. But the debate suggests the need for stability and relationship, not the need to be knocked into shape by the male.

The conjunction of stars and the fluffy bit of chaos recur in *Look! We Have Come Through!*, not surprisingly, since the early stages of Lawrence's struggles and successes with Frieda are told both in *Women in Love* and in these early unrhymed poems. The fluidity of poetry, and of this free verse in particular, has its advantage over the fixities of the prose fiction. Its dialectic is more shifting, its impersonations less hard, its moods less tethered to history and personality. Irony and comedy are happily absent, for Lawrence is not at his best in either. *Women in Love* is a novel which refuses to be linear. It resembles poetry in its reliance on lyrical and symbolic statement, but it still has the novel's characteristic continuity. When Birkin gives up a mood or a thought in exhaustion, irony or bewilderment, it is still registered in continuous and casual patterns, whereas the poems dealing with similar ideas and feelings jump without link or explanation from one mood to another. One result of this discontinuity seems to be a greater freedom from male and female stereotypes. In the fiction, even imagery may be attached to character and therefore to gender. In the poetry, the emphasis can be placed on states of mind and passion.

Sometimes, of course, the poetry simply fills out the novel's outline. When Lawrence retreats from the woman's gratified praise of his body's fineness and function, we see precisely what he meant by that subservience to the ego of which he accuses Ursula in *Women in Love*. The poetry is fuller of feeling and so more lucid than the novel, with its commitments to history, debate and character. The risen Christ's *noli me tangere* and Birkin's stoning of the reflections of Aphrodite are explained in the poems, which ruminate lengthily on the retreat into solitude, on the sense of independence and separateness, and on the conjunction of separate persons. This poetry is about persons rather than about men and women, or man and woman. It is true to those feelings which are common to all the sexes, and proves what the novels asserted and dropped. It is the poetry, not the fiction, which really destroys the old ego of sexual difference. What the novel does is to show the attempt to break, and its difficulty.

'Song Of A Man Who Is Loved' may at a glance—especially a Freudian glimpse—look like the ineffaceable mother's image, but it develops a particularity, physical and emotional, which makes it larger and newer. The lover is secured by permanence and conjunction from the surrounding space, hardness and chaos. Here is a guarantee of rest and peace:

> So I hope I shall spend eternity
> With my face down buried between her breasts;
> With my still heart full of security,
> And my still hands full of her breasts.

The abstract concepts of security and permanence take on the definite forms of solid bone and its soft covering, both needed, bone for a lasting support, flesh for something softer than the world outside. That world's hardness and evasiveness are both present, too, in sensation and sound:

> Having known the world so long, I have never confessed
> How it impresses me, how hard and compressed
> Rocks seem, and earth, and air uneasy, and water still ebbing
>   west.

But the hard things are human, as well as natural, including 'Assertions! Assertions! stones, women and men!' Lawrence's unpleasant qualities, his hating and his superiority, allow him to sound aggressive about human beings as well as assertions and stones, but his more endearing need for stability links him with Ursula and the stray cat. He is not simply a provider of peace, he knows chaos too, and it is a chaos sensuously realised as it never was in the debates and arguments of the novel:

> And the chaos that bounces and rattles like shrapnel, at least
> Has for me a door into peace, warm dawn in the east
> Where her bosom softens towards me, and the turmoil has
>   ceased.

When conjunction has happened, the gains can be demonstrated by man or woman. The knowledge cannot be simply reflexive. The man uses for himself the image of chaos and in 'One Woman To All Women' lets her use his star symbol, the 'other beauty, the way of the stars', which is also now, as Coleridge might say, attached to the reality it represents, brought into the sensuous area of sexual rhythm, motion and propulsion:

> If you knew how I swerve in peace, in the equipoise
> With the man, if you knew how my flesh enjoys
> The swinging bliss no shattering ever destroys.

Admittedly, the last splendid line which Donne-like, brings the cosmos into the lovers' bed is diminished by the refrain and title of the poem, 'You other women'. The ultimate boast and gratification can seem (immediately) rather pettily feminine and (ultimately) pettily masculine, though the poem is concerned to dismiss conventional beauty, and its rejections of cosmetic and narcissistic devices conveniently express the ego-binding of aesthetic vanities, and perhaps explain—if not excuse—the unattractive competitiveness.

In one of the best poems in the volume, 'New Heaven and Earth', there is a refusal to differentiate, a nervous-seeming but ultimately confident glancing from what seems a man's experience to what is felt also as a woman's. The song becomes that of a human being who is loved. Lawrence's usual way is to impersonate the woman or to speak as the man, but here he shifts from the one to the other, as he does again, momentarily, in 'Both Sides of the Medal' where he insists and shows that she has a passion for him as he has for her. 'New Heaven and Earth' is a poem which most clearly deals with the proof of sexual knowledge, with the knowledge of self, or otherness, of newness, of strangeness. It creates an exotic sexual landscape which achieves something less frequently found in Lawrence than in Donne, the sweet and violent jolt through a conceit into fresh experience, the shock given to mind through senses, here creating and re-creating the twinned delights of finding the self in finding the other human creature:

> I am thrown upon the shore.
> I am covering myself with the sand.

> I am filling my mouth with the earth.
> I am burrowing my body into the soil.
> The unknown, the new world!

This landing of the desperate castaway is followed by the sudden shock of translation. The man and his reader are grounded, in a new impact:

> It was the flank of my wife
> I touched with my hand, I clutched with my hand
> rising, new-awakened from the tomb!
> It was the flank of my wife
> whom I married years ago
> at whose side I have lain for over a thousand nights
> and all that previous while, she was I, she was I;
> I touched her, it was I who touched and I who was touched.

Lawrence does better here than in *Women in Love* with the sense of eternal *rapport*. His image of the past is in several senses more solidly persuasive than the novel's statements about the future, in a new version of the traditions of amorous pre-knowledge and eureka-feeling. The woman's flank is the strand of the new world:

> White sand and fruits unknown and perfumes that never
> can blow across the dark seas to our usual world!
> And land that beats with a pulse!
> And valleys that draw close in love!
> And strange ways where I fall into oblivion of
>   uttermost living!—
> Also she who is the other has strange-mounded breasts
>   and strange sheer slopes, and white levels.

The erotic and exotic geography works brilliantly: whiteness, curves, scents and foreignness belonging plainly to the human body and the new world, beating pulse and closing valleys transferring an amorous life to the land, and making it more extraordinary and intense. The rapturous poem—perhaps the most Whitman-like of Lawrence's poems—delights in conjunction, separateness and joy, with vividness which shows what the novel's debate is about.

It shows this more intricately than I have suggested, because it begins with a sense of self-nausea, itself related to the various hatefulnesses of war, the tomb, and imprisonment in self. We move to that sense of rapturous landing from an unpleasantly striking image of a man making love to himself, and of a loathsome hermaphroditic fruitfulness, 'begetting and conceiving in my own body'. The slopes are breasts, the valleys close in, the images belong to female physiology, but Lawrence can also force a sharing of the image which makes ever clearer the common experience of sex, for both man and woman, as he does in 'Wedlock' which uses more obvious domestic distinctions, to make the same point about common experience. It starts with the sense of the man protecting the woman, wrapping her round, but almost immediately refuses to preserve the vital and phallic images for himself:

> Do you feel me wrap you
> Up with myself and my warmth, like a flame round the wick?
>
> And how I am not at all, except a flame that mounts off you.
> Where I touch you, I flame into being;—but is it me, or you?

The imagery of flame ceases to be phallic, passes from the obviously male candle and wick to something larger and less differentiated, 'a bonfire of oneness, my flame I flung leaping round you/You the core of the flame, crept into me'. The image is shared, like the passion. The poem stretches to take in both lovers, itself an act of love.

The outlines, actions, arguments of the novels are not only blurred but self-consciously blurred in the poetry. In 'Wedlock' Lawrence wonders what will come of their love,

> Children, acts, utterance,
> Perhaps only happiness.

and this is most precisely true, the question given poignancy by our knowledge of the final answer; only acts and utterance did come of it. The utterance comes from the experience of conjunction and of discovery. Lawrence's straining and blaming in *Sons and Lovers*, his instrumental use of the women's characters in *The White Peacock*, and his re-interpretation of Helen Corke's novel, *Neutral Ground*, for *The Trespasser*, all pre-date *The Rainbow* and *Women in Love*, which argue, if less sensuously and fluidly than the poetry, the sense of freedom in the break with the ego. Lawrence's *eros* makes no claims to generosity, let alone renunciation, but in its claim for discovery through respect for itself and respect for other life, it seems to have some affinity with *agape*, after all. It is certainly a love that rejects the sacrificial nature of Christian *agape*. That rejection is what *The Man Who Died* is about, but although Christ/Osiris has to leave Isis to bear her child alone, the story of two restored and separate people is not a simply erotic fable of transient therapy. The Preface to *Look! We Have Come Through!* is argued almost entirely in sexual imagery (spasms, plasm, nudity, jetting, Aphrodite, rose) and the benefits it claims for the freedom of free verse were perhaps qualities erotically learnt, fluidity, momentariness, release, resting in the present. This poetry is the utterance created by sexual conjunction; it reveals a release into the present, an ability to accept flux and resist stereotype, a respect or imaginative recognition for the other creature. Free verse fully and warmly dramatised Lawrence's sense of union and individuality, and in so doing paid its debt to the attachment which created its pulse, flow, and motion.

Of course Lawrence did not always succeed in writing from and to the moment, and it would be peculiarly stupid to claim for him a permanent realisation of freedom, joy and conjunction. He was not able to maintain a freedom from sexism or the pains of sexual difference. But Lawrence's late phase included not only *Lady Chatterley's Lover*, where both book and title at last make room for the human couple, (at a certain expense, in the refusal to imagine Clifford) but 'The Ship of Death', where he finds the final version of the new voyage, the new country, the new solitude, and the new discovery, not in any form of love, but in death.

Lawrence's sense of human liberation is realised when he forgets the 'he and she', in a way undreamed of by Donne. This is most fully achieved in the poems, but even in the constraints of the prose fiction there emerges some sense that women and men share the same struggle. The woman in *The Woman Who Rode Away* is, as a woman, the best equipped human being for submission and sacrifice, society having after all freely encouraged female masochism. The women at the beginning of *The Rainbow* not surprisingly resemble their sisters (and fictional contemporaries) in the novels of George Eliot, who also look ahead into history and out into the public world. The Brangwen women look because they have windows to look through, children to plan for, the doctors and parsons to talk to, while the men of the agricultural community work with the animals in the fields behind. Ursula, like Dorothea Brooke, Isabel Archer, Little Dorrit and Tess, is an appropriately female image of Victorian aspiration. Lawrence couldn't sympathise with the suffragettes, but he could sympathise with Ursula's attempt at liberation, permitting her to do such unVictorian things as reject her college education for its irrelevance, choose and use the wrong lover then leave him, become pregnant then have a symbolic and convenient miscarriage. Ursula, like Dorothea and Amy Dorrit, rebels and protests against social limits which are oppressive to the woman but also oppressive to the man. Just as George Eliot moved from Maggie to Tom, from Dorothea to Lydgate, to show not only the woman's limitations but the man's, to achieve not only a feminist plea but a larger human one, just as Hardy moved from Jude to Sue, so Lawrence moves from Ursula to Birkin. I would not want to exaggerate the success of his analysis. George Eliot, a woman who had to put on the indignity of a male name, for reasons both sexual and literary, and Thomas Hardy, least chauvinist of all nineteenth-century male English writers except Meredith, were capable of achieving and maintaining a balance between the plight of man and woman. But when Lawrence moved on that hinge between *The Rainbow* and *Women in Love*, his heroine became more orthodox, less introspective, forgot some of her past, changed to become more conventionally in need of an education from the man.

At the beginning of *Women in Love* Ursula and Gudrun are not making a narrowly female plea when they question marriage and the family. In the episode of the chair, both Ursula and Birkin are together, man and woman, in rejecting the furniture and fittings of family life, despite their will to permanence. Their atypical freedom has of course been observed by several critics, including Leavis and Vivas, as coming straight from Lawrence's own situation. Only in *Lady Chatterley* did he fully admit that the problem of sexual freedom and fulfilment was bound up with property, family, households and children. Only Connie is actually allowed the urge to conceive, perhaps as a belated reflection of Frieda's maternity. She is to have a child as well as acts and utterance, though off stage. Lawrence 'neglects' the family, perhaps because his marriage was sterile, perhaps because his attachment to his mother was sterilising, perhaps because it is the man, rather than the woman, who occupies the centre of the novel. The result is that he often pays man and woman the compliment of valuing them as particular persons, not as parents and ancestors.

Lawrence set the human couple together at the end of *Lady Chatterley's Lover* in an abstract social world, almost as far removed from the average daily life as the Mexico of *The Plumed Serpent* or the Australia of *Kangaroo*. But throughout the novels there are moments when the human being can be set in her environment, to represent not only a woman's life, but something larger. In *Sons and Lovers*, where the women are subordinate to the picture of the man's development and growing-up, there is the remarkable social detail of the scene in Clara's house when Paul Morel finds her and her mother at their lace-making:

> That was a little, darkish room too, but it was smothered in white lace. The mother had seated herself again by the cupboard, and was drawing thread from a vast web of lace. A clump of fluff and ravelled cotton was at her right hand, a heap of three-quarter-inch lace lay on her left, whilst in front of her was the mountain of the lace web, piling the hearthrug. Threads of curly cotton, pulled out from between the lengths of lace, strewed over the fender and the fireplace. Paul dared not go forward, for fear of treading on piles of white stuff.
>
> On the table was a jenny for carding the lace. There was a pack of brown cardboard squares, a pack of cards of lace, a little box of pins, and on the sofa lay a heap of drawn lace.
>
> The room was all lace, and it was so dark and warm that the white, snowy stuff seemed the more distinct.
>
> 'If you're coming in you won't have to mind the work,' said Mrs. Radford. 'I know we're about blocked up. But sit you down.
>
> . . . .
>
> Clara began to work. Her jenny spun with a subdued buzz; the white lace hopped from between her fingers on to the card. It was filled; she snipped off the length, and pinned the end down to the banded lace. Then she put a new card in her jenny. Paul watched her. She sat square and magnificent. Her throat and arms were bare. The blood still mantled below her ears; she bent her head in shame of her humility. Her face was set on her work.
>
> . . . .
>
> Clara broke in, and he told her his message. She spoke humbly to him. He had surprised her in her drudgery. To have her

humble made him feel as if he were lifting his head in expectation.

'Do you like jennying?' he asked

'What can a woman do!' she replied bitterly.

'Is it sweated?'

'More or less. Isn't *all* woman's work? That's another trick the men have played, since we force ourselves into the labour market.'

'Now then, you shut up about the men,' said her mother. 'If the women wasn't fools, the men wouldn't be bad uns, that's what I say. No man was ever that bad wi' me but what he got it back again. Not but what they're a lousy lot, there's no denying it.'

'But they're all right really, aren't they?' he asked.

'Well, they're a bit different from women,' she answered. (Ch. X)

Clara is a suffragette, and Lawrence (and Paul) eventually pack her off again to crude old Baxter Dawes, settling that bit of Paul's *Bildung*. But to say that, even though it is true, ignores the powerful life of those scenes where full weight is given to sensuous and emotional truth, where the tale can be trusted. We see precisely why she was a feminist, perhaps also why she could go back to her bad marriage, liberated as she is into the imprisoning world of work. The white lace smothers and blocks the room. Humiliations of labour blend with humiliations of sex. It is the men who sweat the women, it is an employer and a lover who watches: 'her throat and arms were bare. . . . she bent her head in shame of her humility. . . . To have her humble made him feel as if he were lifting his head in expectation'. Here are traces of that peculiarly Victorian perversion, the gentleman's excitement at the woman's drudgery. But it is a moment which doesn't belong only to a problem of women, but links with the whole world of work.

Paul Morel felt the humiliation of the factory too, though Lawrence toned down some of the more brutal aspects of his own experience. The miners are smothered and blocked also. Lawrence had a clear understanding of the tedium and brutality of industrial work for men and women, and when we think of his own domestic zest for washing up saucepans or laying tables, with care and creativity, we should remember that it was a free and chosen work that he delighted in. He is quick to seize what joy there is, even in the mines, and does so in Morel's marvellous stories, which have their part to play in casting that fatal and transient glamour over Gertrude Morel. He also realised, or showed, that woman had to get into the man's world of work, that the domestic drudgery of Miriam's mother had no zest, was all grind and service, and that Miriam was desperate to learn, to move up and move on. In her story too, for all its distortions, we see the most explicable moments of humility as she struggles to enter the desired and difficult world of learning. Her desires are Mrs Morel's for her sons, Paul's for himself. In the world of work some escape into the rare creative chance, others are imprisoned by the routines of the inhuman machine Lawrence was to indict, fight, and escape. The pressures of that world form the most striking part of Lawrence's argument against capitalist industry and science, and as he shows them in action, as he remembers and imagines, he sees the continuity of human feeling. It flows through love and labour, links men and women, calls on their energy and sometimes defeats it.

Lawrence never faced the question of the identity of man and woman's political predicament, except intuitively, but he recorded their common struggle to survive in the capitalist society. Even writing which uses women as instruments in the male artist's *Bildung* has moments which show the women, like men, as human beings, individuals, persons.

First published in *D. H. Lawrence: Novelist, Poet, Prophet*, ed. S. Spender (Weidenfeld and Nicholson, London, 1973).

Note

1.   Helen Corke, *D. H. Lawrence. The Croyden Years* (University of Texas Press, Austin, 1965).

16. Form as End and Means in James Joyce's *Ulysses*

It is not common for Joyce critics to stand back from detailed analysis and consider *Ulysses* in relation to other novels so it is probably inevitable that the novel should have been so often regarded by those who disliked it as a freak, and by those who admired it as extraordinary, in a class by itself. Robert Adams, for instance, in *Surface and Symbol. The Consistency of James Joyce's 'Ulysses'* (O. U. P., New York, 1962) tells us that it is a book which encourages the critic 'to transcend the formulas of criticism' and that 'it is literature but it is not just literature'. My only quarrel with Adams's book is that it does not make it clear whether critical formulas are to be transcended because this is a unique novel or whether the same critical formulas may have to be transcended when we deal with other novels. He speaks of 'the ordinary novel' which keeps consistently within one angle of vision. Some of us may feel that the flexibility and surprise and change within *Ulysses* might be paralleled by other novelists in similar or different ways. I am not convinced by Adams's arithmetical accuracy here: he speaks of the 'eighteen angles' of the eighteen sections of *Ulysses* and tells us that Joyce shocks us 'into awareness of the act of authorial choice, seventeen times more than the average novel'. Since we have little discussion of the 'average' novel it is not possible to argue with this conclusion, but Laurence Sterne, Emily Brontë, George Eliot and Tolstoy, while not affording us the violent shifts in 'tonality' found in these eighteen sections, may be thought of as providing the same kind of shock and flexibility. I quote Adams in order to agree with him on the general principle that Joyce cannot be fitted into our schematic principles of simple symbolic structure and total relevance. Adams insists that 'one of the preconditions' of the greatness of *Ulysses* is precisely 'its readiness to fracture and escape all closed and formal patterns', and though he makes his case in relation to some of the factual patterns and historical references of *Ulysses* I do not think his conclusion is fully backed by evidence. I do not believe we can say that Joyce fractures and escapes 'all closed and formal patterns' but this may turn out to be a mere objection to terminology, since the case I want to put in this short chapter is one which supports Adams's view of the freedom and discord of the novel. I should like to put it rather differently, by saying that the paradox which confronts us in *Ulysses* is that of a highly schematic form which does not make an abstract or reductive impression.

Joyce does not sacrifice human particulars to aesthetic or intellectual schematism, like Henry James at the end of *The Ambassadors* or E. M. Forster in *Howards End*. Yet he cannot be said to use his main structural device, the Homeric analogy, waywardly or inconsistently. I think it is difficult to say what Joyce does do, as a formalist, without comparing his novels with 'ordinary' novels, and I should like to begin with some reference to a novelist known to Joyce and quoted by Adams as an instance of an 'ordinary' novelist.

I do not think Joyce's critics have observed that in *Harry Richmond* George Meredith uses the same analogy as Joyce in *Ulysses*. The hero's search for maturity is outlined and symbolised by a lavish use of the *Odyssey* as model, with Harry as Telemachus, his father Richmond Roy, as Ulysses, and Janet, his faithful love who stays at home while he goes on his wanderings, as Penelope. The analogy is used with elaborate and flexible irony: the heroic reference is sometimes appropriate and simply illuminating, sometimes ironically deflating. Though the novel is of special interest to students of Joyce, and though the symbolic analogy seems to me more elaborate than anything in other Victorian novels, I want to bring it forward not as a special case but an example of the free and tangential use of analogy to be found in such earlier novels. We could find other instances, like the use of Ariadne, in *Romola*, and less elaborately, in *Middlemarch*, or the use of the *Medea* in *Daniel Deronda*. We should of course mention Fielding's more generalised use of epic analogy in *Tom Jones*. How do these novels differ from *Ulysses* in their use of epic parallel?

They do not differ in their use of several analogies, for Joyce relies on the Icarus-Dedalus model and the Hamlet reference, though it is true that he uses his Homeric parallel in a more elaborate way than any of his predecessors. They do not differ in flexibility: like Joyce, both George Eliot and Meredith use parallel to achieve a double effect of reinforcement and deflation. In all these novelists, the irony is sometimes there to elevate the model, sometimes to elevate the copy. But they do differ in one respect, with the possible exception of Fielding, in using the analogy for the persistent end of illumination. Joyce uses his analogy so persistently that at times it becomes self-assertive play. We may see this as an extraordinary discipline which he imposed on his material, or a source of virtuoso-display, or both. In action and character and language, the reference to the original model is persistent and, considered from conventional standards of 'organic' form, superfluous. We cannot argue that *all* the Homeric parallels exist in order to control our response to the society and people acting out their destinies on Bloomsday. When we recognise Scylla and Charybdis in Section 9, The Library, or Aeolus in Section 7, The Newspaper, the recognition does not have a highly significant part to play in our response to the material in the episode. We feel pleasure in the ingenuity with which the pattern is sustained, and this may be compared to a delight in a social pun, in the case of the Aeolus episode, but I do not think these scenes depend on the recognition of the model in the way the Hades episode, the Eumaeus, Ithaca, or Penelope sections do, where in every case we respond in a special way to the twentieth-century scene because we read it as a modern copy of the original. Some scenes are freer than others.

This element of free play and virtuosity extends beyond the Homeric parallel, and in the pattern of art, colour and symbol which links each episode, there is sometimes a feeling of appropriateness, often a feeling of superfluous ingenuity and decoration, occasionally a feeling of illumination. Joyce's decision to make his pattern consistent and symmetrical in these ways may be compared with the decision to write in a particular verse-form: we sometimes feel that a form is the best possible mode of expression, sometimes, less forcefully, that it is an appropriate choice, sometimes that it is arbitrary and ingenious, displaying form as end rather than means. Within the intricate structure of *Ulysses*, Joyce uses various devices for unity, symmetry and illumination, and our response to them varies from the delight in playful ingenuity to the delight in the illuminating choice and, finally, the acceptance of what appears to be the necessary form.

Most 'ordinary' good novels use the middle way: we feel neither a conspicuous play of structure nor an assertion of structural relations which appears to be the sole vehicle for meaning, but the wedding of form and content in appropriate choice. The paradox of Joyce's formal choice in *Ulysses* is that form is at its most conspicuous when it is least arbitrary and most arbitrary, when he is playing with links and repetitions but without illumination of the material, and when he is doing something which is indeed rare in fiction, depending on our recognition of structure for our recognition of meaning. In this novel we have form as play, form as the 'ordinary' appropriate form of meaning, recognisable but not forcing analysis upon the reader, and form as essential notation, form which must be grasped in analysis before we can see the human material of the novel. When Myles Crawford snubs Bloom and we recognise Aeolus's capricious conduct towards Ulysses, there is play—the pattern is neatly completed. We do not see the snub more clearly or differently because we see its model, and its importance is the importance of all the rebuffs Bloom suffers. When we see John O'Connell, the caretaker of the cemetery, in the shadow of the model of Hades, there is a sinister darkening and ordering of our response, though O'Connell is a sinister and dignified figure even for readers who do not see through him. But when Bloom and Stephen make direct contact, it is essential to analyse the scene in terms of the structural components proffered by the model: we have to see them as Ulysses and Telemachus. When Bloom returns to Molly at the end, it is essential that we see them as Ulysses and Penelope.

The form—the structural relations provided by the model—has in such places to be grasped as essential notation. In these places the human actions and reactions, seen without the structural underpinning, are trivial or simple or obscure. We must not forget that these episodes come at the end of the novel, when we have learnt the notation. (The novel has taught the reader how it should be read.) They come too after the novel has made its impact, like an 'ordinary' novel, by its weight of human particularity. In most 'ordinary' novels the human particulars make their point, and the symbolic accompaniment or structural comparisons illuminate or extend or generalise. At the end of *Ulysses* the symbols carry an unusual weight, but they have not been doing this throughout the novel. Stephen Dedalus, Bloom, and Molly are built up by the human notation of thoughts, feelings, actions, in the medium of interior monologue, which Joyce uses as a means of dramatic demonstration. If we were to select moving moments from *Ulysses* they need be no different from moving movements in 'ordinary' novels: Bloom's memory of his early love, or of the day when Rudy was conceived (no less moving for having the status of life remembered); his jealousy of Blazes Boylan, seldom explicit, but no less moving for being dramatically acted out in gesture; his pity for Dilly Dedalus and the seagulls, and his moment of courage in the pub, where he is attacked because of the misunderstanding about the tip for Throwaway. It is the moments of emotion and the moments of moral action, accompanied or unaccompanied by the Homeric model—important in the last example, not in the others— which bring this novel close to all great novels. And it is the substantial presence of such emotion and action which allows Joyce, at the end, in his three last episodes, to make the model work in a different mode.

It is at these points of formal notation that the novel becomes ambiguous and has been most variously interpreted, and it is at these points that it is at its most difficult. (The difficulty is also an effect of language, and my arguments about arbitrary formal play, appropriate form, and essential formal notation, could also be applied to the language of the novel.) The final encounter of Stephen and Bloom has been described as emptiness or fulfilment, frustration or discovery, separateness or connection. This ambiguity exists because of the absence of complete realistic notation. The moment is moving, whichever way we interpret it, less because of our response to the human foreground than because of the invisible felt presence of the background. All the analogies meet: this is Shakespeare, his son (also his rival) and Ann Hathaway; this is the meeting of Ulysses and Telemachus—to choose one small and one large analogy out of several. Remove the analogy and the meeting will be trivial but neither movingly empty nor movingly loving. It is analogy—and primarily the Homeric analogy—which enlarges these figures into gigantic mist-shadows. The enlargement seems to some to contrast the Homeric meeting with the copy at the expense of the copy; to others to bring out, by resemblance, the moment of generous and loving affiliation. I do not suggest that we can isolate these moments or episodes from the fully human notation that has gone before. Stephen's relationship with his father and mother and country, Bloom's relationship with his wife and children and country, make them fit the role offered by the mythical form. They need the encounter: Stephen's exile needs no emphasis, nor his guilt. Bloom's alienation has been demonstrated throughout the Dublin day, and by now we are are familiar with his yearning for the dead Rudy and have glimpsed his affectionate but unsatisfactory relation with his daughter (unlike himself and Molly, he thinks, she has no taste, and on another occasion he takes 'it is a wise child knows its own father' to himself). It is only in relation to the dead son that he feels securely paternal. We have seen also evidence for and against both views of this encounter: Bloom has made many efforts in loving-kindness which have met with rebuffs, Stephen has been cold and aloof. Because the human notation here is slight—the making of cocoa, the micturition—the use of the model here appears to hold our interpretation in suspense.

The same non-committal and ambiguity is present in the final episode of the return to Penelope. Once more the human and particular notation is slight, inviting us to see great significance in Bloom's request for breakfast in bed. Once more there is a suspension between two poised alternatives: we may see the return of Bloom diminished and degraded by the Homeric model: *this* is scarcely an equivalent for the return of Ulysses. We may see it as enlarged and affirmed: for these two, even *this* is something. Molly is either degraded by the comparison with Penelope (Samuel Butler's views may seem relevant to some scholars but do not appear within the novel) or elevated. We may say: *this* is the Penelope figure! We may say: in her way, she too can be compared with Penelope. We must say both and neither.

This movement between two opposing alternatives of pessimistic or optimistic interpretation is the result of a shift which forces us to decide on model-preference or copy-preference, then temporarily to infer that decision itself is impossible.

If the human notation had been more powerful, giving us the impression from speech and action that this was really the beginning of friendship or a cold trivial meeting, or in Molly's soliloquy, placing more or less emphasis on the tie with Bloom, then the material would be making up our minds for us, as it usually does in novels. But by suspending the importance of the human action and throwing it on to the Homeric analogy, which has already been shown in two-way action, the novel confronts us with a human complexity which, like shot silk, can be seen in two ways, pessimistically and optimistically. We cannot call this a failure or a success; the ambiguity need not be an uneasy hovering between choices, but the admission of paradox. Love can be compatible with infidelity and impotence, the past glow is not entirely lost in the present staleness, human generosity and pity and protectiveness— we may say love—can be shown in the brief encounter even if action is trivial and the future empty. The analogy allows Joyce to present the human particulars without emphasis, and we feel the complexity which defeats our categories of success and failure, optimism and pessimism.

The effect is not unique. It is what faces us in *Henry IV* and *Antony and Cleopatra*, in *Middlemarch* and *Wuthering Heights*, where the writer refuses to make moral judgment easy, and where critical response is frequently defeated by confusing artistic ambiguity with human complexity. What is original in *Ulysses* is Joyce's method of confronting us with this complexity. He adopts a formal model, one element of which I have isolated, which can have a loose and arbitrary relation to the human story, an illuminating appropriateness of the kind found in most great novels, and a conspicuous responsibility at the climax. Even the playful appearances of Homeric correspondence have a more than playful function. It is essential for the final effect that the analogy should be sustained to become as habitual and expected as rhythm in poetry, so that it can carry its burden of complex statement.

First published in *Orbis Litterarum*. International Review of Literary Studies, Copenhagen. Vol. XIX, No. 1, 1964.

17. Love and Sympathy in Virginia Woolf

The novel is an affective medium. Not wholly so, because it argues and discusses as well as expressing feeling. Indeed, its mode of inquiry cannot be separated from its expression and manipulation of feeling, since its medium is mixed, conducting experiments and inquiries in ways which are impassioned, personal and particular. Its expression of feeling, conscious and unconscious, personal and social, is controlled and checked by its habits of investigation. It expresses and meets affective needs in author and reader, but also questions the nature and function of the affections. As it creates character, in the forms of symbol or realistic image, it erodes and modifies myths, fictions, and conventions about feeling and passions. In the novels of Virginia Woolf, fictitious characters are equipped with a reflective intelligence which analyses their affective experience; she creates dynamic models of feeling which are experimental and questioning. Like our first novelists of sensibility, Richardson and Sterne, she also uses explicit comment, generalisation, and interrogation. In *Jacob's Room* (1922) for instance, she observes that though we have maps of London, the passions remain uncharted (Ch. VIII).[1] Like her contemporaries, D. H. Lawrence and E. M. Forster, she insists on our ignorance of feeling and passion, and this awareness brings her art close to Lawrence's own declared effort to use fiction to educate the feelings.

She uses the traditional form of the love-story, and like many novelists, rebels against its constrictions and conventions. In her first novels, *The Voyage Out* (1915), *Night and Day* (1919), and *Jacob's Room*, analysis of feeling is expressed through authorial guide and dramatised characters. The guidance comes to be replaced by the analytic drama of characters, which itself becomes more fragmented until it is undermined by the lyricism and self-questioning of *The Waves* (1931), where Bernard's doubts as to whether there can really be 'a story' reinforce the breakdown of narrative patterns of feeling. The seeds of such doubt appear from the start. Even her early characters feel, then mistrust what they feel, alert to puzzles of love and sympathy. They feel, act, meditate, act again, undo action, and make provisional decisions and ties. They reveal, hide, express, suppress, darken, clarify, misunderstand and understand what they are, as feeling creatures. Sometimes they sound the ancient theme—older than the novel—of reason's conflict with passion. They are up against the difficulty of using our inadequate language for feeling—what are these things called love, hate, anger, jealousy and fear? The passions may appear in their traditional guise, calling attention to their nature and function, to question received opinions. Virginia Woolf has special interests within the common stock of human passions. She tells and changes the story of desire, union, and separation, but enlarges this story, seeing romantic and sexual love as aspects of creativity and sympathy. She is especially alert to the influence of social roles in the life of feeling, analysing the emotions of parent and child, mother and father, man and woman.

One of the central themes in her novels is the collision between what we are expected to feel and what we do feel. She conceives characters whose social and sexual self-awareness creates new stereotypes, like Lily Briscoe and Miss La Trobe, artists whose modes of love and sympathy bring new questions and discomforts. She is good at blurring the lines between defined roles, showing unexpected or incongruous motions of feeling, like Lily's blend of aesthetic imagination with reluctant and acculturated 'womanly' sympathy, or Mrs Ramsay's private rebellions against the demands of maternal and wifely love. Her sense of socially determined patterns of feeling seems to lead Virginia Woolf to an awareness of a conscious tension between freedom and determinism. She can catch her characters in the very act of withstanding or succumbing to their roles. Indeed, she can show them catching themselves in the act of feeling more or less than the social role requires. Mrs Ramsay's inner life is seen as larger and vaguer than the social selection and reduction which is on public view. Virginia Woolf is sensitive to the strange stop-go of passion, the instability of the emotional pulse, the irregularity and complexity of loving compared with the regularity and singleness of loving in love-stories. She is alive to the nuances of public appearances and private experiences. She shows how affective roles display themselves, in language and act, as distortedly hard-edged and definite. She is too intelligent not to know and show that patterns of feeling may seem clear and secure and defined at one moment, blurred or dark at the next. The inner life is inspected, dramatised, and scrupulously placed in the environment of external constraints.

Manner and matter are welded together: the artist's mode of presentation is her mode of analysis. She creates characters who question sympathy, and who awaken the reader's sympathy. She promotes various types of aesthetic continuity in her narrative and drama, yet questions the nature of continuity. She uses the traditional tropes of metaphor, metonymy and allegory, to define, fix and excite, in a rhetoric which works on the reader, but is internalised to make visible the generation of feeling.

As the characters act out and act in love-stories, they examine the nature of love. As her artist-characters respond, invent and imagine, they examine the process of perception and making. The methods and materials shift as her art moves through a noviciate into maturity. Her novels examine the nature of feeling in a constantly re-created variety of affective forms.

In her first two novels, *The Voyage Out* and *Night and Day*, Virginia Woolf follows a long tradition of the analysis of love. She inspects conventions and assumptions of feeling, in carefully defined environments of society and nature. In *The Voyage Out* Terence reads a passage from a silly novel, making Rachel ask 'Why don't people write about the things they do feel?' and 'What are the things people do feel?' (Ch. XXII). One of the things people feel in good novels is that they aren't sure what they feel. Stendhal, Thackeray and Hardy raised the question of uncertain, ambiguous, amorphous and malleable feeling, in a social and psychological analysis of individual lives and specified environments. Julien Sorel, Pendennis, Blanche Amory and Eustacia Vye feel that they can change and influence their affective life by taking ambitious thought. Through the characters' efforts, successes and conflicts, their authors unravel a tangled process of moving from feelings which seem sincere or genuine, to feelings which seem illusory, imagined, provisional and assumed. What they recognise and show in these characters, their social contexts and their social movements, is not simply the distortion of the life of feeling. *Le Rouge et le noir*, *Pendennis*, and *The Return of the Native* show that performance and assumption can move an act into reality. These novels brilliantly undermine what may seem a hard-and-fast distinction between sincerity and insincerity. They also contemplate social circumstance. Virginia Woolf's analysis of feeling is not always as radical or as subtle as that of these great predecessors. It is, however, freshly enterprising. She is not a socially innocent novelist, but her social analysis tends to take place in a narrow space, and that space does not expand, like Jane Austen's narrow spaces. When Virginia Woolf looks at conventions and restrictions, they tend to belong to a class rather than a cross-section of society. This is no reason to be ungrateful for what she does, but she is narrower than Stendhal and Thackeray: their great subjects of social movement, class conflict and class aspiration, lie beyond her scope.

She is, however, aware of society's power to restrict and falsify the emotional and erotic relationships of men and women. In *Night and Day* Katharine Hilbery is cleverly placed in a bookish environment, but deprived of conventional literary misdirection. Neither a Catherine Morland nor a Maggie Tulliver, she helps her mother write a biography and takes refuge (not wholly convincingly) in the secret pursuit of mathematics. She is sickened by the great theme of literature, 'that perpetual effort to understand one's own feeling, and express it beautifully, fitly, or energetically in language' (Ch. III). This literary antipathy may act as authorial disguise in a fairly autobiographical novel, but it is not merely a mask. Disliking literature makes Katharine ignorant of what literature might have shown her—a girl who had read more mightn't have been so amazed by the irregular pulse of love. The antipathy makes her so impatient of self-examination that she adopts the most conventional course open to a young woman of her class and time, and gets engaged with a perversity almost worthy of Edith Dombey. (But Katharine is milk and water compared with Edith's fire and ice.) She is so doubtful about love that she decides to do without, until her author puts her in the way of the real thing.

The second stage in her sentimental education is the process of confusion, identification and anxiety. The novel analyses a complex consciousness, for instance, as Katharine only half-listens to the story her lover relates, and infers love from a state of happiness. The narrative rhythm reveals any lapses of feeling, when desire and affection switch off. The characters are perhaps taken too seriously—not comically enough—as they dash round and analyse their erratic rhythms; and as usual in Virginia Woolf, the course of love gets rather oddly, because sexlessly, done. But the novel faces the disconcerting experience of real feeling, as opposed to expected feeling. It puts out tentative antennae into possibilities of new forms of relationship.

The third novel, *Jacob's Room*, is not an analysis of affection and sentiment but takes a place in the history of feeling in fiction because of its delicate and sympathetic understatement. The narrator adopts a tentative, exterior view of her characters, sometimes vouching for their inner lives but usually presenting them as persons to be read, like most people outside novels, from a distance. They are inferred through objects, rooms and houses. The narrator is not 'a character' like Conrad's Marlow, but fully fleshed in feeling, like the narrator in George Eliot's late novels. The commentary is written in a personal voice which speaks only in general terms, like the tones of an autobiographer who can express feeling only without narrative causality. The feeling often emerges from a character's feeling, as in this passage, which is provoked by Clara Durrant's entry in her diary, 'I like Jacob Flanders' (Ch. V), and by several other opinions, indifferent or warm:

> It seems then that men and women are equally at fault. It seems that a profound, impartial, and absolutely just opinion of our fellow-creatures is utterly unknown. Either we are men, or we are women. Either we are cold, or we are sentimental. Either we are young, or growing old. In any case life is but a procession of shadows, and God knows why it is that we embrace them so eagerly, and see them depart with such anguish, being shadows. And why, if this and much more than this is true, why are we yet surprised in the window corner by a sudden vision that the young man in the chair is of all things in the world the most real, the most solid, the best known to us—why indeed? For the moment after we know nothing about him.
>
> Such is the manner of our seeing. Such the conditions of our love. (V.)

Granting the substantial differences between a novel written in

1859 and one written in 1922, this sympathetic narration can be put
beside George Eliot's narrative commentaries. Like them, it speaks
with anonymity, impersonality and authority, on behalf of a
common attitude, in tones of love. Virginia Woolf's commentary is
more melancholy and sceptical than George Eliot's, but at times
there's only a hair's-breadth between them. That hair's-breadth
lies, I think, in Virginia Woolf's disclaimer of full knowledge: here
the narrator gives a conventional bit of dialogue and inner
monologue, and comments that 'though all this may very well be
true—so Jacob thought and spoke—so he crossed his legs . . . there
remains over something which can never be conveyed to a second
person save by Jacob himself' (V.). This is the modern novelist
speaking, admitting not only the fictional nature of the fiction, but
the difficulty of her enterprise. She admits, too, all the things that go
to make up a character, which we can't assess, or don't want to put
in, or must distort:

> Moreover, part of this is not Jacob but Richard Bonamy—the
> room; the market carts; the hour; the very moment of history.
> Then consider the effect of sex—how between man and woman it
> hangs wavy, tremulous, so that here's a valley, there's a peak,
> when in truth, perhaps, all's as flat as my hand. Even the exact
> words get the wrong accent on them. But something is always
> impelling one to hum vibrating, like the hawk moth, at the mouth
> of the cavern of mystery, endowing Jacob Flanders with all sorts
> of qualities he had not at all—for though, certainly, he sat talking
> to Bonamy, half of what he said was too dull to repeat; much
> unintelligible (about unknown people and Parliament); what
> remains is mostly a matter of guess work. Yet over him we hang
> vibrating. (V.)

This passage is typical of her affective medium of narration. Its cool
tones are part of a complex and varied notation, coloured by
appropriate feeling according to the occasion, as in some Victorian
narrative commentaries. Yet the registration of the characters'
feeling is entirely modern. It presses lightly where Dickens and
George Eliot pressed weightily, using understatement, suggestion
and implication. The pity and love of bereavement are whispered.
The novel ends with the mother holding out a pair of Jacob's old
shoes and asking Bonamy, the friend who loved him, 'What am I to
do with these, Mr Bonamy?' (Ch. XIV). The moment vibrates. Its

resonance is created by understatements and undiscerned anticipations, which have brought the war so suddenly upon the characters and the reader, at its end. Jacob goes to war on the penultimate page, and we do not see him go. We only hear the thought of his mother, reported in free indirect style, that her sons are fighting. There is muted report, a fragile object's appeal, a quiet question. The feeling behind the novel is one of compassion and anger, and the novelist has carefully prepared the shock of its ending.

The last page is unlike any Victorian death-scene, but it uses some ancient effects. There is incantatory language and repetition, making the scene lyrical. The motif of the empty room, 'Listless is the air . . .' is repeated and consummated. Feeling is bounced off objects: letters, bills, armchair are resonant. There is a little sympathetic nature: 'leaves seemed to raise themselves'. A casual street-cry is made fully appropriate, 'A harsh and unhappy voice cried something unintelligible.'

Mrs Dalloway (1925) deals in emotional extremities. They are emphasised in the contrast of Clarissa Dalloway with Septimus Warren, where similarities of vitality and goodwill are balanced by dissimilarities of disintegration and harmony. The oscillation of extremes is also present in the narrated track of feeling. Clarissa herself veers from loving to hating, in her feelings about life in general, and in some particular sentiments. For instance, she sees Miss Kilman as a monster when she is absent, because then—as she knows—she is possessed by the power of the idea. In Miss Kilman's presence, the sense of monstrosity dwindles. Virginia Woolf uses the allegory of feeling in order to represent the disconcerting experience of being overpowered by feeling, amazed by the perceived action of the affections. The characters perform their own analysis of feeling, because it is the very experience of division and abstraction which they feel. The allegory is appropriate machinery. Rhetoric and psychological analysis are perfectly matched, for instance, when Clarissa's hatred of Miss Kilman is imaged as a spectre:

> For it was not her one hated but the idea of her, which undoubtedly had gathered in to itself a great deal that was not Miss Kilman; had become one of those spectres with which one battles in the night; one of those spectres who stand astride us

and suck up half our life-blood, dominators and tyrants.. . .
(pp. 14–15)*

Hyperbole is seen in the making. The exaggeration itself creates a
powerful image, lucidly and consistently inflated; the character
feels both a monstrous enlargement of dislike and a rational
awareness of the enlargement. The figure is an objective correlative
of violent passion and a measure of internal reflection and diagnosis.
The defiance and recovery in the 'Nonsense, nonsense' (p. 15)
which follows is characteristic of the character's resolute self-
rejection and resilient grasp of the solid world. It is within Clarissa's
mind that the monsters are made, but she is aware of the occasion
and process of making and can throw off the passion. She can clearly
distinguish between the outer and inner world, and command her
passions. On a later occasion, the process and pattern are repeated,
as Clarissa feels the presence of the monster, less as a personification
of her own feeling than an image of Miss Kilman, 'stand she did,
with the power and taciturnity of some prehistoric monster
armoured for primeval warfare' (p. 139). She loses malignity,
'became second by second merely Miss Kilman, in a mackintosh,
whom Heaven knows Clarissa would have liked to help.' Clarissa
laughs at the dwindling of image and passion. But they can and do
return in full force:

> Love and religion! thought Clarissa, going back into the
> drawing-room, tingling all over. How detestable, how detestable
> they are! For now that the body of Miss Kilman was not before
> her, it overwhelmed her—the idea. The cruellest things in the
> world, she thought, seeing them clumsy, hot, domineering,
> hypocritical, eavesdropping, jealous, infinitely cruel and
> unscrupulous, dressed in a mackintosh coat, on the landing; love
> and religion. (p. 139)

Definition and analysis go together. Here again, the course of
feeling is disconcertingly dramatised, in a quickly-moving
trajectory. Within one paragraph, Clarissa's mood shifts from
hating to caring for the old woman opposite: 'Let her climb', then
back again to hating, 'love and religion would destroy that,
whatever it was, the privacy of the soul. The odious Kilman would

*The novel has no chapter-divisions.

destroy it' (pp. 139–40). Then follows the excellently observed magnetism of strong feeling, as even Peter Walsh is seen as a part of the distasteful passion of love, and rejected too. Virginia Woolf uses the free indirect style to register the pressure and growth of feeling. She tears her characters out of their affective privacy, showing how passion is checked and qualified, as it gathers momentum and material from external sensations and events.

A piercing insight shows the difference between the double motion of Mrs Dalloway's strong feelings, constantly moderated by the outside world, and the disastrously single affective action of Septimus Warren, which transforms that outer world into metaphors for his inner vision:

> But they beckoned; leaves were alive; trees were alive. And the leaves being connected by millions of fibres with his own body, there on the seat, fanned it up and down; when the branch stretched he, too, made that statement. The sparrows fluttering, rising, and falling in jagged fountains were part of the pattern; the white and blue, barred with black branches. (p. 26)

Once more, rhetoric and analysis blend. The heightened and bizarre sensibility of Septimus has the advantage of brilliant vitality and originality, and the danger of distortion and solipsism. The counterpoint of Clarissa and Septimus creates an implicit commentary on the affective life. Two strong sensibilities are contrasted, the one placed and controlled by a sense of the world outside, the other split off from external constraints. And the obsession of Septimus Warren has social implications, in its doctrine of love and peace, its anti-militarism. Its terrible honesty makes a moral plea, especially conspicuous in a novel about the aftermath of the First World War. It also kills him.

If *Night and Day* showed signs of moving the inquiry about feeling into an inquiry about marriage, the later novels do not. They introduce an important new love-theme, the need to rest from negative capability. Love is not shown as tireless. Virginia Woolf provides images and definitions of love which depend on images and definitions of what love is not. Mrs Dalloway's excess of empathy is the other side of Septimus Warren's schizophrenic isolation, and in *To the Lighthouse* (1927) Mrs Ramsay's radical loving of husband, children, friends, must be arrested and allowed to fall back into the darkness of self-repose:

one shrunk, with a sense of solemnity, to being oneself, a wedge-shaped core of darkness . . . this self having shed its attachments was free for the strangest adventures. (The Window, XI)

There is another darkness, too. The vitality and radiance in Virginia Woolf is presented in a melancholy, sometimes hysterical, medium. It makes its presence felt in different ways. In *The Voyage Out* the enquiries of Terence and Rachel are checked; Rachel's eager question, 'tell me about the world' (Ch. XXII) is soon answered. Barbara Bodichon wrote to George Eliot that she found the first part of *Middlemarch* unbearable, because of the sense of what was to come for Dorothea, 'like a child dancing into a quick sand on a sunny morning'.[2] Virginia Woolf's novels have a similar effect, shadowed as they are by death. Even the ones who don't die in the novels, are shown as decidedly mortal. (Not all characters in fiction are.) Their love of life, people, and self, have a special urgency. It is sometimes said that the Victorian preoccupation with death has been replaced by the modern preoccupation with sex, but this is not true of the Georgian novelists.

Abrupt deaths in Virginia Woolf and E. M. Forster give an edge to sentimental history, and both novelists are good at conflating the shock within the novel and the shock without. In the telling of Mrs Ramsay's death, for instance, there is suddenness and foreshortening. The presentation of feeling is not naive; the novelist knows that the reader was brought up to expect deaths in fiction to be signalled by early warnings. Sudden death—in literature alone—is novel, leaving us, like Mr Ramsay, unexpectedly empty-handed.

[Mr. Ramsay stumbling along a passage stretched his arms out one dark morning, but, Mrs. Ramsay having died rather suddenly the night before, he stretched his arms out. They remained empty.] (*To the Lighthouse*, 'Time Passes', III)

Death in *To the Lighthouse* is introduced in the prevailing medium of melancholy, a melancholy present in the quality of the characters' beliefs and feelings, in the incantatory rhythms and images, in the central symbols, and in the very act of understatement. Virginia Woolf does not use simple understatement, and the bereavement is narrated after three pages of intensely imagistic and rhythmical language, introduced by the bridge passage 'Well, we must wait for the future to show', at the beginning of 'Time Passes'.

Five people put out their lights, and disintegration continues in the landscape of night, rain, compounding darkness, winter, storm and destruction. One night's darkness and breakdown is extended into many. The understatement occurs in a heightened and portentous context. Its narrative brevity, its brackets, and its abruptness, link the widower in the book with the reader of the book.

Mr Ramsay is conceived as a very Victorian character, responding conventionally and expecting conventional response. He performs the part of a grief-stricken husband (which he really is) and expects sympathy from Lily Briscoe. The only moment when the novelist leaves his response to his wife's death uncriticised, and accepted as spontaneous as well as genuine, is within the square brackets. They make a brief space for the pang, performed in the stretching out of his arms. (A similar gesture from a widowed husband in *The Years*, is not accepted as sincere: Colonel Pargiter's daughter comments grimly on his self-dramatised exit from the death-bed with arms outstretched and fists clenched.) What is especially interesting in Virginia Woolf's analysis and drama is her recognition of the transcendence of social roles. The sympathy Lily Briscoe feels she should feel for Mr Ramsay is the feeling she knows is demanded by men of women, and provided for men by womanly women like his dead wife. Even as a guest at the Ramsay table, Lily had felt the impulse to do the proper womanly thing by feeding men with interest and sympathy, and the counter-feeling to resist Mrs Ramsay's direction of the love-feast. Lily is Mrs Ramsay's opposite: epicene, independent, professional. She is equipped to question, criticise, appreciate and redefine a woman's protective role, and comments clearly on its attraction and repulsion. Unlike the reader, she has not had access to Mrs Ramsay's inner darkness or to the interruptions and constraints of her love. Lily's commentary, sensitive as it is in its effort to imagine Mrs Ramsay's imagination, simplifies Mrs Ramsay's affective life. Lily sees it only in its public appearances and projections but the reader has larger access, and can see the ironical appropriateness of Mrs Ramsay's apparition, which provides Lily's picture with a wedge-shaped darkness. It was precisely that inner dark which gave Mrs Ramsay strength to give and imagine. It is the necessary darkness of the imagination which these two women share. Mrs Ramsay was less role-determined than Lily knew.

Lily's attempt to do the womanly thing and sympathise with Mr Ramsay is also a parallel to Mrs Ramsay's inability to say 'I love you'. Lily is less unlike Mrs Ramsay than she thinks, both in this inhibition, and in the discovered symbolic language. Mrs Ramsay had thought 'Anything will do,' when looking for an image or anecdote to replace 'I love you' ('The Window', XIX). Lily finds that praising Mr Ramsay's beautiful boots can replace condolences. Mr Ramsay himself accepts the substitute with pleasure, his self-dramatised and indulgent demand falling away into a simple human gratitude for simple human communion. The indirect and understated language of the affections is delicately exhibited and explained.

In her last three novels, *The Waves* (1931), *The Years* (1937) and *Between the Acts* (1940), the analysis of emotion continues, but the subject of love and sympathy becomes displaced by concerns with time, history, mortality, and the breakdown of art and relationship. The novels are pierced with insights into the irregularity and discontinuity of human feeling and the social calls or needs for regularity and continuity. In *Between the Acts* the awkwardness and fragmentariness of the village pageant create a new version of Lily Briscoe's insight into collaborations of art and nature. The comic mooing of the cows fills a gap in art, and provides for the audience within the novel a bizarre continuity which parallels the novel's own emotional continuity. The last important contribution to the analysis of emotion comes in *The Waves*, which like its successors, fights against narrative fullness, development and continuity. Like the novelist, Bernard is always looking for a story but comes to give up the search as artificial, false, and arbitrary. More clearly than the other characters, he mirrors and contemplates the affective life. Two of his insights into feeling express and perhaps explain the novelist's discontent with her analysis. As Bernard mourns the death of Percival, whom he has loved, he explicitly rejects language as an affective register:

'But for pain words are lacking. There should be cries, cracks, fissures, whiteness passing over chintz covers, interference with the sense of time, of space; the sense also of extreme fixity in passing objects; and sounds very remote and then very close; flesh being gashed and blood spurting, a joint suddenly twisted—

beneath all of which appears something very important, yet
remote, to be just held in solitude.' (p. 187)*

He confronts the problem which exists for the person and the artist.
As a human being he has to experience sympathy, and even plans
carefully the time and place: 'Now in this drawing-room he is going
to suffer' (p. 178). Death had 'crashed' into a time of happiness, so
there is a conflict of feeling. Bernard has to carry forward his grief
and love, into 'the first morning he would never see', stating the
need for continuity and change in images which wring sympathy
. out of the reader, 'the sparrows were like toys dangled from a string
by a child' and 'Madonnas and pillars, arches and orange trees, still
as on the first day of creation, but acquainted with grief' (p. 178).
The Biblical echo 'acquainted with grief', makes its point: rhetoric's
traditional generalisations are examined as they are expressed. 'For
pain words are lacking,' is an insight stated in words.

The other powerful example comes earlier where Bernard is
commenting 'in the midst of . . . anguish' on Susan, who makes her
own emotional judgement of emotion in her repeated 'I love; I hate'
and her comment that love and hate are identical. Bernard sees
himself observing and narrating even in agony, dramatising and
inventing a story for Susan in which 'some witless servant could be
heard laughing at the top of the house as she whirred the wheel of
the sewing-machine round and round.' He quotes the snippet of
story, deducing that we are incompletely 'merged in our own
experiences':

'On the outskirts of every agony sits some observant fellow who
points; who whispers as he whispered to me that summer
morning in the house where the corn comes up to the window,
"The willow grows on the turf by the river. The gardeners sweep
with great brooms and the lady sits writing." Thus he directed
me to that which is beyond and outside our own predicament; to
that which is symbolic, and thus perhaps permanent, if there is
any permanence in our sleeping, eating, breathing, so animal, so
spiritual and tumultuous lives.' (p. 176)

The analysis blends image and commentary, marking flux, the
attempt to wrest moments from flux, and the awareness of the
attempt. Like the novelist, Bernard sees that there is always the

*The novel has no chapter-divisions.

'fringe of intelligence' which catches those undifferentiated materials on which art works. The unwinnable race between form and material, order and disorder, past and present, emerges as a major theme in the last novels. Bernard's statement of his grief and sympathy, undercut by the very act of analysis, at once expresses and analyses a truth about love and imagination.

Virginia Woolf is engaged in a continual debate which is reflected in the interior debates of her characters. Their puzzles and interpretations are impolite beneath a facade of politeness. The sense of an indeterminate world redeemed only by fellow-feeling, is persistent. And the feelings which redeem are themselves scrupulously subjected to doubt, attack and qualification, through rigours and nuances of imaginative essays.

First published in *The Uses of Fiction. Essays on the Modern Novel in Honour of Arnold Kettle*, ed. D. Jefferson and G. Martin (Open University Press, Milton Keynes 1982).

Notes

1. The text of quotations from the novels of Virginia Woolf is from the Uniform Edition published by The Hogarth Press London.
2. *The George Eliot Letters*, ed. Gordon S. Haight (Yale University Press, 1978), Vol. IX, p. 34.

18. A Note on Mrs Ramsay's Stews and Stockings

Virginia Woolf's Mrs Ramsay in *To The Lighthouse* is compounded of the love, impatience, reproach and guilt we feel for our mothers. She is designed to disarm feminist criticism by having the epicene Lily Briscoe as her satellite, convert, and mild critic. Lily reduces maternity to a dark patch in an abstract painting, but is romantically grateful to Mrs Ramsay's unreconstructed ghost for coming back to sit and solve yet another problem by motherly magic. When we begin to feel strangled by her tentacular affections, her daughter-author cleverly decomposes her maternal role, dissolving her into the splendid darkness of the unconditional where we can't criticise her for bossiness and sexism. She matronises the artist, the servants, her husband's lower-class graduate student, and all the unmarried. But the guards are up. If we dislike the way she tells people to open their windows, there's the Swiss maid who has healthy Swiss habits and leaves hers open. If we are repelled by her match-making, so is she sometimes, in ironic flashes, and her author carefully makes the match disastrous. (If only she read *Emma* instead of Shakespeare's sonnets.) She tells her daughters not to laugh at Tansley's ties, but is insufferably Lady Bountiful when she lets him go sick-visiting with her. She's fifty but beautiful, collecting good marks for a whole cluster of doubtfully privileging merits, aesthetic, social, moral. She infantilises her husband and brings up her daughters for marriage.

She's a domestic fraud, getting credit for being able to afford a cook and inherit recipes, but having odd ideas about that *Boeuf en Daube*, which must not be kept waiting. 'The beef, the bayleaf and the wine—all must be done to a turn'. If only it had been a soufflé.

Even less plausible than her stews is the stocking she knits for the lighthouse keeper's son. Erich Auerbach, in his famous book *Mimesis*, converted this brown woollen stocking into a sacred object in fiction and a holy writ in criticism, but did not observe its singular nature. Had she finished the other stocking, she would have measured the unfinished one against it, not needing James's reluctant leg. But had she not, no wonder she was worried about getting them both done in time for the morning expedition, without a knitting machine. (So much for Mimesis, neglected by the character, the novelist, and the theorist of realism.) (If the lighthouse-keeper's son had had only one leg, Mrs Ramsay's compassionate sensibility would have bled.) She has the makings of a great slut, but her feminist daughter was too eager to create a subtle apotheosis for the mother-figure and missed her chance. Worst of all, she comes off, one of the most irritating successes in modern fiction.

This first appeared in *The Fiction Magazine*, January/February 1987.

19. Form in Joyce Cary's Novels

It is no coincidence that two novelists of this century whose popularity may be called both highbrow and middlebrow[1]— Graham Greene and Joyce Cary—have attempted the same kind of experiment. They have both made a transformation of a popular genre, a transformation which their admirers may greet as making the best of two worlds and their detractors as a fall between two stools. Graham Greene's adoption of the thriller is at once more obvious and more self-conscious than Joyce Cary's adoption of the less lively but no less popular form of the pseudo-saga, the chronicle of family life. One does not have to exaggerate Cary's talent in order to recognise the order he has restored to a shapeless literary tradition.

The popularity of the endless shapeless serials of Galsworthy, Walpole and, to go a little lower, Mazo de la Roche, is as mysterious as it is certain. The formula is simple and unvaried: birth, love and death, and in all their less interesting aspects. Marriages are made, babies born, there is some allowed variety in the way of litigation, adultery and house-building, the babies grow up, marry, build, beget and die. The saga itself does not die, and it is its immortality, I suppose, which gives it the attraction of a specious realism. The kind of imagination which feels the need to pursue Beatrice and Benedick beyond the formal inevitability of their curtain has the repeated reassurance of a curtain which rises again and again. The kind of life which needs a substitute or a compensation for living has the satisfaction of a continued accompaniment almost as long as life itself. And to these extra-aesthetic pleasures is added the esoteric delight of recognising familiar faces. The minor characters of one novel reappear as the heroes and heroines of another, not independently and reticently as in Zola, but often accompanied by baffling references to their earlier incarnations or, worse, by ill-disguised exposition of the past. What is a minor pleasure in reading Balzac, Zola and Thackeray where the recurring characters are an essential part of a creation of a world with the realism of flux and diversity, becomes a major pleasure or a major distraction in Trollope and Galsworthy and all the less distinguished others who have helped to demonstrate the truth that where there is no form there is indeed no reason why there should ever be an end. This is the death of naturalism, the disappearance of the curtain.

Galsworthy, of course, is making an attempt to do something as serious as Balzac or Zola, but his portrait of a social organism, growing, changing, inheriting, decaying, enduring, fails where Zola's succeeds because it puts an impossible weight on the external life. The attempt to shift the emphasis from the individual to the group seems to have been most successful where it has given a balanced prominence to individual sensibility and the distanced view of social process. The mere act of repetition from novel to novel is far less convincing as it is forced to bear the thematic burden in Galsworthy than the much less pretentious portrayal of family life in Ivy Compton-Burnett where a single novel can convince us of the life of a group: of the moral insulation of a family which can absorb the individual evil within itself. The serial of family life tries to substitute accumulation for symbolism and the game is hardly worth the candle.

The importance of length in the novel is certainly not a thing to be ignored, and the serial-sagas are attempts to compensate for the lack of distance which is so often the fault of the compression of many generations into one story. Even Virginia Woolf's *The Years* suffers from jerkiness and overdistancing and in Rose Macaulay's *Told By An Idiot* or Margery Allingham's *Dance of The Years* there is the maddening sketchiness of the bird's eye view without Virginia Woolf's compensating flashes of perception. The compressed saga depends on a reversal of the telescope. We never see enough of the characters to be sufficiently moved or involved. The slowly unrolled saga gives us time to be involved but, except for rare cases, has no form and therefore no significance. These two flaws of overdistancing and shapelessness are not inherent in the attempt to show the process of history or the social organism. *War and Peace* and *Middlemarch*, in their different ways, combine the microscopic view of the human heart with the larger view of a community or a country. *Ulysses* moves from the flux of the mind to the flux of the Dublin crowd—the individual sensation is laid bare and then merged in the anonymity of the city. But Joyce Cary, a minor talent to be mentioned in the same breath as these three, treats the historical process in a way which is worth some mention.

Cary, like Galsworthy, sets out to show the flow of a family's life, but he has the initial advantage of a more assertive theme. In his most successful novels he has his eye not on the family but on the age. The conflicts, losses and gains of social change are criticised as they are chronicled, and the criticism is made directly through character and obliquely through form. The age is represented by a generation, the generation by two or more characters. Cary's representative characters are usually repeated and reinforced like Marlowe's and Jonson's humours, but they represent tendencies and not, like Zola's, varying social experience. As units of a social survey these repeated characters present too limited a vitality to make a carrying social symbol, but if we recognise the validity of an expression of opinion which does not pretend to be a complete document they make their point.

Cary's power of spawning characters has often been praised, rather oddly, for there is not a great deal of variety in his persons, either within single novels or in his work considered as a whole. One kind of sensibility is made to work overtime in Cary's novels and this is presented in terms of his visual preoccupation which enables him to show a crowd without losing the sense of the single lives which make up crowds. In some of his books, *Castle Corner* or *A Fearful Joy* for instance, vitality is not presented as a painter's joy of the eye but as a child's or a woman's joy in the living moment, but the evidence and method which establish the vitality is almost always visual. In these novels the sensibility gives life to a not greatly varied world—the lack of variety is perhaps unimportant, and I should not mention it if it had not been praised as the opposite of what it is. It is the dominant sensibility which gives order and simplicity to the novel, though in *Aissa Saved* and *An African Witch* it is not enough to triumph over a crowded and episodic form. But at his best—in *To Be A Pilgrim, The Horse's Mouth,* and *The Moon- light* there is not merely a painter's vision but the power of organising the shifting life of pictures and conversations into a formal order which is both aesthetically pleasing and morally significant.

To Be A Pilgrim and *The Moonlight* share a theme and a pattern. In each book there is the conflict of human relations which have some socially representative force, and in each the action is carried on in counterpoint. Cary is showing the flow of generations not consecutively but contemporaneously, and thereby gains in compression, shape and thematic clarity. This formal transformation of the traditional saga is brought about by the use of another literary tradition, and not by experiment. Cary takes the flashback, the most overworked cliché, in the film and the novel, and uses it realistically and functionally.

It is true that conventions do not need the excuse of realism, but the flashback is a necessity rather than a convention in Cary. It is the only way of making a certain statement. Wilcher in *To Be A Pilgrim*, and Ella in *The Moonlight*, must be presented in flashback. Their life is the life they have lived rather than the life they are living. They participate in the past and look on in the present. The pattern of the novel is the intersection and interruption of past and present, the theme a fight between past and present.

The significance of the pattern is the significance it gives to the material it forms. If it is accompanied here by too much explicit reference to make it comparable in any fundamental sense to the suggestive accumulation of contrapuntal action in *Anna Karenina* and *Middlemarch* there is the same kind of assertive pattern left in the memory. All four novels have individual form, order as rigid and simple as that of a triangle, and as individual as a human face. It seems that novels need not have this formal assertion—it is an extra, though not a superfluous, pleasure of fiction.

Cary's world in these novels is small, and his use of form fairly simple. He is an excellent example of a writer as interested in form as the painter or musician, and it may be the influence of his painting which makes this conspicuous pattern-making. He seems to look on single characters and events with that double vision with which Jimson looks at his Adam and Eve. They are expressions of humanity: Eve leans away from Adam to fend off his first pass. They are also units in a pattern: Eve leans back because the composition demands it.

The counterpoint in *To Be A Pilgrim* and *The Moonlight* is obviously a source of psychological realism. It gives the characters that three-dimensional solidity which Cary hoped to create in the trilogy—*Herself Surprised*, *To Be A Pilgrim* and *The Horse's*

Mouth—by showing the characters as they see themselves and as they see each other, as he explains in the prefatory essay to *Herself Surprised*. In practice, as he admits, this did not come off. Cary thinks that his plan may have failed because it imposed on Sara a consciousness of art and history which would have diluted her character, a consciousness which might be reconcilable with her character in reality but not in the limited world of the novel. But there is, I think, another reason for this failure.

When a major character in one action becomes a minor character in another he becomes an entirely different character. He may retain the given 'characteristics' but he changes his relation to the reader. Such a shift can perhaps be workable only within one novel, as it is in *Middlemarch*, where it has many critical functions, or within one play, as in Shakespeare's romantic comedies where both unity and parody are achieved by the use of the major characters in the romance as the minor characters in the comedy, and *vice versa*. Where the change takes place between books it is more difficult for the reader to retain the relationship with the central character, and this relationship is particularly intimate in Cary because of his use of first-person soliloquy and the more immediate stream of consciousness. C. P. Snow maintains his constant narrator as his actions shift but even so I doubt whether the reader can read more than one novel at a time. Both Cary and Snow seem to expect there to be more of a carry-over from one novel to the next than the formal completion of a good novel—not to mention lapse of time and shortage of memory—can permit. It may be that the novelist gains from a sustained but shifting exploration of a single world but the reader, for practical aesthetic purposes, has to read one book at a time.

The solidity which Cary hoped to achieve by the relation between the three novels of his trilogy has been achieved in a different way by the internal formal relations of the novels. The critical counterpoint, like Huxley's jugglings with time in *Eyeless in Gaza*, gives us ironical portraiture. Personality is seen as growth and as constancy. The doddering old man who misbehaves in parks was once an uncertain child, once an excited innocent wondering how one set about getting a mistress. And the reader sees them all at the same time. Both in Wilcher and in Ella continuity is given more emphasis than change. Age is only youth in a different body.

Indeed, age is often younger than youth in Cary's novels. The old man watches Ann, his niece, the old woman watches Amanda, her illegitimate daughter, and their critical interference with the lives of the young is explained less by their own comments than by the silent commentary of their own interrupting youth. And not only Wilcher and Ella, but Ann and Amanda too are given definition and dimension by the novel's pattern. Their unsatisfactory loves, occupying months where the remembered past in the flashback occupies decades, are seen in ironical contrast with the flux of years. This time-scale has almost a symbolic function for while the new generation drifts and vacillates (desires and acts not, and breeds pestilence) the older generation, presented only at moments of selected crisis, is rushing with gusto through the cycle of birth, copulation and death.

The critical pattern is not merely the contrast between the slow day and the rapid years, between selected excitement and naturalistically displayed triviality. The counterpoint makes the criticism. The presence of the ghosts defines the living. The real action is not the attempt of the aged to force the past on to the young, nor Ann's pathetic imitation of the past, nor Amanda's dispassionate attempt to place herself in situations where circumstance will take the place of desire. Nor is it in their relations with Robert and Harry, two versions of Cary's almost Lawrencian farmer-hero whose lack of cerebral activity contrasts with the heroine's disastrous cerebral excess, and whose gross vigour contrasts, with shifting significance, with the departed grace and grandeur of the past. This is the stuff of the plot but the real action is the oblique criticism of the present by the past. What the present lacks, vitality, passion, grace, the past is shown to possess. Love, seduction, marriage, maternity, all are shown in past and present, the circumstances similar but the actors different. Again Cary provokes the comparison with *Middlemarch* where contrasts and parallels between persons and actions do much of the work of definition, and, more important, of judgement.

Cary is not a George Eliot and he sometimes makes judgement too explicit. Past and present show up each other's light and shade in a moving dance, but since the past is presented as memory it is hard for Cary to avoid explicit comparison. The pattern could say it all but since the past is contributed by Wilcher's memory, and since Wilcher, unlike Sara, is given the intelligence and the experience which can carry the weight of historical consciousness, his direct criticism is constantly supplementing the oblique comments of the juxtaposed actions. This is not true of *The Moonlight* for here there is no fixed *point d'oeil* and the reader does not receive criticism and impression through the sieve of an intelligent mind. And his use of a not particularly intelligent woman instead of an intelligent man has two advantages: there is a closer contrast with the heroine of the present, and there is no character within the novel who is in danger of drawing the reader's conclusions for him.

But in both novels there is yet another method of making the critical point, and this method is an obvious product of Cary's interest in painting. This is his brilliant use of scenic contrast, though once more he sometimes seems to err on the side of explicitness. He can make an almost symbolic use of scenes which are in the same contrapuntal relation as that in which the two actions are presented; as in *To Be A Pilgrim*, where Ann and Robert and the farm-girl carry patched lanterns to the mended boat on the lake which has shrunk to a pond and are faded-out while Wilcher's memory restores the grandeur and glitter of light, bowers, crowds and music which was the past they are trying to imitate. And he can turn to the facile symbolism of the threshing in the Adam room. Such scenes make just the visual point which the camera can make but in the novel it is extremely hard to make them direct, without annotation. It is only fair to say that if Cary's theme were cruder his visual symbols might seem more subtle. For his interpretation of the scenic symbol is often a modification. It is no simple measuring of bad new days by good old ones and he hastens to blur the simple boldness of the visual contrast. Perhaps the old grandeur, thinks Wilcher, was only another kind of make-believe. The water-parties and the crumbling Adam room cannot be left as suggestive scenes. Wilcher is made to accept the present, to accept the thresher's vigour and destruction.

The Horse's Mouth, like *To Be A Pilgrim*, has a similarly articulate mouthpiece, who is at times too explanatory, who puts the unnecessary words in the balloons when the picture has already said it all. It has a similar use of scenic symbol. The painting of Jimson's *Creation* on the chapel wall which is being demolished by order of the local authority sounds stagey when extracted from its context but it is, like the sonata in *The Moonlight* which becomes the expression of romance and passion, a private symbol, having accumulated its significance internally and gradually. Symbol is indeed a word I use with reluctance since Cary's symbols are not literary symbols, not imposed on the characters by the novelist, but are made by the characters out of the stuff of their living and working. The huge picture on the crumbling wall is too literally expressive of the fight of a man and an institution to be called a symbol. The wall and the Moonlight sonata are only symbols in the sense in which a gun is a symbol of death. They are symbols in so far as they are agents. But unlike the gun they have validity and intelligibility only within the novel. They are too particularised to be called symbols.

The crumbling wall-painting is only the sign of Jimson's vitality (he has desire and acts) and of that conflict which is the theme of *The Horse's Mouth*. Like *Mister Johnson*, the best of the African novels, and *Charley Is My Darling*, this book is about creative power and creative lawlessness. The emphasis varies. Mister Johnson is cheat first and poet after, Jimson is painter first and lawbreaker after, and Charley is both juvenile delinquent and infant prodigy. The characteristics are constant though the proportions vary. Johnson, Charley and Jimson all create, all destroy, and all have power, a power which is less the product of genius or courage or lawlessness than of vitality. Vitality was what Ann and Amanda lacked, and if we reduce the themes to the common element, this is it. What interests the novelist's imagination, Cary says in the preface to *Aissa Saved* is whatever makes man tick. His novels are not only dissections of some of the causes of human ticking—love, religion, politics, art—but are revelations of the nature of this ticking. Its intensity he demonstrates by showing us the Anns and Amandas whose vitality is missing.

Mister Johnson and *Charley Is My Darling* are portraits rather than pictures. *The Horse's Mouth* is both. Here Cary shows Jimson's ticking by a formal contrast very like that used in his chronicle novels. Once more the formal arrangement is carried out by an experimental use of someone else's experiment. What the revived cliché of the flashback does for *To Be A Pilgrim* the stream of consciousness or interior monologue does for *The Horse's Mouth*.

One of the excitements of *Ulysses* is the intersection of perception and action. Stephen and Bloom are shown in the normal human state of interrupted consciousness. Eye interrupts eye, memory interrupts experience and friends and strangers force human intercourse and interrupt the private drift of thought and sensation.

Most novelists have assumed, as a necessary selective premise, that the life of their characters shall be an unrealistic cooperation of perception of life and participation in life. Cary, following Joyce and Virginia Woolf, accepts and emphasises the interruption and bittiness of life. Once more he has a double purpose. Jimson's interrupted consciousness creates a personality and a thematic pattern.

Jimson's vitality, his genius and his lawlessness put him in conflict with the law, with institutionalised man, with the Philistines who hate him and the admirers who love him at the wrong period or for the wrong reason. Like Wilcher he is intelligent and perceptive and acts as a sieve which deprives the reader of some of the pleasure of breaking the lumps for himself. Cary's direct method is too direct. But oddly enough it is once more employed with the oblique method. The interior monologue tells but it also shows. The monologue, or visual stream, provides an indirect expression of Cary's recurring theme of conflict, for the extractable plot is counterpointed, not against another plot, as in *To Be A Pilgirm* and *The Horse's Mouth*, but against Jimson's visual preoccupation. Everything which 'happens'—Coker's attempt to get him to pay the money he owes her, the return of Sara, the occupation of the millionaire's flat by Jimson and the sculptor, Jimson's flight—all this is superimposed on the visual stream, whether this is Jimson's concern with the picture in hand or his perpetual falling in love with clouds, bits of body, spilt coffee or anything which makes pattern and colour. Everything in the book which is outside this visual preoccupation is made to define it. The story of the deaf girl is translated into form and colour, and things which defy translation point the struggle. Jimson is a character who is struggling against all the other characters, and the human struggle is narrated by the formal conflict between the stream of perception and the life of dialogue and action. It is a book which is a series of significant interruptions of character by character, of monologue by dialogue, of imagery by incident. It does not do to say that Cary is a painter writing novels; it is musical analogy which seems more relevant than any other. It is the shaping of theme and character which states and proves visual sensibility, conflict, energy and change. The organic shaping is the thing which gives to the best of his novels the rare enough aesthetic pleasure of assertive form.

Cary's last novels, *A Fearful Joy* and *A Prisoner of Grace*, seem to show the dangers of suggesting that he is preoccupied with form. *A Fearful Joy* has a naive enough structure of continuous flow. Past and present are there in two separate blocks since the point is less the life of past in present than the death of the past. *A Prisoner of Grace* has no formal assertion at all. Both novels, like *Herself Surprised*, are studies of the power and vitality of women, a power whose mystery and innocence he sentimentalises. But like *Charley Is My Darling*, they are not novels which force a pattern of conflict. The themes, more complex than I have suggested since they are also concerned with the innocent maker and spectator of history, demand and get a simple almost lyrical treatment. The only disadvantage of this in Cary is that it draws attention to the sameness of the human existence he is studying. The causes vary but the vitality and the consciousness do not.

The important thing is the absence of formal assertion, an absence which does not destroy so much as draw attention to a deficiency. It is not a deficiency which concerns me here, and I do not want to suggest that form is the life of fiction. Some novelists seem to need the pressure of forming a complex pattern. Others do not. Some themes force a conspicuous pattern, some do not. Cary's form-making is expressive in so far as it is necessitated by his theme of historical process. This has an inevitable emphasis of change and conflict and an equally inevitable shift from individual to environment, and it forces a formal correlative, but it is not the powerful thematic assertion of the counterpoint of *Anna Karenina* and *Daniel Deronda* where the shape of the narrative makes a statement which the characters are too blind to make and the novelist too reticent. This is not to belittle Cary's achievement, merely to attempt to put it in perspective, and, since analysis seems more important than judgement, to discriminate between two very different uses of form. Perhaps the most significant thing is the recurrence, in great and minor talents, of a double aspiration of narrative, the aspiration towards the free life and flux of reality and the aspiration towards a formal order which has fixity and clarity.

First published in *Essays in Criticism*, April 1954.

Note

1.   I no longer think this is true, but it seemed so thirty years ago. The
      words 'highbrow' and 'middlebrow' are as dated as my judgement.

20. The Dubious Consolations of Samuel Beckett

Beckett's people are not so unlike the rest of us as to fail to look for solaces of various kinds in art, love and nature. What these solaces may be, and to what extent they sustain the mind, to what extent deepen its suffering, are subjects upon which Beckett is intent. His world is an extraordinary one, but not so remote from other human worlds as to lack these sources of sustenance. Art, love and nature are sources of meaning, and sources of pleasure, though meanings and pleasures are frail, transient, scarred, scotched and annihilated in Beckett's fiction. Even though and even as they disappear or are discredited, these so-called solaces give his strange world a familiar density.

I

In a few of Beckett's stories love has diminished to dream or doubtful memory, and in others the habitable universe gives way to an invented construction. In those, such as *Imagination Dead Imagine*, *Ping*, or *The Lost Ones*, art is always present, a subject as well as a medium. Beckett's art is an unflaggingly self-reflective activity, and the arts he is chiefly concerned with are theatrical and literary. His plays dramatise and discuss dramatic forms like dialogue, entertainment, scenes, continuous action, performance, exposition, and final curtains. Just as *Waiting for Godot* strangled such theatrical conventions as continuity and conclusion, so some of the novels and stories attack the narrative convention of autonomy, completeness and steady action. His fiction is concerned with its own genre, of narrative. It illustrates and inspects the need and nature of storytelling, in many forms and guises, and tests the bare possibility of doing and going without. Plays and stories push their genre as far as possible in the direction of self-destruction, of silence and inactivity, partly out of sheer imaginative zeal and curiosity, partly in admission of defeat, partly as preparation for dying. They also take a close look at forms, conventions and language.

Towards the end of *The Unnamable*, Beckett's most taxing long narrative, the narrator is trying hard to do without story in order to be his naked, silent self. As he struggles he ponders what fiction can teach us about emotion and reason. After the narrator has for a little while managed to escape his narrative function and to meditate on silence, doing without the narrative elements of 'a little nature, and a few names, and the outside of men', he lapses into narration. He does so reluctantly, and involuntarily, pushed as usual by forces beyond his control, and it is typical of Beckett that he should in the same breath demonstrate unconscious pressures and efficiently produce a narrative exemplum. We are presented with a story-lesson.

The story is almost but not quite an anecdote. It is a kind of narrative skeleton, an outline with four unnamed characters, space, time and objects. The history is a sketch, compressed into one long sentence, but allowing for visible improvisation as it develops, prolongs itself, and manages with elasticity and wisdom to contain not only narrative but analysis of narrative, as Beckett's longer stories always do. Each breathless and rushed narration of event is accompanied by an inference about emotion, and eventually by an inference about rational inference. It moves fast, and also slowly. We are told what happens, then why it happened. We are told what is happening to the characters, what is happening to the narrator/listener, and why events and characters are what they have been seen to become in the course of the narrative:

They love each other, marry, in order to love each other better, more conveniently, he goes to the wars, he dies at the wars, she weeps, with emotion, at having loved him, at having lost him, yep, marries again, in order to love again, more conveniently again, they love each other, you love as many times as necessary, as necessary in order to be happy, he comes back, the other comes back, from the wars, he didn't die at the wars after all, she goes to the station, to meet him, he dies in the train, of emotion, at the thought of seeing her again, having her again, she weeps, weeps

again, with emotion again, at having lost him again, yep, goes
back to the house, he's dead, the other is dead, the mother-in-law
takes him down, he hanged himself, with emotion, at the thought
of losing her, she weeps, weeps louder, at having loved him, at
having lost him, there's a story for you, that was to teach me the
nature of emotion, that's called emotion, what emotion can do,
given favourable conditions, what love can do, well well, so that's
emotion. . . . (*The Unnamable* p. 410)[1]*

It is a stunning piece of controlled and compressed lyricism,
irony and analysis, a model of inching and speeding. Self-
consciousness comes along to shake, scrutinise and question a story
that has appeared out of nowhere, apparently to break the silence, to
raise once more, most crucially, the problem of narrative needs and
urgencies. The continuous inferences, and the two violently
clinching affirmative 'yeps' mark off, underline, structure, frame,
punctuate, revise and criticise the happenings. They mark off,
underline, structure, frame, revise and criticise the structures and
revisions. The self-analysis is perfectly compatible with vivacity, is
indeed part of that vivacity, not a burden it carries. The brutal
reduction of story is perhaps intended, so the narrator thinks, to
remind him of the old world of fable, though actually it doesn't
remind him of anything. But as he shows in his admissions and
explanations of irony and compassion, he feels its impact. The story
high handedly breaks a rule of emotional writing, stating abstractly
instead of simply dramatising emotional cause and effect. But
feeling is dramatised as well as summarised: the writer's, the
listener's and the reader's feelings are breathed out pantingly, the
namings and inferences and generalisations. My god, yes, it
breathes, breathlessly, that is what we do in order to be happy, this
is love, yes, it is repeatable, we even do these things over and over
again. The little fable about falling between two stools dares us to
laugh, forces its irony gaspingly upon us, so that we can't smile or
sneer for gasping:

well well, so that's emotion, that's love, and trains, the nature of
trains, and the meaning of your back to the engine, and guards,
stations, platforms, wars, love, heart-rending cries, that must be
the mother-in-law, her cries rend the heart as she takes down her

*The novel has no chapter-divisions.

son, or her son-in-law, I don't know, it must be her son, since she cries, and the door, the house-door is bolted, when she got back from the station she found the house-door bolted, who bolted it, he the better to hang himself, or the mother-in-law the better to take him down, or to prevent her daughter-in-law from re-entering the premises, there's a story for you, it must the daughter-in-law, it isn't the son-in-law and the daughter, it's the daughter-in-law and the son, how I reason to be sure this evening, it was to teach me how to reason, it was to tempt me to go, to the place where you can come to an end, I must have been a good pupil up to a point, I couldn't get beyond a certain point, I can understand their annoyance, this evening I begin to understand, oh there's no danger, it's not I, it wasn't I, the door, it's the door interests me, a wooden door, who bolted the door, and for what purpose, I'll never know, there's a story for you, I thought they were over, perhaps it's a new one, lepping fresh, is it the return to the world of fable, no, just a reminder, to make me regret what I have lost, long to be again in the place I was banished from, unfortunately it doesn't remind me of anything.
(pp. 410–11)

This last story, like so many, is being told and also heard, apparently at the same time, so that the provisional status of the bolted door and the in-laws speaks of the nature of invention and the ignorance of the narrator/listener. I'm not sure whether the 'lepping fresh' is a bonus for attentive readers who will, unlike the narrator, remember a moment in the old world of Beckett's fables, when Belacqua in 'Dante and the Lobster' (*More Pricks Than Kicks*) didn't understand the fishmonger's use of the epithet 'lepping' to describe the lobster's freshness (though he came to understand all too clearly by the end of the story). The self-consciousness is witty and ramifying, fulfilling the earlier description, just before the mediation on silence of 'just one thing more, just one space and someone within', a laconic but accurate forecast of the house with only one loving somebody in it. Its constant self-checking not only makes the irony, but also draws attention to the procedures of reasoning, the interest in objects (especially door, so important at the very end of *The Unnamable*), and the refusal to stick with generalisation.

If we learn about emotion we are also learning about 'trains, the nature of trains, and the meaning of your back to the engine, and guards, stations, platforms, wars, love, heart-rending cries', the meaning of the particulars as well as the generalisations, of the persons, journeys, objects and emotional utterances. The self-analysis makes a seemingly random survey of the main narrative elements of symbol, surface, particularity and themes. The sad and ludicrous self-destructiveness of the passions is certainly instructively set out in this special piece for a special occasion, of terminus, frustrated silence, minimalism. It is a story which is in a hurry to get itself told, because he wants to get it and the whole business of narrative over and done with, yet knows he has to be patient too.

As usual there is some light in the story, things which are entirely lucid, and some darkness, things which aren't certain and have to be teased out. In an odd and admirable way, it is slightly self-preening. Odd, because we are put off by what admires itself. Admirable, because the almost throw-away pace and comment imply self-deprecation. It is after all a reduced telegraphic refusal to be sentimental, using that breathless, fast, and laconic style which expresses ruthless salesmanship in Dicken's Jingle and sharp, quick, fond imagination in Joyce's Bloom. The speed not only suggests the narrator's wish to be done with it, but also shows the story and its meaning being lapped up, with a wit that commands and ensures a further quick response on the part of the reader outside the novel. Though Beckett's insistence on the narrator as listener, on his provisionalities, dilapidations and reluctance, all make the reader of Beckett probably less outside than he usually is—Beckett blurs the aesthetic borders. He ought to make it impossible for critics ever again to use the terms reliable or unreliable narrator, without smiling. Of course all narrators are unreliable. If we didn't know it before, we know it after reading Beckett.

The story is apparently thrown away so as to be more candid, more startlingly eloquent. But it is a story, wrung from the narrator just as he begins to think he may have got clear of the obligation to tell stories out of a need to find or lose identity and meaning. An impatience with story betrayed itself in *More Pricks Than Kicks*, most Joycean of Beckett's books, in the uses and criticisms of Dante, Shakespeare and various literary modes of description and narration. Elaborated in *Watt*, it finds its most thoroughgoing expression in the trilogy. Molloy only wants to say goodbye, to 'finish dying' but is forced reluctantly to write his story, even though the writing doesn't work so well any more. He is pretty good-tempered about it, 'I began at the beginning, like an old ballocks, can you imagine that?' Moran is much less good-tempered and open for most of his story, and sulkily remarks that he has to submit to 'petty scrivening'. But he rather quickly starts imagining a time when he may be reconciled to the writing, and may even be helped to endure pain by the 'memory of this work brought scrupulously to a close'. Malone is less passive and more prolific than Malloy or Moran. The reader had to piece together the oddly related, interconfused and ambiguous narratives of Molloy and Moran, but Malone's impatience with continuous story is under his own control, as he shows in his brilliant device of stopping and starting, planning, doing, and undoing, naming, unnaming, and renaming. The problems of all three earlier narrators are included and exacerbated in the situation of the narrator of *The Unnamable*, who pushes even further those problems of meaning and progression, which are at once epistemological and novelistic. Story, plot, action, actions, character, relationships are provided but broken down, by a mind like the one which its owner describes in *From an Abandoned Work* as 'always on the alert against itself'. There is no doubt that such breakages convey depression and despair with terrifying success. There is also no doubt that the attacks on art derive from artistic zest and power. There have, after all, been plenty of instances of genuine silence in literature, brought about in many ways. The mind that keeps on attacking literature also loves it, can't stay away from the page and pencil, must go on. It is necessary to recognise the versatility of Beckett's dilapidations. Story is pitted against story, character against character, word against word, and the result is a virtuoso proliferation of the literary acts. We get more not less and a new kind of narrative, in which the actual act of writing, failed or successful, becomes action and theme.

Successful narration is brilliantly apparent in the long narratives, particularly *Watt*, the second and third pieces in the trilogy, and *How It Is*. But he does of course offer also failures, stories that haven't developed or exfoliated. *Molloy* seems to be a contribution to the theme of failure. I see *From an Abandoned Work*, *Imagination Dead Imagine*, and *Ping* as limbs or cell-clusters from ravaged, diseased or deficient longer works. *Imagination Dead Imagine* and *Ping* seem to stop because they are attempting something inhuman, something done from the outside, breaking off or breaking down because humankind can't bear so little story, so little character, so little action, so little time and so little space. The extraordinary, static and careful descriptions of these two fragments seem almost to do what Alain Robbe-Grillet keeps requesting the novel to do, while failing to do it himself, namely, to render the visible world without subjectivity. Beckett properly recognises this aim as an imaginative impossibility, which would show imaginative failure, not success. The description of the human pair in *Imagination Dead Imagine* and of the man in *Ping* are so close to being exclusively visual that they eventually convey a painful confinement of the object by and in the medium. But the couple in *Imagination Dead Imagine* are at last allowed to share with the narrator and reader the complicity of 'the infinitesimal shudder instantaneously suppressed' and of the valedictory adjectives 'sweating and icy'. The restriction of sight in *Ping*, associated and conveyed through our own different but similar restriction, is also eloquent of pain. These two pieces seem to confront Robbe-Grillet with the suggestion that to confine narrative to what the eye sees is appropriate only for the description of confinement, and to recognise confinement is, humanly speaking, to express pity. Beckett always speaks humanly.

From an Abandoned Work does not quite imagine the death of imagination. It seems to be an abandonment of something that really could have gone on, or still goes on. Its narrative vivacity is a fine instance of Beckett's self-reflection. As usual, he gets there before his critics, and this fragment illustrates not only the painfulness of the reflective process, which shows the medium becoming the message in a way that wonderfully mocks the sterility of MacLuhan's tag, but also the total awareness of process and effect:

> The questions float up as I go along and leave me very confused, breaking up I am. Suddenly they are there, no, they float up, out of an old depth, and hover and linger before they die away, questions that when I was in my right mind would not have survived one second, no, but atomized they would have been, before as much as formed, atomized. In twos often they came, one hard on the other, thus, How shall I go on another day? and then, How did I ever go on another day. Or, Did I kill my father? and then, Did I ever kill anyone? That kind of way, to the general from the particular I suppose you might say, question and

answer too in a way, very addling. I strive with them as best I can, quickening my step when they come on, tossing my head from side to side and up and down, staring agonized at this and that, increasing my murmur to a scream, these are helps. (p. 16)

Beckett seems at times to be miming the ghastly non-stop analysis found in some pathological states, but he is also the controlled critic, chafing at his victimisation by language. He draws attention to the text, as when he says he is moving to the general from the particular, but his generalisation goes beyond the intellectual processes clearly demonstrated on the page as when he speaks of answers where there are only questions. Directly and indirectly, he draws attention not only to his figures and forms, but to their effects. The self-conscious narrative is a solace and a pain. Screaming helps, the swaying self-reflection disturbs, the dash from question to answer, or from story to analysis, is like the painful tossing of a head.

Beckett is writing in the tradition of comic self-consciousness; his self-analysis is like that of Swift's *A Tale of a Tub*, or of Sterne's *Tristram Shandy*, though these are satiric deflation of literary pretence or posturing. Swift's Grub Street author and the unfortunate, battered Tristram are the disturbed or ineffectual authors of addled narratives, and the 'real' author's irony and travesty set the ideal and structure at a comic remoteness, implying some superiority, some norm of rational discourse or value. In Swift, the dislocations are criticised as irrational and 'modern', in Sterne, the dislocations are defended as imaginative criticisms of simply rational and classical unities. Beckett's self-analysis, like that of these eighteenth-century ancestors, is funny, witty, and extremely clever, but is the language and form of self-laceration, not of satire.

Bergson defines comedy as depending on 'the momentary anaesthesia of the heart' and his metaphor applies to Sterne, at times to Swift, never to Beckett. Even in Swift, the comic anaesthetic doesn't work perfectly: in *A Tale of a Tub* the aggressive deflations and degradations end by undermining Swift's Anglican middle way as well as the fanatical extremes of Rome and of Dissent. Beckett knows what his anguished comedy is up to; instead of laughing, as Beaumarchais says, so that he may not cry, he laughs and cries at once. The comedy is like an operation without anaesthetic, as in Swift's terrible joke about the flayed woman, where the beau's surprise at the effect of flaying works momentarily like humour but carries such incredulity as to violate irony and give us the thing itself.

What is exhilarating or even entertaining in Beckett's wit and literary criticism is also painful, and certainly not without precedent. Donne, for instance, had shown wit as a medium for agony, just as he shared Beckett's impatience with his craft, 'whining poetry'. Beckett's most conspicuous interest in the stories is in narrative form. He manages to toss about agonisedly and alertly, running through all the possible reasons for writing stories. We write them to pass the time, to kill it, to find ourselves in others, to get greater clarity and light, or to try for them. We write because there seems to be someone or something urging us or forcing us. Sometimes we write willingly, sometimes hating every minute, sometimes beginning reluctantly but expecting to feel better, especially when we've finished. Our acts of writing and telling are related to all those acts of everyday or every-night life, dreaming, remembering, planning, anticipating, anticipating memory and remembering anticipation. We may go into a story or an act as into a game, play it badly or well, go on, stop short, give up because we forget or are confused, too hard-pressed or too depressed. We may play according to set rules, try to approximate art to science, description to measurement, human relationships or actions to sets and series, quality to quantity. As we play, obey, create, suffer, we may feel addled or desperate. We may even feel enlightened about the nature of feeling and reasoning.

Beckett is interested also in inspecting the word. His self-consciousness about the literary forms that tradition has set up, codified, and analysed extends also to the way language works. He interrupts that interrupting story at the end of *The Unnamable*, and constantly interrupts his sentences, to comment and criticise, looking hard at words, phrases, clichés, metaphors, even punctuation marks. 'How hideous is the semi-colon', comes the observation, mad no doubt (whatever that means), and the reader of *Watt*, exhaustedly alerted to sentences, paragraphs, and larger patterns of event, turns to realise that the page bristles with semi-colons. Beckett calls minute halts, makes us travel as slowly and painfully as his one-legged, crippled and mud-slowed travellers. He divides his characters into travellers and paralytics, and his readers share the experience of both kinds. Like Belacqua, and so many other Beckett people, we are bogged down in the stories and the sentences, can't speed as we usually can through prose fiction, are made to see how difficult it is, are made to feel 'how it is', to meditate bewilderedly on present time, are sent back to read again (more grimly punished by the return than Sterne's lady reader). We emerge, unable to feel the same again about hundreds of well-worn, useful little words and phrases, like 'on my way', 'roughly speaking', 'get off with my life', 'this time', 'that's the way it was', my life', 'all (all!)', 'it seemed to me', 'I had the impression', 'go on thinking!'. Molloy says, 'from time to time (what tenderness in these little words, what savagery)'. The end of *The Lost Ones* says: 'So much roughly speaking for the last state of the cylinder and of this little people of searchers one first of whom if a man in some unthinkable past bowed his head if this notion is maintained.' The familiar phrase 'roughly speaking' asserts both its cold glib everyday connotation and a newly learnt precision which strips familiarity, remakes metaphor, and admits the provisionality of speech and fantasy. 'This notion is maintained', proffers a customary dryness but has to be received afresh. Sometimes, of course, the minute halt calls attention to the word and the experience that the word conveys, as when the Unnamable discourses on the eye:

> This eye, curious how this eye invites inspection, demands sympathy, solicits attention, implores assistance, to do what, it's not clear, to stop weeping, have a quick look round, goggle an instant and close forever. It's it you see and it alone, it's from it you set out to look for a face, to it you return having found nothing, nothing worth having, nothing but a kind of ashen smear, perhaps it's long grey hair, hanging in a tangle round the mouth, greasy with ancient tears. . . . (p. 378)

The verbal wit alerts us to the deadening acts of language, in the marvellous joke about organs and homonyms: 'And the face? Balls, all balls, I don't believe in the eye either.' Although it is to the forms of story and drama that he directs attention, he also looks closely at diction with solicitude for familiar and for unfamiliar words, sending us to the dictionary, sometimes severely, sometimes amusedly. His 'gentle skimmer' can't skim, or he will miss the point, not only of fairly accessible jokes like Belacqua feeling 'a sad animal', but smaller essential ones like Malone's 'There I am back at my old aporetics. Is that the word?', followed later by the Unnamable's '. . . how proceed? By aporia pure and simple?' and six sentences later, '. . . I say aporia without knowing what it means.' Dictionary work is soon forgotten, perhaps indeed intended to provide exercises in self-chastening scholarship and amnesia, but here at least is one word that many Beckett readers must have learnt for good from reading Beckett.

I need not labour the entertainment to be derived from such exercises and riddles. We can't skim, we are required to work. Such work is amusing and exhausting. Readers of fiction expect a certain licence to skim a bit. Beckett doesn't grant it. He knows that literature is a game, but not just a game. It is rewarding but laborious. The reader participates fully in this most precious human solace, works at it and plays with it, understands but is sometimes muddled, loves it, gets fed up, is inspirited but then bored. In this Beckett is not doing anything new, but writing in the old tradition of literary self-consciousness, shared by Shakespeare and Keats as well as the eighteenth-century novelist. Shakespeare broke both comic and tragic tension by dispelling his own figments, admitting that the old mole was in the cellarage and that Cressid had indeed become a type of infidelity. When Theseus in *A Midsummer Night's Dream* reminds the audience, on stage and off, that 'the best in this kind be but shadows' he disturbs more than the dramatic illusion in a *memento mori* for actors, author and audience. In *The Fall of Hyperion* Keats dispels our belief in artistic unity and our faith in the present by the line 'when this warm scribe my hand is in the grave'. He makes us remember the act of writing in a way very like Beckett's insistence on those pencils and bits of paper. He anticipates Beckett even more precisely and profoundly in 'Ode to a Nightingale', as he attempts to stabilise a vision of art's permanence and joy despite the facts of age, sickness and death. This imagery is like that of Beckett, though not so minutely particularised:

> Fade far away, dissolve, and quite forget
>   What thou among the leaves hast never known,
> The weariness, the fever, and the fret.
>   Here, where men sit and hear each other groan;
> Where palsy shakes a few, sad, last gray hairs,
>   Where youth grows pale, and spectre-thin, and dies;

> Where but to think is to be full of sorrow
> And leaden-eyed despairs;
> Where Beauty cannot keep her lustrous eyes,
> Or new Love pine at them beyond to-morrow.

At the end Keats has to admit, with a self-conscious scrutiny both of word and form, that the lyric effort of imagination can't last, hasn't lasted, and has forced him to doubt the enterprise in and of the Ode. He too looks not only at the act of imaginative invention and identification but at language. He repeats his own word 'forlorn', moving it out of the enchantment of faery lands into the more apposite context of his own solitude: 'Forlorn! the very word is like a bell/To toll me back from thee to my sole self!' Keats knows that fancy cheats, that its figments are dispelled in time and space, that we can't always distinguish vision from daydreams. The vision is checked, but also placed and licensed by the act of self-reflection.

II

Keats attempts to find meaning and stability through poetry and through love. Beckett too is concerned with a world in which Beauty won't keep her lustrous eyes. Beckett's people are mostly extremely ugly, often sick, crippled, impotent. But they still need and make love, after a fashion. That fashion makes us look hard at the same facts of mutability and morbidity which Keats faced, knowing from personal experience that women had cancers and that consumption was killing. Beckett sets such knowledge down in detailed imagery. The result is the least romantic treatment of love offered by English literature, a far cry not only from Keats but from everyone else.

Beckett's people love things as well as other people, and at times seem to find them more satisfactory objects of affection. Most of the things in Beckett are needed for survival, like bicycles, exercise books, pencils, jars, sawdust, mud, sacks, tin-openers, tins and biscuits, and this survival is frequently related to love. He also likes things because they are silent. But things sometimes offer some sensuous pleasure, as they do for Molloy, who finds that a pebble in the mouth 'appeases, soothes, makes you forget your hunger, forget your thirst'. Objects may be substitutes, but their solace does at times assume surrogate sexuality. Malone sets out his attempt 'to begin to understand, how such creatures are possible', plans to write one story about a stone, but realises that where there are men there are invariably things too. The stone doesn't get a story to itself after all, but comes into the human story, sometimes as a love object. Malone is urgent about his possessions, but makes it clear that the need isn't simply a need for instruments:

> And I loved, I remember, as I walked along, with my hands deep in my pockets, for I am trying to speak of the time when I could still walk without a stick and a fortiori without crutches, I loved to finger and caress the hard shapely objects that were there in my deep pockets, it was my way of talking to them and reassuring them. And I loved to fall asleep holding in my hand a stone, a horse chestnut or a cone. . . . And those of which I wearied, or which were ousted by new loves, I threw away, that is to say I cast around for a place to lay them where they would be at peace forever. . . . (*Malone Dies*, p. 249)

Although Malone feels pity and affection for objects, as for people, and although they are, like people, eventually ousted, it is plain that he knows they aren't quite the same as people. He seems to excuse his attachment to objects by explaining that he hasn't really 'evolved in the fields of affection and passion'. I think Beckett sees a love for objects, however sentimental, as an improvement on masturbation, which is pretty severely put in its place in the stories as an uninteresting satisfaction of appetite, like eating, and an overrated pleasure, 'the alleged joys of so-called self-abuse'. The love of objects shows the minimal caring for something else. Instead of providing a contrast to the great importance of human relations it rather signals a common and simple need and satisfaction, something like Auden's 'Love requires an object/Almost I imagine/Anything will do'. Sometimes objects, but more usually human beings, of either sex, will do in Beckett.

At moments sexuality, like language, seems to be regarded for the first time, in a way that combines extreme matter-of-factness with sympathetic sense of need:

> I did all he desired. I desired it too. For him. Whenever he desired something so did I. He only had to say what thing. When he didn't desire anything neither did I. In this way I didn't live without desires. If he had desired something for me I would have

desired it too. Happiness for example or fame. I only had the desires he manifested. But he must have manifested them all. All his desires and needs. When he was silent he must have been like me. When he told me to lick his penis I hastened to do so. I drew satisfaction from it. We must have had the same satisfactions. The same needs and the same satisfactions.

('Enough', *No's Knife*)

There are worse accounts of human connection. Beckett's wit is quietly at work in the pun of 'I drew satisfaction from it'. But the love, if we may call it so, in 'Enough', is not qualified only by the matter-of-factness of style and the cooling reasonability of inference. The relationship itself is restricted, not only by its one-way traffic of desire, which lies within the experience of most of us, one way and another, but by extreme fetishisms and phobias. The older man who leads and instructs the narrator wears gloves, because he dislikes the feel of human skin (though not necessarily of mucous membrane). He leads the narrator, touching him 'where he wished. Up to a certain point'; and the last sentence says, 'Enough my old breasts feel his old hand'. Since the affair began when the narrator was six, it has indeed been a long outing, part walked, part remembered. It seems stupid or indecent to over-analyse this story, compounded as it is of fairly ambitious movements of sexual love, like mutuality, compliance, desire, and the sharing of a past, with the grotesque and comic details that it has in common with dirty jokes, like the gloved love-making.[2] Still, as title and last sentence say, it is enough.

We may remember Longinus's strange comment that pity is not a sublime emotion, in attempting to express an awkwardness about using the term to describe some aspects of loving in Beckett. While his avoidance of pitying tones might be taken as a strong way of invoking pity, I have come to think that pity is the wrong word, carrying with it some complication of superiority, some inclination, however kindly, from high to low. It is as if Beckett refuses to feel compassionate about bestiality or other so-called sexual perversions, recognising them as not only human but compatible with tenderness and fondness, besides signalising common need and gratification. He humanises the dirty joke, or the *graffito*, by giving full particularity, however repugnant this may be or seem to be, then daring us to be disgusted. Joyce shares with Beckett this refusal to outlaw certain modes of sexual connection. Bloom's masturbation, his fetishistic correspondence with Martha Clifford, his rump-licking near-impotence in bed with Molly are all thoroughly understood and affectionately presented. In Joyce and Beckett to understand all is to make pity redundant or inept. Joyce is good at comprehending impotence, fetishism, various reduced states of sexual connection, but diseased and ageing sex lie outside his story. Even the excesses of humiliation are reserved for nighttown. It is as though Beckett brought nighttown into the daylight. Joyce invokes the awful image of a 'grey sunken cunt' to express an uncharacteristic moment of depression in Bloom's day, and it is no wonder that he swiftly invokes the healing counter-image of Molly's warm flesh, however far removed from it Bloom may have to be. Beckett takes that grey sunken cunt and gives it character, name, story.

Many times, Malone kisses his mother's 'old grey pear' (breast, I suppose) and may have pleased her a little. His lovers, usually heterosexual, and often said to be in love, are old, impotent, diseased, crippled, smelly and ugly. It is as if he took those images of dying and sickness and sparse-haired age, from Keats, and particularised them in action, recognising, over and over again and without making too much fuss, that the old, the ugly and the sick may desire, be gratified, love, take and give sexual pleasure, and that the 'healthy' reader should admit his likeness. Sex ticks on, however minimally, in sickness and in health. In *More Pricks Than Kicks* the sexual kicks are indeed few, for though Belacqua is certainly not impotent he is a rather unwilling lover. Watt, too, finds coupling an exhausting business. Murphy's is probably the nearest we get to energetic love-making in Beckett, but although he enjoys the pleasures of the serenade, nocturne, and albada, he dislikes the part of himself that loves Celia. But even for Belacqua and Watt, love exists, and is a solace, however scotched or slighted.

Watt's relation with Mrs Gorman, the fish-woman, isn't really love, and he finally decides that he may have liked her just for the fishy smell, and she him for the stout. But their affair is played out with more affection and consolation than this rude explanation suggests:

Then he would have her in the kitchen, and open for her a bottle of stout, and set her on his knee, and wrap his right arm about her waist, and lean his head upon her right breast (the left having unhappily been removed in the heat of a surgical operation), and in this position remain, without stirring, or stirring the least possible, forgetful of his troubles, for as long as ten minutes, or a quarter of an hour. And Mrs. Gorman too, as with her left hand she stirred the grey-pink tufts and with her right at studied intervals raised the bottle to her lips, was in her own small way to peace too, for a time. (*Watt*, Ch. 2)[3]

This affair bears a strong family resemblance to the later loves, also described comically, but with total acceptance, without repugnance for what might be found repugnant by the average insensitive reader. Murphy divides jokes into those that have once been good and those that have never been good, and most of Beckett's comic love-affairs are instances of life's bad jokes, though their badness is tender and heartening, and conveys the message that love like this is, at worst, better than nothing, and, at best, very like more salubrious, young and elegant love-making. He stresses weakness, silliness, inefficiency, lack of good looks, pressure of time, fatigue and age, all problems that everyone must experience or anticipate. As with the story of the gloved lover, the silliness and innocence of some of Beckett's people—Watt, Molloy and Malone, for instance—may remind us of the fool in traditional dirty jokes, and the three subjects of innocence, ignorance and impotence are, as the groundsman in 'Draff' might say, classical. Beckett's sending-up of high-flown languages also makes its contribution to the amusing treatment of sexual half-heartedness:

> Further than this, it will be learnt with regret, they never went, though more than half inclined to do so on more than one occasion. Why was this? Was it the echo murmuring in their hearts, in Watt's heart, in Mrs. Gorman's, of past passion, ancient error, warning them not to sully not to trail, in the cloaca of clonic gratification, a flower so fair, so rare, so sweet, so frail? (*Watt*, Ch. 2)

In the trilogy there is more love and more sexual energy. Age is the problem, but they do their best. Molloy possibly pleases his mother by kissing 'that little grey wizened pear'. He admits her terrible smell, and while he says 'Pah' realises that she may also have said 'Pah', for, as he insists, he doesn't 'diffuse the perfumes of Araby'. Molloy's willingness, pliancy, frankness and tolerance remind us not too grimly of the rotting flesh and his matter-of-factness is both funny and insistent:

> And if they had removed a few testicles into the bargain I wouldn't have objected. For from such testicles as mine, dangling at mid-thigh at the end of a meagre cord, there was nothing more to be squeezed, not a drop. (*Molloy*, pp. 35–6)

Molloy probably knew true love, though he isn't absolutely sure:

> It was she made me acquainted with love. She went by the peaceful name of Ruth I think, but I can't say for certain. Perhaps the name was Edith. She had a hole between her legs, oh not the bunghole I had always imagined, but a slit, and in this I put, or rather she put, my so-called virile member, not without difficulty, and I toiled and moiled until I discharged or gave up trying or was begged by her to stop. A mug's game in my opinion and tiring on top of that, in the long run. But I lent myself to it with a good enough grace, knowing it was love, for she had told me so. She bent over the couch, because of her rheumatism, and in I went from behind. It was the only position she could bear, because of her lumbago. It seemed all right to me, for I had seen dogs, and I was astonished when she confided that you could go about it differently. I wonder what she meant exactly. Perhaps after all she put me in her rectum. A matter of complete indifference to me, I needn't tell you. But is it true love, in the rectum? That's what bothers me sometimes. Have I never known true love, after all? (pp. 56–7)

He isn't quite sure but, as usual, he reasons quite acceptably. The discourse on the needs and nature of true love contains more than irony. Molloy says it is characterised by the acceptance of poor conditions (flying 'High above the tight fit and the loose'), and by superfluous, supersexual attentiveness, like cutting the beloved's toe-nails and massaging the beloved's rump. His explanation for refusing to repeat the experience is suspect but plausible, based, I suppose, on a sense of its uniqueness and perfection, which makes him want to keep the memory 'pure of all pastiche'. There is no one quite like Beckett for having it both ways, for doing what he says women do, giving the cake to the cat and eating it as well. It doesn't seem right to say that all the customary exalted definitions of love's value are here satirised or deflated, since Beckett insists that if they mean anything at all, they apply to all human conditions. Beckett certainly makes romantic definitions take a beating, from grotesque, brutally detached and ferocious humour. But he forces the extension of romantic value with plausibility. Rank as love is, for Beckett's people, it behaves remarkably like love: suffers like love, consoles like love, and is not exempt from dirtiness, ugliness, smelliness, sickness and death. Love is thus particularised and related to traditions and human experience. On at least two occasions there is an uncertainty about the name of his true love, part of the total slipperiness of names in the trilogy, but part also of the weakness of amorous memory.

The other member of the trilogy who knows true love is Malone's Macmann. His idyll resembles Molloy's but has its own special features. Macmann has an affair with his keeper, Moll. They are not unsuccessful, in spite of impotence, 'summoning to their aid all the resources of the skin, the mucus and the imagination, in striking from their dry and feeble clips a kind of sombre gratification' (p. 261). The course of their intimacy is made to conform to traditions of love. Macmann learns the right language, 'the yesses, noes, mores, and enoughs that keep love alive' and he writes love poems while she writes love letters. They say the usual things, wish they had met while young, are grateful for finding each other, know what they have is a protection, company, and a solace when the wind blows at night. The conventions are of course changed by the age, impotence, and revolting aspect of the lovers. They are consoled for not having met sixty years ago by the elaborate argument that whereas they were very ugly in youth now they're scarcely worse than even their 'best favoured contemporaries'. Impotence gives new meaning to those 'mores and enoughs' as to the 'heart's labouring'. The account of the affair, with its shifting balance of feeling from one love to the other, and details of decline and death, is an off-hand and nasty way of describing something that has given shape and interest to thousands of romantic novels.

Beckett is insisting, as Moll insists, that sexual love can be nasty but still help. Love finds its warranty in the repulsive as in the sublime. Macmann's explanation of human need is remarkably sane, despite his insanity:

When you hold me in your arms, and I you in mine, it naturally does not amount to much, compared to the transports of youth, and even middle age. But all is relative, let us bear that in mind, stags and hinds have their needs and we have ours. (*Malone Dies*, p. 262)

Or, as Malone puts it earlier:

> For people are never content to suffer, but they must have heat and cold, rain and its contrary which is fine weather, and with that love, friendship, black skin and sexual and peptic deficiency for example, in short the furies and frenzies happily too numerous to be numbered of the body. . . . (p. 243)

Love is sometimes romantic, beautiful, even associated with nostalgia and dreams. This romantic image of love, however, gets discredited. The sense of beauty and youth, which it invokes or which is added to give it extra glamour or value, is permitted only in dreaming. Even memory sets it too firmly in the solid earth of experience. One of its purest appearances, set easily and obviously in dreaming, is in *From an Abandoned Work*, which is filled with odd but brilliant images of the past, the image of his mother, the image of blue, brightness, and the image of beloved objects:

> Love too, often in my thoughts, when a boy, but not a great deal compared to other boys, it kept me awake I found. Never loved anyone, I think, I'd remember. Except in my dreams and there it was animals, dream animals, nothing like what you see walking about in the country. I couldn't describe them, lovely creatures they were, white mostly. (p. 142)

Insubstantial, but charming. Charming, too, is the off-hand and good-tempered lack of fuss and competitiveness. The narrator of this fragment is violent, given to sudden rages, but there is something very cool and calm about his account of his love-life, and the tacked on observations, 'I'd remember' and 'lovely creatures they were' have a nonchalance which combines with the inexplicable passions to create his character and his story. Even the dreams are given individuality.

But they have something in common. Where sexual love has charm, it is given a remoteness. In *Lessness* the remembered or imagined love has the calm melancholy of assured loss, 'Old love new love as in the blessed days unhappiness will reign again' and perhaps, 'Never but in dream the happy dream'. There is also the image of the lovers' shadows watched by Malone, who shares with several of the narrators a pure innocence about some sexual activities. He can't quite make out what is happening over the road, as he looks from his window, from his bed, at the shadows that move, come together, separate, join, stand up against the curtain, clasp, rub against each other. He describes the encounter with the precision and abstractedness of the eye that doesn't recognise what is happening, either because he is too old, or too remote, and then comes the sudden identification:

> . . . it is clear we have here two distinct and separate bodies, each enclosed within its own frontiers, and having no need of each other to come and go and sustain the flame of life. . . . Perhaps they are cold, that they rub against each other so, for friction maintains heat and brings it back when it is gone. It is all very pretty and strange, this big complicated shape made up of more than one, for perhaps there are three of them, and how it sways and totters, but rather poor in colour. But the night must be warm, for of a sudden the curtain lifts on a flare of tender colour, pale blush and white of flesh, then pink that must come from a garment and gold too that I haven't time to understand. So it is not cold they are, standing so lightly clad by the open window. Ah how stupid I am, I see what it is, they must be loving each other, that must be how it is done. Good, that has done me good. (*Malone Dies*, pp. 238–9)

This must be one of Beckett's most beautiful voyeuristic descriptions, and the forms, colours and movement make the encounter as balletic as it is mysterious, for not only does Malone not know for a long time what they are doing, he doesn't even know if it is dawn, late night, or evening, only that they move together in the suddenly lit window which shows him that there really are people outside, that the terrifying Magritte-like image he has of the black night being painted on his pane, is not real. But after the delicate beauty, comes the reduction: 'they have loved each other standing, like dogs. . . . Or perhaps they are just having a breather, before they tackle the titbit. Back and forth, back and forth, that must be wonderful. They seem to be in pain.' It is the voice of experience now, added to that of innocence. And the knowing ends the beauty, rather as Alice and the fawn can only companion each other when they do not know they are girl and animal.

There is the other beautiful image in *Imagination Dead Imagine*, carefully drawn and measured, each white body lying in the white semicircle, vanishing and reappearing, freezing and heating. They do not move but the mirror shows breath and the eyes open and 'gaze in unblinking exposure', but only once overlapping, 'for about ten seconds'. Shudder is suppressed, but they are sweating and icy. And there is the shattering understatement, 'the bodies seem whole and in fairly good condition'. Perhaps there is no ground for including this as an image of sex, but it is an image of the human couple, locked in a position of non-embrace, and of non-sleep. They are all too successfully imagined, and their lovelessness seems imaginable when imagination has died.

Imagination creates the terrible embraces in *How It Is*, where the couples, unsexed, behave aggressively in order to make contact, invent and develop a code and a language, compel each other to sound and even song, use the same instrument, the tin-opener, to nourish, wound, speak to each other, and touch. *How It Is* presents a dimension of love in the light, associated with brightness, flowers, blissful nature, but the force of the embraces and aggressions in the mud, of those awful arse wounds, is finally shown when they too are revealed as too good to exist, part of a terrible and terribly reduced dream of love that might be supposed to be awful enough to exist. Perhaps the most sickening displacements in all Beckett come in the hell-like life or life-like hell of this novel, where even the tormented contact is finally dispelled, and everything except mud and solitude said to be fictitious. To be made to regret such encounters and wounds is to have imagination stretched into a knowledge of isolation. No wonder such an imagination can create Malone's astonished gaze at copulation, Watt's embrace of Mrs Gorman's single breast, Macmann's tolerance of Mag's vomit, the compliance with every wish of the old man who didn't like to touch skin.

III

The *Texts for Nothing* are eloquent on the subject of the third solace, nature. The clerk or scribe of the fifth text wonders if he will ever see sky again and be free to move in sun and rain, but he then immediately discredits the nostalgic imagery as mere literary props:

The sky, I've heard—the sky and earth, I've heard great accounts of them, now that's pure word for word, I invent nothing. I've noted, I must have noted many a story with them as setting, they create the atmosphere. Between them where the hero stands a great gulf is fixed, while all about they flow together more and more, till they meet. . . .

And the sixth text has the narrator trying again to write a little story, 'with living creatures coming and going on a habitable earth crammed with the dead, a brief story, with night and day coming above . . .'. Beckett imagines solitude like no one else, he also transforms the sense of time and place, but he cannot usually dispense with some kind of natural habitat. He tries, to be sure, but the attempt to create a measurable and visible exterior in *Ping* only shows up the naturalness of the other invented places. And even the cube of *Ping* depends for its claustrophobia on a nature implied outside. The place and space of *How It Is* has a memory or dream or tradition or fiction of light, sun, air, but even its admitted actuality has mud, a mud in which no flowers grow. *Imagination Dead Imagine* has temperature and light, though tormentingly. But most of Beckett's people do relate to nature, if only across the gulf described in the fifth text, and do a certain amount to create setting and atmosphere. These solitaries, in pain and doubt, ignorant of meaning and identity, trying to make out the point of human existence through reports and stories, then trying to stop, trying to shut up, trying to die, do mostly live on an imaginable earth, with imaginable air, water and fire. Beckett usually accepts an irreducible minimum of air, movement and nourishment—the absence of such a minimum, its reduction through fantasy and abstraction, in *Imagination Dead Imagine* and *Ping*, is terrifying. But he generally needs the elements of earth, air, water and fire to provide the minimal living conditions, though living would not be his term. So his people tend to have a response to nature, often the acceptance of an elaborately described habitat. Like literature, and like sexual love, nature, interrogated for meaning, sometimes offers one, sometimes doesn't. The effect of meanings and lack of meaning is not only helpful in creating people, it also helps the reader get some bearings, though getting them is not by any means a simple process of reassurance. Nature does not offer, as in the *Lyrical Ballads*, a familiar landscape transformed by the moonlight of imagination. Though Coleridge's use of suns and moons in 'The Rime of the Ancient Mariner' does sometimes come to mind when facing those dubious moons in *Molloy*. But our notions of familiarity and strange transformations have been moved on by surrealist art, and Beckett, like Henri Michaux, whom he occasionally resembles, is doubtless affected by the flora, fauna, and things of surrealist landscapes and seascapes. *Imagination Dead Imagine* and *Ping* owe something to cubism, too, and non- or semi-representational painting and sculpture. Beckett's landscapes are marvellously original and bizarre, but his nature is transformed by the people wandering through it (his travellers) or bogged down (his paralytics) more often than by visual inventiveness.

The first sentence of *Imagination Dead Imagine* says contemptuously that it is easy to imagine nothing, 'no trace anywhere of life', but hard though necessary to imagine a death or afterdeath of imagination. The first thing to go is landscape: 'Islands, waters, azure, verdure, one glimpse and vanished, endlessly, omit'. Beckett's natural landscape never had a very impressive presence even before imagination died. As early as *More Pricks Than Kicks* he was showing displeasing scenes, like the Hill of the Wolves in 'Fingal', with a 'ruin of a mill on the top, choked lairs of furze and brambles passim' or the view from the Hill of Fingal, 'its coast eaten away with creeks and marshes, tesserae of small fields, patches of wood springing up like a weed, the line of hills too low to close the view'. It lacks charm, though it certainly has visible life. In the story 'Walking Out' nature is more than unpleasant, and beauty is conferred only to reveal horror, as in the sheep-and-lamb-crammed landscape which Belacqua criticises for its lack of horses, where 'the grass was spangled with scarlet after-births, the larks were singing, the hedges were breaking, the sun was shining, the sky was Mary's cloak, the daisies were there, everything was in order'. E. M. Forster had to move to an Indian sun and landscape in order to destroy the pastoral sweetness of our fertile spring myth, Beckett successfully attacked an Irish pastoral while staying in Ireland. In 'A Wet Night' the rain which is falling in 'a uniform untroubled manner' evokes, in order to annihilate, Joyce's sympathetic snow at the end of 'The Dead': 'It fell upon the bay, the littoral, the mountains and the plains, and notably upon the Central Bog it fell with a rather desolate uniformity.'

No more could be expected of rain which is Beckettian, Irish, and

purgatorial. The very last landscape in *More Pricks Than Kicks*
presents a problem of classification to the groundsman:

> What with the company of headstones sighing and gleaming like
> bones, the moon on the job, the sea tossing in her dreams and
> panting, and the hills observing their Attic vigil in the
> background, he was at a loss to determine off-hand whether the
> scene was of the kind that is termed romantic, or whether it
> should not with more justice be deemed classical. Both elements
> were present, that was indisputable. Perhaps classico-romantic
> would be the fairest estimate. A classico-romantic scene.
> ('Draff', *More Pricks than Kicks*)

Nature is certainly there, but put in its place, with whatever
attributes that muted admiration, irony, or satire require. (Beckett
would probably exclaim at the presumptuousness of putting nature
in its place.) It is more accurate to say that Beckett does not allow
natural landscape to have the part it generally has in previous
literature. But he obviously has an eye for its dubious charms, as for
those of literature and sex, even as he meditates its abolition. The
existence of nature, diminished and subdued, is of some
importance, both to Beckett's people and Beckett's readers. Where
nature is almost obliterated, in *Imagination Dead Imagine* or *Ping*,
the reduction of the now unnatural landscape is painful, like the
reduction of human vitality for which it provides a constricted
space. None of the longer works can get along without nature. It
seldom commands an enthusiastic or admiring response and it is
extremely unstable, but it does provide welcome landmarks. (The
plays can do without its richness, for it remains rich in most of
Beckett's fiction, never as impoverished as Winnie's heap of sand in
Happy Days, or the tree in *Waiting for Godot*. The habitat of his
fiction tends to be more sensuous and elusive than the simplified
symbolic settings and objects of the plays.) To like nature need not
be a virtue. Moran likes nature, but he is one of Beckett's nastiest
people, a pedantic Christian and a horrible father, and his romantic
response to nature is part of his obnoxious certainty, and soon to be
lost, since he has to come out of his domestic garden into Molloy's
harsher and wilder territory. But his response to nature is plainly
discreditable. First, he is misled by nature. About to leave, on the
'threshold of the Molloy affair' he sees in the sun's beams 'the
sabbath of the motes' and wrongly concludes that the weather is

fine. Earlier when Gaber is about to announce the Molloy quest, he enjoys nature, in spite of its internal discomfort, partially and selfishly inhaling 'the scent of my lemon-verbena' and listening to the blackbird and thrush, 'their song sadly dying, vanquished by the heat, and leaving dawn's high boughs for the bushes' gloom' as the contented spectator himself will soon do. On a later occasion he moves straight from an appreciation of sunset—'in the west scarves of fine red sheen were mounting the sky'—to his dinner, an unsatisfactory shepherd's pie. He has already remarked that the great joy which surged over him at the sight of the red sky ended in a sigh, 'for the joy inspired by beauty is often not unmixed', though what the reader observes as the mixture—the straight move from the shepherd's sky ('Red sky at night is the shepherd's delight') to the shepherd's pie—is not in his mind. He has a foreboding about leaving his province for Molloy's, and his own is largely described in terms of his neat and possessively enjoyed garden, 'my house, my garden . . . my trees . . . my birds of which the least is known to me', where the Biblical echo manages to cast a slur on both Moran and the Almighty (like the Mary-blue sky in 'Walking Out'). Once he starts on the Molloy country that slight nastiness we find in 'Fingal' creeps in:

> But the principal beauty of this region was a kind of strangled creek which the slow grey tides emptied and filled, emptied and filled. And the people came flocking from the town, unromantic people, to admire this spectacle. Some said, There is nothing more beautiful than these wet sands. Others, High tide is the best time to see the creek of Ballyba. How lovely then that leaden water, you would swear it was stagnant, if you did not know it was not. (pp. 134-5)

Much later, disintegrated and reduced in the Molloy country, he has a surge of the old romantic and heroic nature-feeling; he thinks gratefully of Juno's milk as he looks at the night sky, which promises an 'evening that brings out the lights, the stars in the sky and on earth the brave little lights of men'. This sounds a sublime consolation, but in a sentence or two the light goes out, he is alone and not liking it. At the end he returns to his garden, and it is emollient but dubious; something sinister about it makes his response shift and sway:

There was a bright side. They were lovely days. The winter had been exceptionally rigorous, everybody said so. We had therefore a right to this superb summer. I do not know if we had a right to it. My birds had not been killed. They were wild birds. And yet quite trusting. I recognised them and they seemed to recognise me. But one never knows. Some were missing and some were new. I tried to understand their language better. Without having recourse to mine. They were the longest, loveliest days of all the year. I lived in the garden. (p. 176)

The change in Moran's language is accompanied by a change in his feeling for nature. He is wary of cliché, of the language of fixity, expectation, and justice. He is less possessive of his territory. He has been in the Molloy country, and comes back more like Molloy and less like the Moran he was.

Molloy's attitude to nature is much closer to the usual one (I hesitate to call it a norm) in the stories. It wobbles from a sense of beauty to a sense of repulsion, from a romantic straining after a natural sublime to a rejection of such spuriousness. Molloy's word 'strains' is nicely ambiguous; early on he tells us his soul 'strains wildly' after certain things in nature,

the fields, whitening under the dew, and the animals, ceasing from wandering and settling for the night, and the sea, of which nothing, and the sharpening line of crests, and the sky where without seeing them I felt the first stars tremble.. . . (*Molloy*, p. 11)

Apart from the warning refusal to speak of the sea, Molloy seems to strain after a pleasant calm and freshness, but it soon becomes clear that the natural description acts as a clumsy aid in Molloy's attempt to talk about things other than himself, for instance, cows and sky. It is also evident that nostalgia for nature can't be credited. The different bits of remembered landscape are at times dismantled, having been arbitrarily assembled by memory and fiction, for the putting together of cows, sky, sea and mountains is all part of the admittedly tiring heaping up of things until there is no more room and no more light. At times the image is kept pleasantly before him but not for long, and not without being undermined, as in the description of him springing along rough sunlit quiet streets (on his crutches, of course), giving himself 'up to that golden moment, as if

I had been someone else'. Warmth, light, calm, silence and languor are all appreciated, and have an emotional impact, 'I didn't feel unhappy', but it is evident that there is something wrong. Molloy is indeed acting like someone else, having an untypical response, and it may be one of those moments when his experience is contaminated by the experience of Moran who finds it easy to be warmed and consoled by nature. After a while Molloy reverts to the early image of straining and depreciates it, 'I was straining towards those spurious deeps, their lying promise of gravity and peace from all my old poisons, I struggled towards them, safely bound. Under the blue sky, under the watchful gaze.' This isn't simply a rejection of romantic nature, but the invocation of something menacing, as if the spuriousness were a real trap, the blue a hopeful gaze turned towards a victim. But the response to nature wobbles, as suits Molloy's self-styled 'long emotional confusion' and he can speak of the affection he feels for the surface of his 'way', 'bright or dark, smooth or rough, and always dear to me, in spite of all, and the dear sound of which goes and is gone, with a brief dust, when the weather is dry'. Molloy can list and reduce the items in a landscape, but he can also attend most closely to sights and sounds, as he does when he gets a little too close to his 'way', and lies with outstretched arms under a hawthorn:

> The white hawthorn stooped towards me, unfortunately I don't like the smell of hawthorn. In the ditch the grass was thick and high, I took off my hat and pressed about my face the long leafy stalks. Then I could smell the earth, the smell of the earth was in the grass that my hands wove round my face till I was blinded. I ate a little too, a little grass. (p. 27)

Sometimes there is only a little wrong, as here, but sometimes there is a violent rejection, as with the sun and the moon, often suspect in Beckett. The Dantean moonspots are a problem for Belacqua, and Watt dislikes both moon and sun, though he has an unexplained lapse in favour of the sun. Molloy's moon casts a bright but far from lucid shine. One night he sees it suddenly, rather as Malone sees the lovers across the street, and describes it with a similar cool precision, in terms of the framing window-bars and the movement across the window, in three segments, the middle staying constant while the 'right gained what the left lost'. This at once gives rise to doubt and relativism, as he reasons that either outside or inside is moving. The reasoning is sound in the abstract but depends on a loss of common ground, so that the one seems as likely as the other, contrary to common sense, experience and scientific knowledge, all of which are occasionally reduced or ignored. The moon is therefore a dubious moon, not to be trusted, even though it seems 'a simple thing . . . that vast yellow light sailing slowly behind my bars . . . which little by little the dense wall devoured and finally eclipsed'. Nature is observed familiarly, but detached and transformed by Molloy's mind, so it seems that the optical illusion that the wall devours and eclipses may not be illusory at all. Molloy's devotion to strict appearances continues with his account of the light and shadows on the wall, 'And now its tranquil course was written on the walls, a radiance scored with shadow, then a brief quivering of leaves, if they were leaves, then that too went out, leaving me in the dark.'

The observation becomes lyrical, splendid, though always wary and provisional. And Beckett makes Molloy say so: 'How difficult it is to speak of the moon and not lose one's head, the witless moon. It must be her arse she shows us always'. The description is undermined first by interpretation and then by rough bathos about science, as it suits Molloy's book. (We are even told here that he has studied astronomy.) The course of the undermining is an intelligible if singular course of thought and feeling, moving from the moon at the window to the quivering light on the wall, from the sensuous response to that quivering to a rejection of lunatic enchantment and power, backed by tradition. 'The witless moon', seems to carry a lingering feeling for the witlessness, but the wild and beautiful word is rudely and cleverly obliterated. If she has no wits, and makes us lose our head, then she is punished by the logic and science which see only an arse. A couple of pages later on Molloy returns to 'this business of the moon', faces the fact that he will have to cope without having all his wits about him, but will 'none the less get done with it, as best I can, at least I think so':

That moon then, all things considered, filled me suddenly with amaze, with surprise, perhaps better. Yes, I was considering it, after my fashion, with indifference, seeing it again, in a way, in my head, when a great fright came suddenly upon me. And deeming this deserved to be looked into I looked into it and quickly made the following discovery, among others, but I confined myself to the following, that this moon which had just sailed gallant and full past my window had appeared to me the night before, or the night before that, yes, more likely, all young and slender, on her back, a shaving. And then I had said, Now I see, he has waited for the new moon before launching forth on unknown ways, leading south. (p. 41)

Soon the feeling that he has unaccountably lost time is replaced by the calm recognition that he hadn't seen any moon at all, new or old, that his nights were moonless, but he has been seeing through someone else's eyes and seeing the sky 'different from what it is' and the earth 'in false colours'. Later on, on a moonless night, when there is no question of a moon or of any other light, the sounds of night are sweetly and gently rendered, in one of the lyrical passages in which Beckett excels:

it was a night of listening, a night given to the faint soughing and sighing stirring at night in little pleasure gardens, the shy sabbath of leaves and petals and the air that eddies there as is does not in other places. . . . And a good thing too. (pp. 48–9)

Some of Molloy's lyrical images are strongly morbid, like the one of a great cloud:

ravelling, discovering here and there a pale and dying sky, and the sun, already down . . . manifest in the livid tongues of fire darting towards the zenith, falling and darting again, ever more pale and languid, and doomed no sooner lit to be extinguished. (p. 65)

Even this description is undermined: he first identifies the 'phenomenon' as characteristic of 'his region', then admits that he isn't qualified to speak of its characteristics, having never left it and so knowing neither its limits nor the regions beyond. This confession is further qualified by the reminder that he is in bed, and remembering inadequately a time when he was on his bicycle, itself jolting and as a 'cycle', 'boundless'. This stroke of wit completes the undermining of the notions of 'region', of space, time, or person. Moon, sun, and also sea are all uncertain in this jolting and perhaps cyclical chronicle, though Molloy's set-piece description of the sea is not so much morbid and undecided as frankly arbitrary and time-consuming:

But in order to blacken a few more pages may I say I spent some time at the seaside, without incident. There are people the sea doesn't suit, who prefer the mountains or the plain. Personally I feel no worse there than anywhere else. Much of my life has ebbed away before this shivering expanse, to the sound of the waves in storm and calm, and the claws of the surf. Before, no, more than before, one with, spread on the sand, or in a cave. In the sand I was in my element, letting it trickle between my fingers, scooping holes that I filled in a moment later or that filled themselves in, flinging it in the air by handfuls, rolling in it. And in the cave, lit by the beacons at night, I knew what to do in order to be no worse off than elsewhere. And that my land went no further, in one direction at least, did not displease me. And to feel there was one direction at least in which I could go no further, without first getting wet, then drowned, was a blessing. For I have always said, First learn to walk, then you can take swimming lessons. (p. 68)

The instability of nature derives from the instability of the spectator, who is only remembered and therefore partly forgotten and partly made up, by an old, sick chronicler, urged on by others who commission and collect his work. What he remembers is of course even more unstable than what he saw, and that was 'naturally' confused and undermined by ignorance, optical and other illusions, tradition, distance and notions of significance. Space is affected by time, vision blurred by being turned into literature. (Beckett is nearly always carrying on a blatant or subliminal argument with Proust about the redemption of time through art.) The attempt to see what is characteristic is a discredited romantic notion, like that in the fifth text, of sympathetic climates and natural phenomena. In Molloy this is a peculiarly interesting question, since character and personality are undermined, Molloy's region being confused with Moran's. The whole tradition of sympathetic nature and pathetic fallacy is not only attacked as Coleridge attacked it in 'Dejection, An Ode', lamenting but insisting that 'Ours is her wedding garment/Ours her shroud', but also attacked by the disrupted sense of personality which makes it impossible to say what 'ours' may be. But despite the various disruptions of nature's stability, she (if she may be so denominated) gives the novels a strongly sensuous dimension, sometimes pleasant, sometimes unpleasant. The aesthetic notion of nature is disrupted like the aesthetic aspect of sex. We are made to see the moon's arse as we are made to see Mag's gums and single tooth.

Nature in Beckett is always uncertain, then, but the uncertainties shift. In *How It Is*, some of the *Texts for Nothing*, and *Lessness*, it joins with sexual love and religion to define the glamour of what is sometimes memory, sometimes dream, sometimes dream masquerading as memory, sometimes fictitious narrative creating all the deceits of dreams and memories. In *How It Is* and *Lessness*, beautiful nature is part of the remembered, dreamed, imagined and never experienced good moments, but it also provides the unpleasant mud or grey sand of the present, which may also be ultimately discredited, as in *How It Is*, but have a firmness of impression and a continuity that the remembered figments or moments never possess. Beckett's sensuous powers create sounds and shapes of great power, like the remembered crocus in the light, the white horse, and the tone-poems of *Ping* and *Lessness*. Although *Ping* is an abstract and 'unnatural' construct, an enclosure shutting off the phenomenal world, it owes much to Beckett's brilliant sense of shape and colour, which in its turn can light and form the figments and moments of the unstable but sensitive language.

Such imagery is significantly promising but reliable in *Lessness*. In the greys and whites and blacks of aridity, lessness and blankness, blue stands out. (It does so also in *Ping* where the eyes whose vision is so limited are light blue.) In the deprivations of the desert the blue is the only colour, belonging both to eye and sky, so suggesting the inseparability of the human sight and the natural scene. The eyes, 'little holes two pale blue', do not exactly see the sky, any more:

> Face to calm eye touch close all calm all white all gone from mind. Never but imagined the blue in a wild imagining the blue celeste of poesy.

> Never but imagined the blue in a wild imagining the blue celeste of poesy. Light white touch close head through calm eye light of reason all gone from mind. (*Lessness*, pp. 13, 19)

Sight and scene share a colour, but that is all. What remains is the contrast of the sightless eye and reasonless mind, with the blueness. The word 'celeste' stands out as another word for the colour blue, possessing also musical meaning (a soft pedal of piano or stop on harmonium) and religious associations. But both 'celeste' and 'poesy' are dignified, exotic and technical words which insist semantically on the dimension of art and imagination. Their effect is rather like that of some of Wallace Stevens's more exotic flowers of language, and like Stevens mingles natural and artistic implications. The colour blue is Stevens's image for the colour conferred on natural green by art, though he too makes the admission that it is impossible to unmake the blue, to imagine dead imagination. Though their sensibility, temperament and personality are strongly opposed, Beckett and Stevens join in many ways in the rejection of metaphysics, in the attempt to establish a provisional and cagey value for art in a world where imaginative powers have been discredited.

A cruel nature is drawn in *From an Abandoned Work*, where the violence of animals, humans and plants joins monstrously at the end, to confirm the abandonment. Like Molloy, the narrator in *From an Abandoned Work* has his 'way', and it is appropriately and personally violent, like his rages, 'And in this way I have gone through great thicket, bleeding, and deep into bogs, water too, even the sea in some moods and been carried out of my course, or driven back.' I think he is the only one of Beckett's people to make his way through fire, the image of his bizarre and murderous irrationality, though this way is only (only!) imagined in a dream,

> And that is perhaps how I shall die at last if they don't catch me, I mean drowned, or in fire, yes, perhaps that is how I shall do it at last, walking furious headlong into fire and dying burnt to bits. (p. 10)

This extraordinary fragment also contains the stark beauty of the white horse, the Schimmel with the red band on its side, 'bright white, with the sun on it', which seems to provoke the blinding savage rage, in one of those entirely original fantasies which present a plausible causality. The strength of the visual stimulus seems a sufficient occasion for the rage, perhaps supported by the thought of the effects of light and patterns in epilepsy. This piece even presents a scene (almost but not quite sublime) of nature's vastness, in the striking sentence, 'One day I told him about Milton's cosmology, away up in the mountains we were, resting against a huge rock looking out to sea, that impressed him greatly' which is cooled by the preceding sentence, 'A very fair scholar I was too, no thought, but a great memory.' Beckett's natural images frequently approach the sublime, but the sublime has to be inhibited, he knows all about it, but we can't have it, it won't do here. The narrator of this story is even slightly comforted by the thought of the natural cycle, which doesn't often cheer up Beckett's people, and sentimentally or Moranically describes the tears he sheds for happiness, 'for love of this old earth that has carried me along so long and whose uncomplainings will soon be mine'. He imagines his recycling, first under the surface, then dispersed through earth and finally, 'a ton of worms in an acre, that is a wonderful thought, a ton of worms, I believe it'. It is such a wonderful thought, though horrid, that it too has to be discredited, 'Where did I get it, from a dream, or a book read in a nook when a boy, or a work overhead. . . .' Even this narrator, who shares nature's violence, in his love of trampling birds, butterflies and slugs (a hostility returned with interest by birds and stoats and ferns) and in his rages and murderousness, makes due acknowledgment to the literary tradition, though in its morbid moments. Both character and nature join here in imagery and action of frenzied savagery, and the few brilliantly lovely fragments are plainly figments and dreams which offer no opposition. Nature is abandoned in both senses, being savage and purposeless, as far as Beckett's people can make out.

Romantic nature is displaced along with romantic love, beautiful nature along with graceful love. And it isn't surprising that nature-lovers like Moran tend to be discredited also as Christians. The men at the end of *Watt* are like Moran, sentimental about nature and so about life, 'It's not a bad old bugger of an earth.' Isn't it though—Watt thinks so. Of course, he is mad, but Beckett was speaking up for the authority of madness before R. D. Laing, though after Shakespeare. For Watt the leaves will soon rot, but his dislike of sun, moon, earth and sky, the lot, isn't simply a dislike of dying but a hostility to the whole bad business. Nature is a fallacious source of benevolence and pleasure, providing less than human love. She is bloody, rank, meaningless. If her earth provides the two distinct hells of *How It Is* and *Lessness*, the unfantastic nature of Watt is every bit as unpromising:

But by this time Watt was tired of the ditch, which he had been thinking of leaving, when the voices detained him. And one of the reasons why he was tired of the ditch was perhaps this, that the earth, whose contours and peculiar smell the vegetation at first had masked, now he felt it, and smelt it, the bare hard dark stinking earth. (Ch. 1)

Art, love and nature do for Beckett's people what they do for everybody: they warm, they chill, they offer and they withhold significance. The heat and cold, the approach and retreat of meaning, may take unfamiliar shapes in these stories, but what they do and do not do for people is utterly familiar. Passions and appetites persist, however attenuated, however absurd.

First published in *Beckett The Shape Changer*, ed. K. Worth (Routledge & Kegan Paul, London, 1975).

Notes

1. All references to *Molloy*, *Malone Dies* and *The Unnamable* are to the one-volume edition of 1959 (Calder, London).
2. For instance, the joke about a fool petting in his mittens. See G. Legman, *Rationale of the Dirty Joke* (Jonathan Cape, London, 1968) p. 119.
3. References to *Watt* are to the edition of 1963 (Calder, London).

21. Alan Sillitoe's *The Lost Flying Boat* (1983) and *Down from the Hill* (1985)

The Lost Flying Boat is ancient and modern, revising myths and forms with daring modesty. It tells of a secret mission, a strange voyage, a treasure-hunt, and a fight between pirates. At every twist of adventure we move through the large complex world of the map and the little complex world of the mind. The storyteller is a wireless-operator, under contract, a professional and archetypal listener and communicator. His company are ex-R.A.F. men, chosen by their old captain and by a bigger private enterprise. The place is the inside of a huge old flying boat. Characters and readers are concentrated and compelled by unities of time and space, inhabiting an environment as rich and vicious as a grand hotel, as claustrophobic and comforting as a womb, as clandestine and militant as a Trojan horse. The machine and the journey offer escape and microcosm. Like the globe itself, the flying boat is a marvel of destruction and creation, beautiful, expensive, lovable, and fragile.

The narration harks back to the post-war early nineteen-fifties, an era recalled after a space of twenty-five years. Battles in the air, submarine war, terrorism in Malaya, post-war austerity, brief encounters of love and marriage, are all sketched with great economy as the characters talk and remember. The plot is elegantly simple, the story told with the minimum of emotional and moral commentary. But Sillitoe's simplicity is a conjuring trick. We concentrate on the technical particularities of the action, take-off and landing, maps, charts, theodolites and guns, and what makes the concentration, in every sense of that word, is the imagination of the long-distance listener and teller.

He tells well because he listens well. He has postponed the story

255

until it compels a telling. And the telling is a *post-mortem*, in a complex but not tricksy sense. At every stroke the story tells a double narrative, of action and reaction. The teller's needs, motives and passions are sometimes explicit, sometimes implicit, but always animatedly present. His austerity is justified by the barren post-war world, by the failures of love, by the gratuitous loyalty of a short-term contract, by his individual reserve and reservations. The hero becomes a member of the quest to escape or solve love's questions, to find a peacetime vocation, to swop one pain for another, to live in a world of men, to survive without passion. The very restriction of the world, not only without women but also without sex, transcends and reduces the problems of relationship. The novel economically dramatises relationships, but they are refreshingly arbitrary, matters of contiguity not choice, brought to abrupt and harsh conclusions.

Language is cleverly used to articulate surfaces and depths. Everyone speaks the old R.A.F. slang, but clichés become vivid figures, refreshed in unexpected contexts, pressed on for resonance and irony. The phrase 'couldn't care less', for instance, moves out of casual realism into a signal we must decode. The operator is not only the narrator but the reader. He can decode but not always understand. In the special circumstances of this book, he must offend against his code, suspend its rules or keep them secretly, listen but not transmit, send false messages, pervert his craft. The radio and the radio operator become cryptic signs. Like the hero, the reader tunes in to the music of the spheres but is assaulted by the roar of static. The book doesn't suspend us between surface and symbol, particularity and parable, but uses characters, images, and events which perform double duty. Like Robinson Crusoe's agriculture and technology, the professional expertise of navigation and radio is exact, informative, enlarged and symbolic. The image of the code delights the code-conscious critic.

Alan Sillitoe's fiction restores traditional forms of realism, social or psychological, as in *Saturday Night and Sunday Morning* or *Her Victory*, tries out modernist dislocations, as in *Raw Material*, combines realism with reflexiveness, as in *The Storyteller*, flaunts humour, laconically withdraws. This novel combines a highly physical adventure-story with intently metaphysical inquiry, never pretentiously or sensationally but harshly and austerely. It has the stylistic and emotional power of *The Loneliness of the Long Distance*

Runner, tensing us between the poles of realism and poetry.

Down from the Hill is an entirely individual novel. Nothing in it could be replaced out of the common box of fashionable spare parts. It is skilfully crafted but looks as natural as leaves on the tree. It revives myth through imagination, not cold imitation. It contemplates love and hostility, inventiveness and flatness, social hope and cynicism, through an intelligent medium which shifts under your eyes, as real art does. It actually seems to have been written out of the self-delighting impulse to think and feel in the language of fiction.

This is a memory novel which doubles the act of memory in a story of two journeys, one in 1945, one nearly forty years later. The un-Proustian research into time past discovers that a journey can't be recovered, though the novelist proves this by imagining both trips and setting them side by side in loving and ironic contrast. The young Paul Morton, a first-person narrator, and his middle-aged self, presented in the third person, are manipulated by the authorial imagination, which can return. Despite the neat antithetical balance, the structure allows for a variety of flashback. The young man remembers, though he does a lot of anticipating. The older man looks ahead a bit, though he has more to remember. The acts of recall aren't simple and single, but manifold. Consciousness is presented as a temporal hodge-podge. The first part of the novel is especially good at the difficult job of presenting time present, through the elated, open, exposed awareness of the seventeen-year-old boy, cycling for dear life through the post-war Midlands landscape.

Alan Sillitoe is very good at the motions and maps of journeys, on foot, in flight or, as here, by bike and car. The bike trip covers the miles slowly, the car moves fast. Both are aptly and wittily varied vehicles for meditation and fantasy. The form is ancient, but it never looks over its shoulder with bookish evocation of odysseys, quixotic trails, or pilgrims' progress. Like Ulysses and Huck Finn, Paul is a storyteller who deals with the people he meets on the road by making up identities for himself and for them. Strangeness is a great stimulus to invention, and imaginary stories are fitted to real people as fast as imaginary people spring into life at a hint from a stab of feeling or a name of a place. Moreover, the other travellers are also storytellers, like the people encountered by Tom Jones and Nicholas Nickleby. The story is comically and richly faithful to its great tradition, crammed with narratives which are socially revealing models, funny and pathetic anecdotes, and images of the hero's consciousness and art. The young Paul creates as he breathes. He is to become the older Paul, writer of screenplays, assertive in his non-stop fantasies and convincingly touched in as a professional. Some of the stories are briefly brilliant, like the fantasies about a vampire or a jealous husband, the latter figment realised in a typical stroke of style, 'And for God's sake get my dinner on the table. I'm bloody starving.'

It's a story about stories. Paul knows that he constructs reality out of lies. Both young and older Paul dream their dreams of fair women, for the story is also about love. Fantasy and reality blur. A real girl called Alice Sands is no more real than a playfully invented one called after a place, Edith Weston. Both stand for an early, pure, and romantically unconsummated love, but they are created and regarded with irony as well as desire, known to be futures as unreachable as the past. Both young and older Paul are open to love, and the erotic fantasies and erotic acts are done with delicacy and the right touch of roughness.

Down from the Hill both is and is not a novel about politics. The young Paul observes that 'All times were historic.' The book suggests that some times are more historic than others in its focus on 1945, after the Labour landslide, and 1983, after Mrs Thatcher's second victory. But the times are not equally represented. The 1983 trip includes an encounter with unemployment, and there is no tolerance of the gloom of our moment now. The 1945 trip includes no image of revolutionary elation, but plays down the Labour victory. One character complains that though there's been a landslide he can't find anyone who's voted Labour. I felt the same about the book, though the reasons for its political images may be autobiographical or ideological. The older Paul speaks out of a political, as well as an emotional loss; his brief observations are effective metonymies, like the mention of anti-Semitism, but there is a gap the novel never fills in, between the middle-aged disguised man and the apolitical young Paul. The rest of the life between the journeys is there, in its professional, familial, and amorous implications, but the story is left backgrounded and incomplete. Fair enough, perhaps. It is a novel, not a history; an uncomfortable one.

First published in *The Times Literary Supplement*, 11 November 1983 and 6 November 1984.

Details of
Previous Publications

These essays originally appeared in the following publications, and I am grateful to the editors for permission to reprint, where this was necessary. Further details of previous publication appear at the end of each chapter.

Novel, Fall, 1968; *Genre*, Winter, 1977; *The Rikkyo Review*, 1986; *Children's Literature in Education*, Spring, 1977; *The Times Literary Supplement*; the *Dickensian*, 1977; *The Sphere History of Literature in the English Language*, 1969; The Penguin English Library *Daniel Deronda*, 1967; *The Novels of Thomas Hardy*, Vision Press, 1979; The Boydell Press edition of *Evan Harrington*, 1983; *Meredith Now*, Routledge, 1971; *D. H. Lawrence: Novelist, Poet, Prophet*, Weidenfeld and Nicholson, 1973; *Orbis Litterarum*, 1964; *The Uses of Fiction. Essays on the Modern Novel in Honour of Arnold Kettle*, 1982; *The Fiction Magazine*, 1987; *Essays in Criticism*, 1954; *Beckett the Shape Changer*, Routledge, 1975: The essay on *Les Liaisons Dangereuses* (Ch. 5) was originally a radio broadcast for the Open University.

Index

Italic type indicates extensive discussion